D0850847

Sharing Executive Power

In many companies, two or three executives jointly hold the responsibilities at the top – from the CEO who relies on the operational expertise of a COO, to co-CEOs who trust in interpersonal bonds to achieve professional results. Their collaboration is essential if they are to address the dilemmas of the top job and the demands of today's corporate governance. *Sharing Executive Power* examines the behavior of such duos, trios and small teams, what roles their members play, and how their professional and interpersonal relationships bind their work together. It answers some critical questions regarding when and how such power-sharing units form and break up, how they perform, and why they endure. Understanding their dynamics helps improve the design and composition of corporate power structures. The book is essential reading for academics, graduates, MBAs, and executives interested in enhancing teamwork and cooperation at the top.

JOSÉ LUIS ALVAREZ (PhD) is Professor of General Management at Instituto de Empresa Business School, where he directs its Center for Corporate Governance. He is a Visiting Professor at INSEAD and has been a Visiting Professor at Harvard Business School.

SILVIYA SVEJENOVA is Assistant Professor of Strategy at ESADE Business School in Barcelona. She is a Visiting Lecturer at the Cranfield School of Management.

Sharing Executive Power: Roles and Relationships at the Top

JOSÉ LUIS ALVAREZ AND
SILVIYA SVEJENOVA

CAMBRIDGE
UNIVERSITY PRESS

CAMBRIDGE UNIVERSITY PRESS
Cambridge, New York, Melbourne, Madrid, Cape Town, Singapore, São Paulo

Cambridge University Press
The Edinburgh Building, Cambridge CB2 2RU, UK

Published in the United States of America by Cambridge University Press, New York

www.cambridge.org
Information on this title: www.cambridge.org/9780521601078

First published 2005

Printed in the United Kingdom at the University Press, Cambridge

A catalogue record for this book is available from the British Library

Library of Congress Cataloguing in Publication data
Alvarez, José Luis.
Sharing executive power: roles and relationships at the top / José Luis Alvarez,
Silviya Svejenova – 1st ed.
   p.   cm.
Includes bibliographical references and index.
ISBN 0-521-84125-9 (hardback) – ISBN 0-521-60107-X (paperback)
1. Corporate governance.   2. Chief executive officers.   3. Directors of corporations.
4. Decision making.   5. Leadership.   I. Svejenova, Silviya, 1973–   II. Title.
HD2741.A59   2005
658.4′2 – dc22   2005   012511

ISBN-13   978-0-521-84125-2 hardback
ISBN-10   0-521-84125-9 hardback
ISBN-13   978-0-521-60107-8 paperback
ISBN-10   0-521-60107-X paperback

To our maestros, with gratitude

Contents

Figures and tables

Figures

Tables

Acknowledgments

José Luis Alvarez would like to thank Instituto de Empresa Business School's former Dean, Angel Cabrera, and Dean Santiago Iñiguez. They, together with Associate Dean Salvador Carmona, have patiently forgiven José Luis' avoidance of academic administrative tasks. Associate Dean for Research Julio de Castro has also been generous in providing the financial aid necessary to support the co-authors' travels as they coordinated their efforts, first, between Cranfield and Madrid, and, later, between Madrid and Barcelona. Instituto de Empresa Business School also provided funds for the research assistantship of Leticia Henar, who was as hardworking and reliable as any authors could wish or need.

During Silviya Svejenova's work at Cranfield School of Management, the head of the Strategic Management group at the time, Murray Steele, and her colleagues, shielded her from excessive teaching and administrative commitments, allowing much needed time for her to write. Nardine Collier, Dee Donovan, and Margaret Hamer should be thanked for their valuable assistance. Having relocated to ESADE Business School in September 2004, Silviya would like to thank Montse Ollé, Director of the Business Policy Department, and her new colleagues for their support and patience with her intense dedication to the book during the first months of her employment there and for the financial aid for her travels between Barcelona and Madrid.

Our appreciation goes to Katy Plowright, our committed editor from Cambridge University Press, for believing in our project and for supporting us throughout the production of the book, and to the two anonymous reviewers.

Nina Colwill and Dennis Anderson deserve special thanks for their splendid help, with industry and diligence, in polishing our writing on successive waves of this work. We also thank Caterina Ciani and Sheila Hardie for their language editing at the early stages of the project.

We would like to express thanks for the suggestions and criticisms offered by participants in meetings and research seminars at the Academy of Management, the American Sociological Association, the Barcelona Gestió, the Copenhagen Business School, the Cranfield School of Management, the ESADE Business School, the European Group for Organizational Studies, the Harvard Business School European Research Center, the Iberoamerican Academy of Management, the IESE Business School, INSEAD, the Instituto de Empresa Business School, the London Business School, the Rotterdam School of Management, the Strategic Management Society, the University of Navarra, and Warwick University.

We extend our thanks to the brothers and co-presidents of Banco Popular, Luis and Javier Valls, for their time in December 2001; and to Juan Vives Ruiz, then HR director of Banco Popular, for making the interviews possible and providing sources of information from Banco Popular's press archives. We are especially grateful to Agustín Almodóvar, Paz Sufrategui, and the entire team of El Deseo for their hospitality during hectic times for them. Special thanks go to Jim Moore, for his help in gaining an insight on the history and management structure of Sun Microsystems, and to Fiona van Haeringen who made our meeting in Palo Alto in October 2001 possible.

We are grateful to Luis Vives for bringing to our attention numerous sources of information on small-numbers arrangements. Jin-ichiro Yamada helped with data on historical and contemporary cases of Japanese partnerships. Mikolaj Piskorski was our "tipping point" for the propagation of our teaching case on Almodóvar, and provided useful insights from his teaching experience.

Carmelo Mazza and Jesper Strandgaard Pedersen, dear friends and colleagues at the Copenhagen Business School, were generous in providing content suggestions and energy. Our current *à quatre* (Alvarez, Mazza, Strandgaard, and Svejenova, 2005) work on independent European filmmakers provided us with the joy of combining work and friendship.

Against all logic or duty, Jackie for José Luis, and Nedko for Silviya, temporarily organized important parts of their lives to support our need for writing time. They are truly our vital contingencies. In the two years of writing and producing our book, Camilla and Adrian were born to Jackie and José Luis. They adamantly and noisily refused to adapt to José Luis' working habits. And that has been both exhausting and wonderful!

Finally, this book is dedicated to our maestros in scholarly work. We have been extraordinarily lucky to have them and to learn from them. With this book we offer them homage and sincere gratitude.

Introduction

T HIS IS A BOOK about corporate political design, and, in particular, about the differentiation and integration of the roles
played in executive committees, CEO offices, and boards of
directors. Our principal argument is that productive interpersonal relationships based on personal and professional trust are the key to the
integration of these structures. Such role integration is particularly visible in what we call small numbers at the top as a mixture of role
separation, role combination, and role-sharing among a reduced number of executives – usually between two and four.

There are few incumbents at the corporate apex in the majority of
organizations (Mintzberg, 1980). Corporate power, like social power,
is always a phenomenon of small numbers. Sometimes the pinnacle of
the organization takes the form of dominant coalitions, as noted by
Cyert and March in their *A Behavioral Theory of the Firm* (1963) and
by Thompson in *Organizations in Action* (1967), or of upper echelons,
as in Hambrick and Mason's (1984) influential piece; sometimes it is
an inner core group, as in Kleiner's (2003) text for practitioners.

Although, as Khurana (2002) reminds us, individualism is assumed
in most concepts of corporate power, rarely does one individual exercise great power in complex organizations. Yet performance is often
attributed to the individual at the top. There are, however, numerous
practices that do not fit that individualist assumption. Increasingly,
two executives are sharing corporate governance roles traditionally
occupied by one person (e.g. co-CEOs), and duos linked by trust are
occupying two vertically contiguous roles (e.g. a CEO and a COO), in
what Kirkpatrick (2004) calls "buddy acts" (p. 44). Sometimes circles
of intertwined executives with the same or different status or job cate-
gory, and with personal or professional trust, or both (what Hodgson,
Levinson, and Zaleznik [1965] called "role constellations"), occupy
the roles that constitute corporate governance.

There are at least two reasons for us to focus the central chapters of this book on these duos, trios, and quartets and other executive constellations based on role separation, role-sharing and other role combinations, and on the trust that jells them: (1) for the inherent interest of the phenomenon of small numbers at the top, and (2) for the lessons it can contain for our knowledge of corporate governance.

First, the occurrence of small numbers is an interesting and important social phenomenon in its own right, one that had been largely neglected for over a hundred years since Simmel (1902a, 1902b). There were some attempts to study small numbers at the top in the mid-1960s (Whisler, 1960; Daniel, 1965; Etzioni, 1965; Hodgson, Levinson, and Zaleznick, 1965), primarily in order to account for the growing complexity of the chief executive office in the multi-divisional organization. These works were followed some thirty years later by Stewart's (1991) lucid piece on the chair–CEO relationship and, in recent years, by the work of organizational sociologists interested in the role of third parties in networks – Burt (1992), Krackhardt (1992), and Gargiulo and Benassi (2000), among others; and, even more recently, by authors interested in roles at the top (O'Toole, Galbraith, and Lawler, 2002; Sally, 2002; Hambrick and Cannella, 2004). The use of small numbers such as dyads, triads, and quartets in executive committees, CEO offices, and boards of directors[1] is the specific focus of this book.

Second, it is hoped that the study of interpersonal ties as integrating mechanisms in the creation and maintenance of small numbers at the top will improve our knowledge of corporate governance, thereby providing us with a stronger base on which to construct effective corporate political designs. For that is the ultimate aim of this book.

---

[1] When we refer simultaneously to these three decision-making loci, we often use the expression "corporate governance." This is, in our view, the system of roles aimed at making key decisions for the long-term welfare of corporations. To avoid too repetitive a vocabulary, we may also refer to them as vertical structures; as decision-making structures (because strategic decisions are the sole responsibility of those who occupy the top structures, whereas implementation responsibility is shared with horizontal structures); or as highly discretionary structures (because they are less bound by rules and procedures than are lower layers of the organization).

We reserve the word "executive" for CEOs or those top managers who may sit on boards as executive directors or take part in executive committees. We use the word "manager" to refer to medium- or high-level employees who are not members of executive committees or boards of directors.

Knowledge has accumulated on the topic of horizontal structure designs – designs in which the differentiation in groups of specialized people and the corresponding integration or coordination of those units reflects the value chain of the company. However, as Tushman (1977), Lewin and Stephens (1994), and others have noted, vertical structures have been much less studied from a design perspective. Although the field of strategic leadership, based primarily on Hambrick's upper-echelons theory, has generated an astonishing amount of high-quality work on top management teams, CEOs, and boards of directors, most of its works have, for methodological reasons, been primarily limited to the demographics of executive teams rather than their deliberate design characteristics and processes, as one of its academic champions has recognized (Finkelstein, 1992).

There are at least four reasons why so little research has been undertaken on the design of vertical structures.

(1) There are methodological challenges in the study of decision-making and decision makers at the top. It is difficult to secure access to the corporate inner sanctum (e.g. board deliberations are confidential), forcing scholars to resort to indirect research strategies, using such proxies as demographics, functional experience, and social networks. As a result, the measurable composition of corporate governance bodies has attracted the most research, but the core of decision-making at the top – in which interpersonal relationships, and trust and affection among executives play critical roles – still eludes academics.

(2) When it is not demographics-based, the study of the incumbents at the apex of organizations has been diluted in the wide field of leadership studies, which mostly focuses on the personal characteristics and psychology of executives rather than on their actual behavior and their activities in performing the tasks prescribed by their roles. Studies of leadership are too often lacking in context, and do not account for the activities reserved for directors, executives, and their specific contingencies – a gap we try to fill with this book.

(3) Corporate governance is, to a significant degree, an institutionalized function. A series of highly publicized business *affaires* have prompted the generation of a variety of norms, either social (e.g. professional codes of good governance) or legal (e.g. criminal law reforms such as jail penalties for CEOs convicted of misrepresenting the accounts of their companies), which have undoubtedly reduced the latitude for the design of distinctive corporate power structures.

(4) Not only are the assumptions, values, beliefs, and rules about corporate governance more institutionalized in today's investor capitalism than in the old days of managerial capitalism, but they are also more widespread across nations and business systems (Aguilera and Jackson, 2003). The demands for similar standards are increasing with the growth in global capital flows and are resulting in a higher degree of convergence in corporate governance.

Despite this stronger institutional logic (Thornton and Ocasio, 1999) and wider convergence, this book argues that current corporate governance reforms are mostly based on weak norms and that there remains a wide range of possible variations in corporate political structures. This diversity (e.g. small numbers at the top) is not widely recognized in the business press[2] and even less so in the academic literature. It has long been acknowledged that executives have latitude in deciding the domains of their jobs and the manner in which they should assume their responsibilities in the face of constraints (see Stewart, 1982; Alvarez, 2000). The integration of roles at the level of corporate governance must be based upon weak structures such as interpersonal relationships because there are no other formal integrating mechanisms or superior hierarchy. Our position is in contrast to the normative environment of today's businesses – an environment in which personal relationships are regarded with great suspicion in all corporate governance reforms. For instance, Blas Calzada, former president of Spain's Securities and Exchange Commission, bluntly expressed these suspicions, declaring that the chair of a board and the CEO cannot be friends.

There is an element of irony in today's normative thinking, in that friendship and personal trust in corporate governance are mistrusted, whereas when considered as components of the social capital that provides the glue for modern societies, their value is positively recognized and even demanded by most analysts of the contemporary social scene (see, for example, Piore, 1995; Putnam, 2000).

In the remaining pages of this Introduction, we first present a string of examples of what we call the "small numbers at the top," in order to illustrate clearly what we mean by that expression. Then, in a section

---

[2] Contrary to this opinion, Hambrick and Cannella (2004) attribute the rapid diffusion of the CEO–COO formula to the role of the business media: "If someone as eloquent as Peter Drucker advocates top-level job-sharing, and journalists and consultants chime in repeatedly, sometimes invoking vivid cases of successful CEO/COO duos, then the bandwagon is rolling" (p. 977).

on the academic aim, we refer to our main theoretical approaches – contingency and role theory – and place them within current academic debates on the design of corporate power structures. We are of the view that organizational theorists have not paid sufficient attention to small-numbers structures, and that, even in recent research on shared leadership, the phenomenon of small numbers is treated only tangentially. In a section on social opportunity, we argue that this topic is especially appropriate and relevant in a period when changes in corporate governance are occurring throughout the world, based primarily upon well-known agency theory postulates, which we believe to be ideologically loaded and limiting for the range of possible governance practices. We conclude this Introduction with a description of the work process that led to this book and a summary of its chapters.

The small numbers at the top phenomenon

Despite a lack of academic acknowledgement, as noted by Stewart (1982, 1991), executive role-sharing and role constellations abound. Tandems, trios, quartets, and variants of these options are seen in a variety of contexts. They proliferate in creative enterprises such as entertainment, advertising, and fashion, where the gap between management and creativity is often bridged by teams comprising artists and managers. The luxury fashion brands of the Louis Vuitton Moët Hennessy Group have been co-run by a designer, in charge of the aesthetic concept, and an entrepreneur, responsible for the product's commercialization. Music recording has long been a favorable place for enduring career couplings: Pairs such as Gloria and Emilio Estefan, the most powerful Latin music duo in the USA, have developed a personal and professional relationship over the past three decades, nurtured by their mutual loyalty and by their roots, their friends, and their troupe (Townsend, 2000). As in other tight partnerships, their joint trajectory is also embedded in their company, Estefan Enterprises, which includes the Crescent Moon Studios and video, TV, and cinema production companies, among other businesses. Film directors often couple their careers with producers who are close to them and who provide them with both autonomy and resources (Alvarez, Mazza, Strandgaard, and Svejenova, 2005). A case in point is the famous Danish film director Lars von Trier, at the core of the Dogme movement, who has teamed up with his producer and friend Peter Ålbæk Jensen (Brorsen and Strandgaard, 2002). Italian independent filmmaker Nanni Moretti works closely with his producer and friend Angelo Barbagallo. Asked how the two prepare a film, Moretti explains:

Rather than a team, we are two people – Angelo Barbagallo and me . . . having our own production company, and such a good partner, enabled me to suddenly decide to make films, . . . to make documentaries or shorts, whatever we felt like . . . when you have a conventional relationship with the film producer, a film will have very clear and distinct stages – the writing of the film, pre-production, the actual shooting of the film, post-production, the editing and all the rest. Whereas in some of these films that I have made in recent years, these stages have become much more blurred. (Wootton, 2001)

Some of these complementary tandems play such an influential role in their firms that the company's stock value falls when they leave, as occurred in the case of the departure in November 2003 of Gucci–Yves Saint Laurent's chief designer, Tom Ford, and its CEO, Domenico de Sole. In creative industries, tandems and career couplings are observed not only between artists and business professionals but between two creative people, such as the filmmaking Coen brothers (De Felipe, 1999). Advertising pairs recurrently team up as well, often for campaigns, or they may move in tandem from one agency to another (Vagnoni, 1997). Similarly, in Nissan Design International, vehicles are designed by some twenty-five couples, each consisting of an intuitive creative and an analytic creative, who have been hired in pairs by the unit's founder, Jerry Hirshberg, in the belief that the odd coupling leads to friction that, in turn, enhances creativity (Cubeiro, 1998). Musicians in string quartets also tend to develop long-term collaborations (Murnighan and Colon, 1991), as do scientists (Zuckerman, 1967). Pierre and Marie Curie, and Irène Joliot-Curie and Frédéric Joliot, are examples of Nobel Prize winners with both scientific and affective ties. Their accomplishments as couples were probably far greater and more lasting than they would have been had each worked individually (Pycior, Slack, and Abir-Am, 1996).

United professional trajectories could also manifest themselves in some hierarchical partnerships at the executive level of creative organizations (e.g. co-Presidents, CEO–COO, co-CEOs). World-class media empires may need more than one person at the top (Grover, 1999). Teaming up in 1984, the creative Michael Eisner as CEO and the financially adept Frank Wells as COO, put the troubled Walt Disney Productions back on its feet. A *Business Week* article portrays their partnership in the following way:

When he first came to Disney back in 1984, Eisner's comrade in arms was Disney president Frank Wells. An accomplished Hollywood lawyer and one-time head of Warner Brothers, Wells was the yin to Eisner's yang. When Eisner got too excited about something, it was Wells who would bring him back to earth. Eisner would want to build a Mickey-shaped hotel, Wells would remind him of how much it would cost. (Grover, 1999)

This pairing ended in an untimely way in 1994, when Wells died in an accident. Despite Eisner's many attempts to find another partner, there has never been another such successful team at Disney.

Michael Barker, Tom Bernard, and Marcie Bloom are co-presidents of Sony Pictures Classics. Before founding the company in February 1992, Barker and Bernard founded Orion Classics in the early 1980s. Marcie Bloom has been their partner since 1989.

Small numbers at the top can be observed not only where internal differentiation is greatest, as in the firms engaged in artistic activities, but also in mainstream businesses. Small numbers at the top abound in the broad domain of family businesses, often with kin sharing management responsibilities persistently over time. In the 1997 Arthur Andersen–MassMutual American Family Business Survey, more than 11 percent of the business respondents reported that they had two or more CEOs and more than 40 percent believed that that would be their situation in the succeeding generation. In the 2002 American Family Business Survey almost 9 percent reported having two co-CEOs, and 3.5 percent having more than two CEOs; more than 35 percent said that co-CEOs are possible in the next generation, and two out of five of those likely to adopt co-CEOs responded that one of the co-CEOs may be a woman (Mass Mutual Financial Group and Raymond Institute, 2003). One common path to such couplings occurs when parents name their children as equal successors to the business. In June 2004, for example, Marc and Manuel Puig became co-CEOs of Puig Beauty and Fashion Group, the family-owned corporation carrying the well-known perfume brands of Carolina Herrera, Paco Rabanne, and Nina Ricci among others.

Pairs of CEOs are also found in such steady and conservative sectors as investment banking. Goldman Sachs has hired co-CEOs for more than two decades: Weinberg and Whitehead, Rubin and Friedman, and Corzine and Paulson. But Goldman Sachs, a case we often refer to in this book, is not an isolated example in the financial sector. Winthrop H. Smith and Charles E. Merrill jointly ran the brokerage house Merrill Lynch for decades (Heenan and Bennis, 1999). In a similar arrangement, Charles R. Schwab served as Chair and David S. Pottruck as President, sharing the CEOship at Charles Schwab Corporation.

There are pairs at the top in other traditional sectors. In the catalog retail company Spiegel, for example, the CEO role is shared by Mike Moran, James Sievers, and Harold Dahlstrand, who together constitute the Office of the President, each contributing different skills and responsibilities.[3] At Ralston Purina, Patrick McGinnis headed the Pet Products Group, while sharing the CEO role with Patrick Mulcahy, CEO of the Eveready Battery Company between 1997 and 1999. The US superstore chain Bed, Bath & Beyond, was founded and led by co-CEOs Leonard Feinstein and Warren Eisenberg. In January 2001, the international news and technology information giant Reuters America Inc. announced the appointment of Alex Hungate and Phil Lynch as co-CEOs – not their first such partnership. And co-presidents Mark G. Parker and Charles D. Denson have served Nike since 2001.

The high-tech industry also provides some pertinent examples, like the case of the co-founders of the Hewlett-Packard Company – Stanford buddies William R. Hewlett and David Packard (Kaplan, 2000). Another example is the introverted Bill Gates and the socially adept Steve Ballmer, who met at Harvard in the early 1970s (Heenan and Bennis, 1999). In the Microsoft duo, Gates was the strategist and Ballmer the tactician. While at the University of California in Berkeley, the technically creative Steve Wozniak hooked up with the marketing whiz Steve Jobs, five years his junior, forming the partnership behind Apple (Kaplan, 2000). This partnership broke up in the early 1980s when Wozniak left Apple.

The leadership of political organizations also provides well-documented examples of tandems at the top, for reasons similar to those found in business: the impossibility of a single individual simultaneously conducting inspiring and disciplining activities, performing external roles (e.g. relations with the electorate) and internal functions

---

[3] This company was having dire financial problems as we were writing these pages.

(e.g. control of the party). Role transitions between such disparate roles are difficult to conduct and can endanger the coherence of public image demanded of politicians (Miller, 2001). In Spain in the 1980s, the long-standing government of the socialist party was headed by a tandem consisting of the Prime Minister and First Secretary of the party, Felipe González, who focused on institutional tasks and securing the support of the voters; and the Vice Prime Minister and Second Secretary of the party, Alfonso Guerra, who had the explicit role of coordinating the efforts of top officials in the administration and of harnessing the party bosses. Similarly, US President Bill Clinton and Vice-President Albert Gore demonstrated that complementary tasks are consistent with differences of character throughout their first presidential campaign, when Clinton picked Gore as his running mate to the end of their second mandate (Williams, 2001).

Tandem leadership is not then a negligible phenomenon that occurs only in small economic sectors and marginal organizations. These and many more examples are scrutinized in Chapters 4 to 6, which focus specifically on duos and other small numbers. For an alphabetically ordered list of selected examples of small numbers at the top, see the Appendix.

The academic aim of the book

This book uses two academic platforms to build its arguments: contingency theory and role theory. We believe that both of these perspectives represent an opportunity to understand the phenomenon of small numbers at the top. Furthermore, neither theory has been sufficiently applied to contemporary vertical structures.

The critical role of interpersonal relationships as an integrating mechanism was present in the initial versions of contingency theory, but was not pursued in its later developments. Yet the examples of small numbers at the top that have been presented in this Introduction could not have been effectively maintained without high levels of trust. In this book, we try to recover and update contingency theory, originally intended for horizontal structures, and apply it to the design of vertical structures – to the system of roles and processes commonly known today as corporate governance. This is the main theoretical strategy of the book, deployed in Chapter 1 on contingency theory and in Chapter 3 on role theory.

Our thesis is that the key to the challenges of designing vertical structures is similar to the one that Tom Burns, pioneer of contingency theory, describes in the preface to the third edition (1994) of his book *The Management of Innovation* (1961), co-authored with G. M. Stalker. As Burns says: "My own preoccupation was with the structure and dynamics of interpersonal relationships, of the various interests pursued by individuals and of the alliances they formed to further them and the social sub-systems observably present in organizations" (p. xiii).

As we argue in Chapter 3, there is a characteristic of roles at the top that explains why interpersonal relationships are such an important integrating mechanism: roles at the top, although increasingly bound by social and institutional regulations, are still subject to the enactment – choices and actions – of their incumbents. There is wide latitude for designing the behaviors, activities, and tasks that roles at the top encompass, and, as a consequence, for the accommodation of interpersonal relationships among the role holders. To give one example, Stewart (1991) claims that the variations available for the division of tasks between a CEO and a chair of the board are numerous (e.g. the latter could be partner, executive, mentor, consultant), and the particular roles chosen depend on the degree of mutual trust and joint agreement about the content of the two roles between the two incumbents. It is for vertical structures, therefore, that the following assertion by Eccles and Nohria (1992), intended for structures in general, is most true:

the best structure often must be compromised in order to adapt to the particular individuals who are available . . . A sub-optimal structure that takes account of people's strengths and weaknesses is almost always better than an optimal structure that makes overly heroic assumptions about what people are capable of doing . . . structure must be designed around and for individuals. (p. 141)

We might add that when designing top structures, both individuals and their relationships should be taken into account.

Small numbers at the top, although existing in the practice of corporate political structures, are not well recognized or even welcomed by some management scholars and managerial traditions.

In a revision of his classic article about the folklore and the reality of managerial work, and even in the midst of an argument emphasizing the vast difference in managerial roles and the enormous challenges of role transitions, Mintzberg (1989) is explicit in his skepticism toward role-sharing:

> Herein lies a clue to the problems of team management. Two or three people cannot share a single managerial position unless they can act as one entity. That means they cannot divide up the ten roles unless they can very carefully reintegrate them. The real difficulty lies with the informational roles. Unless there can be a full sharing of managerial information and, as I pointed out earlier, it is primarily oral, the team management breaks down. A single managerial job cannot be arbitrarily split, for example, into internal and external roles, for information from both sources must be brought to bear on the same decisions . . . in all cases the interpersonal, informational, and decisional roles remain inseparable. (p. 22)

Although praising teams, Richard Hackman (2002) is critical of both the idea of shared leadership and the notion of co-CEOs:

> The idea of shared leadership is generally more attractive in theory than it is in practice. Not to have some single individual who is responsible for making sure things stay on track is to invite coordination problems ("Who was supposed to do what?") and unnecessary interpersonal conflict as those who are supposedly sharing leadership arrange themselves into a hierarchy. Ideas such as "Co-CEOs" and the "Office of the President" sound better than they actually work. (p. 274)

James Schrager, quoted in Ladika (2004, p. 57), expresses his rejection of CEO role-sharing by reversing a typical expression of popular wisdom: "Two heads are not better than one when it comes to leadership. The key to success is a single leader. It's a very powerful pattern that goes back to the beginning of time. It's an immutable pattern."

In a piece jointly written by a scholar and a practitioner (Allen and Berkley, 2003), breaking down the role consolidation of CEO and chair (role-splitting being another alternative for the design of structures with small numbers at the top) is looked upon with skepticism: "Effective firms lodge ultimate leadership and accountability in a single place. A split power structure would reduce the authority of the CEO" (p. 24).

Some executives are highly critical of small-numbers arrangements. Zelleke (2003), for instance, quotes from one interview: "Co-CEOs is a dumb idea. It does not work . . . constituencies . . . will be playing politics between the two" (p. 124).

Counterbalancing these criticisms are the numerous examples of small numbers at the top analyzed in Chapters 4 to 6, and those ordered alphabetically in the Appendix. The business press has occasionally noted their spread (Collet, 2002). Several theoretical positions also back the feasibility of small numbers at the top. Contingency theory and resource dependency theory, for example, openly suggest the possibility of role-sharing. In his landmark book, *Organizations in Action*, James Thompson (1967) states that dominant coalitions, one of the potential embodiments of small numbers at the top, are intrinsic to the running of complex organizations:

Although the pyramid headed by an all-powerful individual has been a symbol of organizations, such omnipotence is possible only in simple situations where perfect technologies and bland task environments make computational decisions feasible. Where technology is incomplete or the task environment heterogeneous, the judgment decision strategy is required and control is vested in a dominant coalition (p. 143).

In the final chapter of *The External Control of Organizations*, Pfeffer and Salancik (1978) discuss how role-sharing schemes in the chief executive office may help corporations to deal with such dualities as autonomy and discretion, stability and predictability, and accountability and adaptability:

If differentiation in organizational structures is useful for dealing with competing demands, it would be logically possible to extend that argument and suggest the usefulness of differentiation even in the chief executive position. Instead of having a single chief executive or chief administrator, the organization might have several, each with his or her own expertise and the ability to cope with some segment of the environment . . . have the actual organization control lodged in a multiparty executive position . . . Of course, such an organizational design is at variance with the traditional prescriptions for unity of command. (p. 276)

Building on these insights and traditions, the thrust of the argument of this book is that the task demands of top management and corporate governance roles make it difficult for executives to exercise power without relying upon a variety of small-number combinations. These arrangements can function only on the basis of interpersonal and professional relationships of trust.

When we were well advanced in the writing of this book, a recent piece by Hambrick and Cannella (2004) on the spread of the

CEO–COO dyadic formula presented a direct challenge to our arguments. They sought to explain the diffusion of that vertical structure in spite of its lower economic efficiency compared to a non-COO executive team structure. After comparing contingency, institutional, and personal preferences hypotheses, they show that contingency theory is the one with the least power of explanation for their data. Although their conclusions may seem, at first glance, to be incompatible with our overall argument, that may not be entirely the case. As Chapter 1 details, within the contingency perspective we conceive of what we call the executive environment – a broad contingency that includes the political preferences and interpersonal relationships of executives and one that we consider critical for the design of vertical structures. The version of contingency theory that Hambrick and Cannella use for the elaboration of their hypothesis, on the other hand, is restricted primarily to what we refer to in Chapter 1 as the external environment – the one that drives the design of horizontal structures. We are separated, then, less by the substance of the argument than by the selection of conceptual boundaries.

Hambrick and Cannella's (2004) piece ends with a request with which we wholeheartedly agree, and try, in fact, to address in this book: "More generally," they say, "our study signals a great need to understand the implications of a host of other top-executive staffing arrangements which so far have escaped attention; these include CEOs . . . and others" (p. 977).

In addition to our application of contingency theory to corporate governance, complemented by our use of roles and relationships as the building blocks of our arguments, we engage in several other academic debates.

In the wide field of leadership studies there is the growing debate over individual versus shared leadership. It is still widely assumed that leadership is exercised on an individual basis. Among the exceptions to this generalized assumption is Heenan and Bennis' (1999) book on co-leaders, which provides a collection of accounts of collaborations between a leader and a leader's lieutenant. Our book differs from theirs in at least three basic ways. We are primarily concerned with the design of corporate governance arrangements; we extend our analysis beyond dyads into threesomes and even foursomes; and although we do examine the leader–lieutenant phenomenon, we also focus on role-sharing at the top among equals.

Recently, another exception has appeared in the volume *Shared Leadership* edited by Pearce and Conger (2003). Shared leadership, which these authors define as "a dynamic, interactive influence process among individuals in groups for which the objective is to lead one another to the achievement of group or organizational goals or both" (p. 1), has two causes in common with small numbers at the top: (1) senior leaders of complex organizations do not usually possess all the relevant information and competencies; and (2) the complexity of the CEO's job means that it is difficult to fill with one person. However, the research on shared leadership does not focus on co-leadership, such as role-sharing at the top, but on leadership distributed throughout both vertical and horizontal structures. Pearce and Conger themselves recognize that co-leadership differs from shared leadership ("a distinct concept", p. 8). In their concluding chapter, they argue that the field of shared leadership is still in its early stages, with plenty of opportunities for more refined understandings. We try to contribute to the field by focusing on co-leadership at the top rather than on leadership distributed across the organization.

Our focus is reflected in two articles on the topic: O'Toole, Galbraith, and Lawler (2002) and Sally (2002). These authors provide splendid accounts of the existence of co-leadership and a wealth of evidence of its spread. Perhaps the main difference between our work and theirs is that we focus specifically on corporate governance structures. And having the length of a book at our disposal, we have been able to embed the explanations of the phenomenon within two traditions in organization theory: contingency theory and role theory.

An influential book by Khurana (2002) contains a sociological inquiry into the excesses of individualism in corporate governance. Khurana uses Weber's notion of charisma to explain the celebrity status of some CEOs in the USA in the 1990s, and some of the gaps between excessive expectations and delivery. Khurana argues that the contribution of people at the top toward the results of organizations is especially susceptible to biases in attributions. Because at the apex the distinction between means and ends is more ambiguous, performance is over-determined, and causalities follow the rule of equifinality, it is executives to whom it is more difficult to give credit for organizational results. As a consequence, giving credit for organizational results becomes a social construction (see also Alvarez, 2000).

Changes in capitalism have encouraged a type of crowd psychology, as Lewis (1989) humorously describes. Investor capitalism has extended ownership rights to a multitude of dispersed small investors who cannot follow the nuances of the evolution of the shares in which they invest; nor can they easily understand the reasons for the performance of corporations or predict their future evolution. Consequently, these non-professional atomized multitudes, fed by an ever-increasingly influential financial press, have no option but to allow themselves to track external signs from which they try to infer the causes for corporate performance. Therefore, a variety of reasons ranging from our genetic cognitive biases through the individualism of Western societies to the role of the press in legitimating business practices (Mazza and Alvarez, 2000; Hayward, Rindova, and Pollock, 2004) feed the attribution fallacy that has enabled CEOs to gradually acquire an aura of causality and charisma. Thus Khurana argues that 'Boards wish to find a new CEO with as much star power as possible, because a high-profile, high status appointment is almost certain to inspire public confidence in the company and immediately boost share prices' (p. xii).

A highly revealing quote in Khurana's book that we cannot resist reproducing here details the mechanisms of attraction that operate in top management selection leading to that gift of grace that is charisma. The quote comes from a head-hunter explaining his criteria for the selection of candidates:

A top executive must have stature and poise. Someone needs to move with focus, crisply and gracefully. They need to make the first move to shake hands (two strong shakes). I know if they are listening if they lean forward when they sit. They should be able to lead with small talk, but quickly get into the heart of the matter. They can't appear to be easily flustered . . . I have to have the impression that someone else – a secretary or assistant – is handling the details of their life . . . [David] did not display any of this, so he was off my list. (p. 154)

Impression management reigns, then, in the selection of executives for corporate governance positions and with it the psycho-sociological mechanisms described by attribution theory.

In this book we build upon the work of Stewart (1991), Heenan and Bennis (1999), Khurana (2002), O'Toole, Galbraith, and Lawler (2002), Sally (2002), and Pearce and Conger (2003), all of whom question two basic assumptions: (1) that executive leadership is a solely individualistic job; and (2) that trust-based interpersonal relationships at the top must be viewed with suspicion.

Many individualist assumptions of leadership are reinforced by the overwhelming dominance of the agency theory, as Daily, Dalton, and Cannella (2003) have recognized. This dominance was especially intense in the 1990s – precisely the years when corporate governance gained academic recognition, and reforms in practice started to spread throughout the world. It was not until the 1990s, for instance, that boards tended to adopt a more proactive stance (Carter and Lorsch, 2004). This theoretical dominance took place in spite of mounting evidence of the importance of process and executives' conduct for board performance (McNulty and Pettigrew, 1999).

Organizational behavior, organizational theory, and economic sociology have created a number of micro, meso, and institutional alternatives to agency theory. Such is the variety of hypotheses, concepts, and variables posed as alternatives to the agency theory constructs, that Zajac and Westphal (1998) have characterized these perspectives as a loose complex of behavioral approaches, defined primarily by what they are not: economic frameworks. Role theory is not usually registered within the behavioral perspectives, but it probably should be (Stewart, 1982). Roles are a collection of behaviors, bundled together as activities aimed at fulfilling certain expected tasks. Roles at the top are the building blocks of corporate political design to which we apply a contingency logic. Chapter 3 is devoted to them.

The social opportunity of the book

In the first years of the first decade of the first century of the new millennium, the ideological, legal, and media contexts are not especially supportive of executives. They have become the usual suspects when a corporation experiences poor results, even though research continues to show that the ability of top management or leaders to influence results is often minor or highly contingent upon the situation or the sector (Wasserman, 2003). And, of course, they are also the public scapegoats of choice in cases of corporate misbehavior, as in the *cause célèbre* of Martha Stewart. A clear example of this anti-top-management feeling was a 2003 front cover of the *Wall Street Journal* caricaturing a group of executives in the typical and stigmatizing striped prison uniform. This atmosphere of distrust is common to both the US and European business systems, signifying that the "CEO's lot is not a happy one," as revealed in the title of an interview with New York Times company president and CEO Russell Lewis (Lewis, 2002).

In the case of corporate governance, the media scrutiny is not merely the result of new developments, but of an ongoing trend that began more than a decade ago. As early as 1995, Margaret Blair was noting four main concerns about corporate governance: the US economy's loss of competitiveness; takeovers, buyouts, and restructuring; huge self-proposed executive salaries; and the success of capitalism.

(1) As early as the mid-1980s, the US economy was experiencing a loss of competitiveness compared to Japan and Germany. One of the reasons posed at the time was Germany and Japan's long-term approach – one in which stakeholders had a bigger say than did US stakeholders.

(2) Market myopia was rampant in the USA: hostile takeovers, leveraged buyouts, and other corporate restructurings, all emphasizing the short-term approach to decision-making among American executives. The debate about the economic and social effectiveness of these practices and the theory that inspired them has not yet been resolved. Jensen (2000) has stated that this debate is not only academic but also political, social, and ideological. In fact, agency theory is one of the most interesting cases in the field of social and economic sciences, in that it generates the hard-core nucleus of an ideology – neoliberalism – that when put into practice gives greater impetus to the theory.

(3) There were large increases in executive compensation packages. In the 1990s, boards of directors were charged with keeping executives in check as a mechanism for stopping the rampant self-awarded salaries. However, the apparent failure of some boards to control the salaries of CEOs and other executives has meant that it is now the shareholders who begin to voice disapproval of the compensation packages in their annual meetings.

(4) The systems and practices of corporate governance have been under intense scrutiny, as if the capitalist system, no longer having a competitive systemic alternative to beat, had turned its destructive energies on itself.

The criticism of executives is still going strong. Yet there is little evidence for system-wide problems, and less evidence yet that executives are responsible for such problems. The most common and better-known criticism, defended by agency theory, is that executives take personal advantage of the asymmetry of information, which they enjoy because of their position as agents, to promote strategies that maximize the values to which their compensation packages are indexed. Or that managers use their personal and professional connections with members of boards, analysts, and regulators to avoid being monitored and checked. It is not surprising, then, that an abundance of professional and ethical criticism has been leveled, above all, at executives and board directors – the very groups upon which we focus in this book. Revealingly, criticisms have not been equally aimed at middle management, employees, shareholders, or institutional investors.

In contrast to this suspicion about the upper echelons of organizations, respected authors such as Kanter, Kotter, Mintzberg, and Pfeffer, agree that executives are answerable to a long list of constituencies, whose interests and pressures must be constantly assessed and balanced. These executives are not, then, the powerful actors that most people assume them to be. Rather, they are less powerful figures, with a perpetual deficit of political capital *vis à vis* the responsibilities and results demanded of them.

There is an irony in that the norms of good governance laid down by the capitalist regulators seem to share with the ideological left the assumptions of the negative consequences of the interlocking relationships among the managerial elite.[4]

The broader expected social repercussion of this book resides in the recognition that interpersonal relationships between governance actors exist, are real, and are essential to corporate governance. This recognition occurs at a time when the regulators and the media suspect all close relationships among the actors of corporate governance, as reflected in the increment in rules and regulations inspired by agency theory that combat these relationships. Of course, we are not the first to have this intent. We again acknowledge a distinguished predecessor, Rosemary Stewart. In her 1991 piece on a topic that a decade later has elicited academic and social debate (the dual versus independent structures of CEOs and chairs of boards), Stewart uses a role-theory perspective, understanding roles as social domains of actions to be enacted by their incumbents with political purposes and seeing positive interpersonal

---

[4] There has never been enough proof of that unity for action, except in specific cases such as the one described by Palmer and Barber (2001).

relationships between CEOs and chairs as the key to successful corporate governance. As we were working on the final version of the book, a piece destined to influence the field greatly appeared, arguing that actual relationships at the top cannot be assumed *ex ante* to follow agency theory postulates (Roberts, McNulty, and Stiles, 2005).

In summary, we employ two basic academic tactics to understand the phenomenon of small numbers at the top and the design of corporate political structures. First, we apply contingency theory to vertical structures. Second, we use roles as the differentiated building blocks of those structures, and claim that sustained interpersonal relationships are the most important integrating mechanism at the apex. In the ambiguous, imperfect, and uncertain world of executives, to use the highly literary three-adjective expression of Coffey, Athos, and Raynolds (1968), it should be no surprise that interpersonal relationships are important mechanisms for coping with the political and psychological dimensions of that job environment. Revisiting interpersonal relationships at the top, and analyzing what constitutes them – trust, affection, partnerships, and emotions – is the best antidote for agency theory.

The work leading to the book

The idea for this book developed during our work on a project on new organizational forms that was related to a multi-national effort on that topic led by Arie Lewin at Duke University. We targeted film production companies for the many insights they could provide: insights into agile structures capable of handling expansion during filming and contraction between projects; into the challenges of collaboration among talented, star professionals like producers, creatives, and technicians; into the uncertainty of what is needed to produce a hit; and into the importance of professional networks.

The starting point for our journey was to conduct an in-depth study of three cases that we believed would provide understanding of the industry drivers for agile organizational design and the basics of professional collaboration. We decided to focus on three Spanish directors and their production companies: José Luis Garci, Fernando Trueba, and Pedro Almodóvar. Garci had won an Oscar for Best Foreign Film in 1982, as did Trueba in 1993, and Almodóvar had been a nominee for his film *Women on the Verge of a Nervous Breakdown*. All were reasonably well known, at least in the world of Spanish filmmaking, had established their own production structures, and had directed very different types of film.

The director who was most open to our request for access was Pedro Almodóvar, despite the hectic schedule that he and his team were experiencing with the promotion of his latest film around Europe and the USA. We were granted access to El Deseo SA, the production company established by him and his brother Agustín. During the period 1999–2001, we made several visits to the company premises, conducting interviews, spending time with the team, and studying the company's archival materials. During our field research, our initial interest was surpassed by a greater one, as our focus shifted to a study of the relationship between the director and Agustín, his brother and managerial *alter ego*. Despite his reputation for seeking control over all the processes and people involved in his movies, we found that Pedro Almodóvar confided fully in Agustín, who was not only the executive producer of his films, but also the CEO of El Deseo SA.

We presented our first results from the Almodóvar study and our first theoretical forays on the topic of role-sharing at the top at a number of academic forums. The reaction we obtained motivated us to continue working on the topic of two or more individuals sharing leadership positions. During our presentations, colleagues suggested that power-sharing was not limited to creative enterprises and that similar phenomena were spread across sectors and countries. The positive classroom reception granted to our teaching case on Almodóvar's production company (Alvarez and Svejenova, 2000) in business schools in Europe and in the USA kept our spirits high. We acknowledge that an important part of the interest in our work may be attributed to the ever-increasing fame of the subject of our main case study. Pedro Almodóvar won an Oscar for Best Foreign Film with *All About My Mother* just weeks after we began our first fieldwork on this project. In 2003, he won another Oscar, this time for Best Original Script for *Talk to Her*. These were exceptional achievements for the filmmaker, and timely events for the diffusion of our research.

In the summer of 2002, two articles appeared in *California Management Review*, one by O'Toole, Galbraith, and Lawler (2002), and the other by Sally (2002). Both dealt with issues similar to those we have chosen for our study, and these happenings finally convinced us to continue the pursuit of our topic. So we embarked on the adventure of writing this book.

We have conceived this text in the genre of an academic essay in the broad field of organizational theory or sociology of organizations. Books have a flow and rhythm different from those of the tightly argued short pieces published in academic journals. Books are less constrained by the protocols of research presentation and leave room for the authors to be more revealing not only in the logic of their reasoning but also in their intellectual itinerary. We have tried to provide sufficient academic references so the reader can easily track the origins of the notions or arguments we develop, but it has not been our intention to be exhaustive. However, in selected cases we have gone to extra lengths to describe or justify essential points (by, for example, emphasizing a long list of potential contingencies and by providing a sizeable table of examples of co-leadership arrangements), in an attempt to underline the significance of the phenomenon at the heart of this book. Where available, we have referenced well-known, high-quality texts to illustrate some developments in the literature, rather than discussing these developments at length in our book. An example is Finkelstein and Hambrick's (1996) book on strategic leadership, which we have cited for further reading on a perspective that is very important to our topic. In some cases, even though the arguments are as well known as the evolution of political theories of organizations or role theory, we discuss them at some length because we believe that the discussion will help the reader to understand our idiosyncratic concerns and intentions.

Considering, as well, that books, unlike journal articles, are often started without an end game prepared in detail, we occasionally make unexpected theoretical *detours* and abandon some expected routes. Now that we have completed this volume, we are more convinced than ever that our chosen topic deserves our efforts and enthusiasm, and, above all, further research. We will be satisfied if our contributions heighten interest in it.

Plan of the book

The book consists of two parts. Part I (Chapters 1–3) advances the conceptual background of the book and deals with the essential contingencies and roles in the structuring of corporate power. Part II

(Chapters 4–6) focuses on the phenomenon of small numbers at the top and examines the nature and dynamics of structures of twosomes, threesomes, and larger executive constellations.

Chapter 1 is our conceptual starting point. In it we attempt to explain the existence of small-number arrangements at the top from the perspective of organizational design. We first justify, through a brief evaluation of structural theories of organization, the application of contingency theory (in conjunction with ideas from political theories of organizations) to corporate governance bodies such as executive committees, CEO offices, and boards of directors. Next, we review the numerous heterogeneous external, internal, and executive contingencies identified by the literature as having importance in the design of organizations as a whole. Finally, after an examination of the task requirements of work at the top, we propose six main contingencies, two each of the external, internal, and executive environments, that we believe to be peculiar to the design of corporate power structures.

Chapter 2 provides arguments for the difficulties of managing solo at the top without the support of a power-sharing structure or any other form of executive constellation. We discuss the consequences of organizational size and environmental complexity for the increasing variety of tasks to be performed at the corporate apex, as revealed in the classic works of Stewart (1967), Mintzberg (1980), and Kotter (1985), among others. These increasingly complex tasks brought, in turn, increasingly differentiated dilemmas, paradoxes, and dualities to executives.

(1) Geographical expansion and technological leaps led to tensions between exploration and exploitation, and between innovation and control.

(2) Size and complexity extended the range of differing dilemmas regarding priorities and actions: external versus internal, management or predictability versus leadership or change, managing up versus managing down, and managing the present versus managing for the future, among others.

(3) The number of roles in the corporate office increased with the division of decision-making rights among the CEO, the president, and the chair of the board.

Chapter 2 also details the political challenges of managers at the corporate pinnacle. In it we maintain that these political challenges cannot be easily and efficiently satisfied without the support of close coalitions and alliances, thus providing further reason for the spread of small-numbers arrangements at the top.

In Chapter 3, we further advance the conceptual foundations of our contingency perspective of corporate political structures. We introduce roles and relationships as two essential parameters of political design that, considered in conjunction, help to explain differentiation and integration of vertical structures. We argue that from a contingency theory stance, roles are vehicles of differentiation, whereas relationships of differing nature and strength are mechanisms of integration. In this chapter, we seek to establish a bridge between the extensive scholarly work on roles and relationships and the literature on corporate governance and top management. It provides a review of pertinent work on roles and relationships that we believe can enhance understanding of the design and dynamics of small-numbers power structures. We discuss the resource view of roles and suggest that roles can be a useful political resource of governance and a means of creativity in the design of vertical structures. Next, we introduce a range of role-related processes, such as creation, consolidation, sharing, separation, and integration of roles, all of which serve to illuminate the variability in the genesis and development of small numbers at the top. Finally, we scrutinize relationships as the mechanisms that help achieve role integration, an underdeveloped yet highly important area in corporate governance, by delving into three essential types of relationship: shared cognition, affection, and trust. We conclude that trust among executives is the distinctive, and often the only, integration mechanism at the top. We argue that trust should be much stronger among executives than it is at lower organizational levels because of the uncertainty, unpredictability, and imperfection of the executive world.

The gist of Chapter 3 is that executives have at their discretion, by tampering with roles, alternative designs for the corporate power structures they inhabit, allowing them to address the critical contingencies they face.

In Chapter 4, we examine the nature and types of professional duos, distinguishing them from the broad and general sociological concept of the dyad. In order to advance understanding on this particular small-numbers arrangement, we interweave notions from the sociological and social-psychological literature on dyads with insights from both historical and contemporary cases of professional duos. Two types of professional duo are differentiated and discussed: the hierarchical type, of which CEO–COO is probably the most commonly recognized, and the partnership, exemplified by co-CEOs and co-chairs.

In Chapter 4 we also scrutinize the processes that can transform a dyad (a basic unit of two individuals) into a professional duo (a dyad with committed working relationships for a given period), which, in turn, can dissolve over time, or increase in commitment to become what in Chapter 6 we label "united careers." As an illustration of the milestones of the process, the case of Sun Microsystems' former hierarchical duo of CEO Scott McNealy and COO Edward Zander is discussed at length. Finally, we comment on the inherent instabilities of professional duos as a vertical structure and the range of decoupling and exit strategies that the partners in the duo might experience or undertake.

The theoretical insight and examples that we advance in Chapter 4 help to explain why duos are the most widespread and resilient of all the small-number options. Thus:

(1) They overcome fundamental dualities in executive work.

(2) Because a dyad is a structure of two often-complementary individuals, it allows for the full deployment of the individuality of the executives within their own domain.

(3) Entering one of these dyads demands strong commitment. Under the scrutiny of the business community and the media, the making and breaking of such commitments may have an effect on reputation and career. Managers must be cautious when ending a duo relationship, because it can have both personal and professional costs.

Chapter 5 presents a definition and analysis of threesomes and foursomes, as small numbers at the top with particular power dynamics. We build upon Simmel's (1950) work on triads; that of Hodgson, Levinson, and Zaleznik (1965) on executive constellations; as well as that of Krackhardt (1999) on Simmelian ties.

Several historical triumvirates are discussed in this chapter, including the consulates of the Roman Empire, the Directorates in Revolutionary France, and the Soviet troikas of the late 1960s and the 1970s. The chapter also provides a basic typology of the games that are played when power is shared *à trois*: Simmel's original *tertius* strategies, such as mediator and arbitrator, the *tertius gaudens* strategy developed much more recently by Burt (1992), and the *divide et impera* game. These strategies are illustrated with contemporary business triumvirates at the helm of Citigroup, Viacom, Google, Loews, and La Caixa, the largest Spanish savings and loans institution.

Triads and larger small-numbers combinations differ fundamentally from duos in three ways. Two of these ways are psychological: triads break the bias toward the preservation of individuality and the exclusivity in the domain of the relationship. A third difference is structural: because triads are composed of too many people for role-sharing to be convenient, role distribution, which reduces the need for trust, is more characteristic. These three mutually reinforcing traits suggest that each member of the triad can more easily be replaced by a new member than can members of a dyad. Consequently, triads may favor the emergence of politics at the top – the development of alliances to overcome the power of the *tertium*. As a consequence, many triumvirates are unstable and transient.

Chapter 6 sheds light on a long-term, committed form of partnership at the corporate apex, one that we have labeled "united career." In that chapter we define a united career as a durable, coordinated task collaboration in the working lives of two or more professionals, in which the career of one individual evolves with that of other individual(s) through a series of joint vertical, lateral, or cross-organizational moves. We distinguish it from other career phenomena and strategies, such as dual career, co-work, and mentor–protégé. We argue that unraveling manifestations of united careers is not straightforward, because the strength of the relationship, as well as the joint career decisions and moves, cannot be easily deduced from job titles.

Chapter 6 provides some examples of united careers in domains in which they are most frequently found, such as the creative sectors, science, and start-ups in general. It examines four cases of united careers from different businesses: Goldman Sachs' former co-CEOs John Whitehead and John Weinberg; Oscar award winner Pedro Almodóvar, film director, and his brother, Agustín, producer and manager; Spain's Banco Popular's co-chairs, the brothers Luis (who stepped down in late 2004, after more than three decades at the top) and Javier Valls; and Sony Corporation's co-founders, Masaru Ibuka and Akiro Morita. Our focus is on the dynamic of the career coupling and the mechanisms used by individuals with united careers to combine their career trajectories successfully. Finally, we explore the implications of such career coupling for corporate power structures and governance, for the individuals involved, and for the organizations where such united careers are housed.

The concluding chapter builds on the arguments developed in the previous chapters and summarizes our assessment of the capability of each of the different small-numbers alternatives (duos, trios, and four-somes) to deal with the contingencies that drive the design of structures at the apex of organizations that we detail in Chapter 1. We propose criteria that decision-makers should employ in assessing and choosing among their options for balancing role differentiation and people integration at the top. We also propose and evaluate three basic general corporate power regimes – Rules, Politics, and Trust. The chapter concludes with a research agenda for further understanding the design and dynamics of vertical structures and co-leadership at the top.

PART I

Contingencies and roles in structuring corporate power

1 | *Contingencies of corporate power structures*

The executive who must work with the
human materials around him must also
work with the human materials in himself.

Glover and Hower, 1963, p. 4

We believe that socio-psychological
attitudes of chief executive officers and
general managers are a critical contingency
in organizational design and strategy that
has not been developed sufficiently in
previous studies.

Lewin and Stephens, 1994, p. 183

IN THE INTRODUCTION we presented some examples of duos, trios, and other constellations at the governance level of corporations. These examples reveal combinations of role separation, role-sharing, and role integration that differ from the standard solo occupancy of corporate governance positions. They also challenge the common assumption held in corporate governance regulations and codes of best practices that affective and trust-based interpersonal relationships among top executives are to be viewed with suspicion. How then we do account for the abundance of small numbers at the top?

If a structure is not congruent with the main contingencies in its internal and external environments, performance results will be less than optimal or unsatisfactory, and will, perhaps, even lead to failure. This is a fundamental tenet of the contingency theory of organizational design. A second fundamental assumption of contingency theory, based on the principle of equifinality (Katz and Kahn, 1978; Gresov and Drazin, 1997), is that any organization can reach the same final state (e.g. a sufficient or satisfactory level of adaptation to the environment) by a variety of paths or, in this case, by different structures. There is no universal way to organize, but some designs are more efficient than others.

According to contingency theory, there could be two possible explanations for the small-numbers phenomenon in executive committees, CEO offices, and boards of directors. Either there are some contexts and some contingencies specific to decision-making structures for which small numbers of executives at the top constitute the best possible arrangement, or small numbers are, if not the optimal configuration, at least good enough to satisfy both business and institutional criteria as well as the personal preferences of executives by, for instance, allowing them to work with people for whom they feel affection or professional trust (Lewin and Stephens, 1994; Hambrick and Cannella, 2004). Corporate political structures are highly discretionary structures. Their incumbents determine not only the architecture of the subordinate non-political layers – horizontal structures such as functions, divisions, business units, and departments – but also the very design, composition, and processes of executive committees, top task forces, CEO offices, and (to some extent) boards of directors. In short, corporate political structures design themselves and this reflective, self-referencing characteristic is a key to corporate power structuring.

The goal of this chapter is to foster an understanding of the reasons for small executive arrangements at the top from the perspective of organizational design. We begin by justifying the application of contingency theory, the conceptual framework unanimously considered to be central to the field of organizational design, to executive committees, CEO offices, and boards of directors. We believe that contingency theory combined with some of the ideas inherent in political theories of organizations as they apply to corporate power structures, is the best way to tackle the academic challenges alluded to in our Introduction to this book. We also review the numerous heterogeneous external, internal, and executive contingencies that have been identified in the literature as drivers for the design of organizations as a whole. Finally, we propose six main contingencies peculiar to the design of corporate power structures. Small numbers of executives at the apex of organizations, we argue in this book, is a viable structural option for adaptation to these contingencies.

Political and contingency theories of organizations

Contingency theory shares some common history with what we consider to be the most fruitful traditions in the political theories of organizations. This section begins with our own interpretation of the fate of these political arguments. We tackle these political theories first because they were developed earlier in the evolution of organizational theories than were design theories. In fact, the first non-economic conceptions of complex organizations were highly political. Although other brief presentations of these developments are available,[1] we summarize them here in order to make patent the theoretical motivations that we bring to the topic of corporate power design.

The emergence of macro-political theories of organizations

Political theories of organizations have had a discontinuous evolution in organizational theory, characterized by periods of strong influence followed by periods of minimal impact. They re-emerge regularly in various forms and with different emphases, but are none the less recognizable in their basic identity – one characterized by three fundamental ideas: organizations as plural systems, organizations as goal-drifting systems, and power structures as *pièces de résistance* of the organizational architecture.

 Perhaps the most important political characteristic of organizations is their plurality and internal heterogeneity; organizations are multigoal, non-unitary systems that depend for their functioning upon the active management of a plurality of social groups that are both internal and external to the formal boundaries of the organization and that represent differentiated interests and competing claims on resources. This pluralistic viewpoint is contrary to that held by the strongly unitary and, as Michael and Hambrick (1992, p. 17) say, "dubious" Barnard and against current economic theories of the firm, which make shareholders' interests the dominant ones. That very plurality is the reason, as Bendix (1956) recalls, for Weber proposing that the specific task of leadership was to promote social ideologies of power and subordination, without which it becomes difficult to hold organizational groups

---

[1] For an insightful summary, see Davis and Thompson (1994).

together. Since Weber, political concepts such as authority, legitimacy, domination, and subordination have been applied to economic organizations.

A second characteristic, organizations as goal-drifting systems, is a consequence of the necessary openness of organizations to their environment. Cooptation, the mechanism employed by organizations to balance the pressures, interests, and influences of the external social groups, results in the transformation of the original organizational goals into new emergent purposes (Selznick, 1957) or in the drift into mindless routines (Snook, 2000). The *corruzione* of original organizational goals, therefore, has striking similarities to an analogous drift which Machiavelli found in other polities such as Italian Renaissance city-states: the *corruzione* of civic conviviality (Pocock, 1975). It also reminds one of the vices, which Plato described as corrupting the basic types of political regimes and bringing about the replacement of one regime by another. Thus, according to the political theses of organizations, these are essentially weak, entropic, and transitory regimes.

A third essential component of the identity of political hypotheses is derived primarily from Michels' work on the leadership of socialist parties in the early twentieth century. The realm in which the most eventful political dynamics occur is the strategic leadership or upper echelons of organizations because it is at the highest strata where organizations encounter the political, social, and institutional environments (Parsons, 1956a, 1956b) and because it is in that domain that executive committees, CEOs, and boards of directors decide on the most important organizational elements. As Glover and Hower (1963) state:

Also determined at the top management level are such matters as the main features of the overall organizational structures, and the principal assignments of personnel, and the major allocations of capital funds. It is at that level, also, that the value system of the organization and the philosophy of management are shaped. (p. ix)

The corporate apex also holds decision rights over its own structure. Burns (1961) says of a CEO:

As the ultimate controller, he sets the goals . . . sets the parameters of the task and activities of groups and persons. As the patron of the concern, he specifies the measure of privilege and rights attached to lower positions.

The system and structure of management are both determined largely by him. Above all, he is the ultimate authority for appointment and promotion. (p. 211)

In the following pages we discuss in more detail the historical development of these three fundamental characteristics of the political view of organizations.

The first of these traits – organizations as plural systems – emphasized the heterogeneity of organizations. Because of that diversity, ideologies of power and subordination holding the organization together and legitimizing hierarchies are critical. Scholars dealing with the transition from traditional to industrial societies were puzzled by the existence of what Bendix (1956) called "good will," what Barnard (1938) called the "zone of indifference," and what Simon (1945) called the "zone of acceptance": the provision of effort, subordination, and discipline by the employees, without explicit coercion on the part of the organization's superordinates. Bendix *Work and Authority in Industry* (1956) confirmed that organizational ideologies must link up with broader social and political ideologies in order to provide corporations with the legitimacy needed to maintain organizational order, the old Hobbesian concern and one of the key tasks of what years later would come to be called corporate governance.

Subsequent to Bendix, it was the work of Etzioni (1961) that was most concerned with the legitimacies that sustain organizational order. His key concept was compliance, which can be divided into two types: (1) the orientation studied by Bendix – that which subordinates hold toward the legitimacy of the organization's institutional powers; and (2) the power used by superordinates in order to control subordinates, a concept closer to the notion of power put forward by French and Raven (1959).

In spite of Etzioni's contribution, the attention to the first political aspects of organizations, namely those centered on their legitimacy to compensate for their internal diversity, lost ground in the 1960s. This was the time when the primary concern of organization studies became the exploration of variables measuring horizontal structures such as specialization, standardization, configuration, formalization, and centralization.

Nearly a decade elapsed before another important attempt was made to conceptualize organizations as political entities. This time it was centered on the second of the three basic political characteristics of organizations mentioned: the displacement of goals as a consequence of the openness of the organizations to their environments.

Building on Michel and Selznick, in an attempt to refocus organization studies toward power realities, Zald (1969) acknowledged the fundamental importance of the question: "Whose goals are maximized and with what consequences?" To answer that question, Zald resorted to the notion of organizations as polities based on constitutions. *A la* Parsons, these constitutions contain:

(1) the rules of belonging or inclusion of individuals in organizations, regulating the dedication of time, energy, and motivation of employees;
(2) the autonomy and decision-making rights of the different groups and organizational levels;
(3) the relationships between the organization and society, or what today would be called corporate social responsibility; and
(4) the business domain of the organization, or decisions about the products or services that should be produced for which clients and with which technologies.

Zald (1970) proposed a "political economy" of organizations: "political," because he understood organizations to be political systems with internal elements (succession mechanisms of the elites, power distribution, and corporate values) as well as external elements (primarily relationships with stakeholders); and "economy," because he considered organizations to be productive systems with both internal elements (such as formal control systems, rules for resource distribution, incentive systems, and division of labor) and external elements (such as production factors and sector dynamics). In a classic institutional study, Zald (1970) applied this model to an analysis of the transformation of the Young Men's Christian Association (YMCA) of Chicago from a missionary religious agency to a secular social services agency that targeted the integration of marginal sectors of the population. Zald describes how the external groups modified the objectives of the YMCA through their influence over its control and resource allocation systems.

Zald did not address the third characteristic of the political view of organizations, which is the critical role of the upper echelons in the social, political, and structural design of the organization: shaping structures, defining common interests, developing coalitions around those interests, and mobilizing resources and profit from opportunities. Both Weber and Parsons had estimated these tasks to be of even greater importance than organizational values.

Micro impulses to political theories of organizations

These works did not make a permanent impact – neither the works of Etzioni and Zald, both of whom were eminently Parsonian in their functionalist emphasis on classification and integration of political, social, and economic dimensions; nor the works of institutionalists who, like Bendix and Selznick, exhibited a preoccupation with aligning ideologies, power, and organizational goals. However, other studies originating in social psychology and linking the power dynamics of micro and macro social levels later elevated the topic of power to a central position in the field of organization studies.

The first study of power in the field of social psychology that greatly influenced the field of organizational sociology was French and Raven's well-known 1959 work on the bases of social power. In 1962 Emerson confirmed French and Raven's logic in another micro and deductive work, making it even more explicit that power should be treated as an attribute, not of social actors, but of their relationships. Emerson's strategy was to strip the discussion on power of any unnecessary political, social, and organizational variables. As a unit of analysis he chose the dyad, whereby each individual tries with calculating rationality to minimize dependence on, or to increase influence over, the other. The result of these motions depends on the power bases and tactical skills of each actor. The power of Actor A over Actor B is the quantity of resistance by B that A can overcome. The dependence that B has on Actor A is directly proportional to the motivational investment of B in goals mediated by A and inversely proportional to the possibility of B's satisfying those goals through relationships other than the one held with A.

The main advantage of Emerson's dynamic framework of power is his logic of action, the human impetus that he uses as the basic mechanism for the explanation of political tactics that can be observed in organizational settings: minimizing dependence. Within this logic are four basic tactics:

(1) the reduction of motivational investment in the desired objectives in order to reduce dependence on the facilitators of those wants (withdrawal or avoidance);

(2) the development of social networks that may facilitate other routes to the achievement of those objectives (bypassing);

(3) the establishment of coalitions by the weaker party to counteract the powerful actor (coalitions); and

(4) the increase of motivational investment by the more powerful party in the relationship by acknowledging the higher status of that party (flattery).

As Hegel well knew, even in the most asymmetrical relationships, there is always a simultaneous give and take of autonomy and dependence, and, hence, some space for tactics by the weaker party.

Emerson's framework fits perfectly into such social systems as organizations because they are, by definition, based on the interdependence of people and units – a concept at the core of contingency theory. However, in order for Emerson to become a real influence in the field of organizational theory, the dynamics of his framework, one intended for dyadic relationships between individuals or between abstract parties, had to be translated into interorganizational and intraorganizational levels. The author who made this leap in levels of analysis was James D. Thompson. As we said of Emerson, it is difficult to exaggerate Thompson's influence in the field. Few works give the impression that a turning point has been reached in an academic field, but Thompson accomplished this with his book *Organizations in Action* (1967), a concise publication of less than two hundred pages (Scott, 2003).

Thompson's fundamental idea is that organizations seek to survive through the rational and instrumental attainment of goals. This rationality is the basic principle of legitimacy for structured collective action in contemporary societies. There are two basic requirements for the rational attainment of goals: (1) to reach an internal alignment among the three common subsystems of business organizations – operative, executive, and institutional – without which there is no organized collective action; and (2) to eliminate or reduce the uncertainty that comes from the environmental contingencies upon which the organization is dependent. Organizations are in the midst of webs of dependent relationships, both internal (among the distinct subsystems) and external (with several environments, e.g. legal, business, and ideological), as well as vertically and horizontally (Gresov, 1990). A rational strategy for reducing dependencies is structural differentiation: organizational subunits become specialized in homogeneous segments of the environment with which they establish the most stable relationships possible. The influence of this argument was evidenced fifteen years later in the publication of Tom Peters and Bob Waterman's (1982) bestselling management book *In Search of Excellence*. They indicated that the key to successful implementation was two alignments. The first was internal to the organization: a search for alignment among Peters and Waterman's seven Ss or organizational elements: strategy, structure, systems, styles, skills, staff, and shared values. The second was external: between the organization and the environment through the choice of the most appropriate tasks and technologies.

Thompson further contributed the point that the challenge of the managerial process lies not only in eliminating uncertainty by fit with existing contingencies but also in providing potential for maneuverability and flexibility for the future. The balance between, on the one hand, the search for certainty or stability through the specialization of tasks, and on the other hand, the flexibility and loose alignment (what Hedberg, Nystrom, and Starbuck (1976) called the "value of imperfection"), is what Thompson called the "paradox of administration." A decade later, Pascale (1990) and Kotter and Heskett (1992) illustrated the success of organizations that managed to sustain both alignment and flexibility in the long run.

The job of top executives is further complicated because each organizational subsystem, in applying itself to distinct tasks and environments, develops differentiated cognitive biases and interests. Thus, the challenge of managing is not merely analytical, but is also one of political accommodation of heterogeneous positions and claims. On this point, Thompson builds on the work of Cyert and March (1963), who emphasized the internal plurality of organizations, our first characteristic of the political view of organizations. Task specialization produces two types of bias, one conscious and calculating, aimed at furthering personal, departmental, or other interests; and another more interesting bias that may work unconsciously to achieve the same aim. Therefore, in order to understand actors' dispositions, decisions and, ultimately, actions, the organizational structure must be factored into the equation.

In order to deal with those biases without losing too much alignment, the executive must be a "superb politician" (Thompson, 1967, p. 143) who recognizes that formal authority is probably insufficient to meet all expectations and fulfill all responsibilities. The establishments of alliances and of an inner circle or dominant coalition are essential resources for the executive. As the next chapter details, compensating for the executive's inherent deficit of political capital is an endless task, and one of the major reasons for the existence of small numbers at the top.

As Tushman (1977) noted, organizational politics and design moved closer together in Thompson's work because he added a micro, internal, and structural argument to the traditional macro-political hypothesis, which was focused on the consequences of cooptation: displacement of goals. Thompson believed that the partition of organizations into specialized units and positions created cognitive predispositions and social dispositions, leading to politics.

After Cyert and March (1963), Crozier (1964), and Thompson (1967) had drawn attention to interdepartmental power, this topic attracted influential scholars, such as the members of the Aston Group, Pettigrew (1973), Pfeffer and Salancik (1978), and Bacharach and Lawler (1980). However, Perrow (1986) criticized several of these authors for their undue focus on measuring the several dimensions of horizontal structures while neglecting to explore vertical structures such as executive committees, CEO offices, boards, shareholders' general meetings, institutional investors, and stakeholders – the key actors in what today constitutes the field of corporate governance. Not even contingency theory, the most influential school of organizational design, was systematically applied to the structuring of corporate power.

Such theoretical voids on important topics invite their filling. In this case, the political structure of organizations, its design and influence, the third fundamental characteristic of the political view of organizations posited at the beginning of this chapter, was not fully addressed by organizational theorists. That vacancy was occupied by agency theory, a political theory in disguise (Finkelstein and Hambrick, 1996).

In the following pages we present a detailed review of contingency theory and attempt to select those of its elements that could apply to the design of the vertical structures. As mentioned at the beginning of this chapter, we believe that this approach is an alternative to the hegemony of agency theory in the field of corporate power structures.

Contingency theory

Reviews of contingency theory (Padgett, 1992; Pennings, 1992; Galunic and Eisenhardt, 1994) often begin with the statement that this school has dominated the field of organizational design from the second half of the 1960s. Scott (2003) goes even further, ranking contingency theory as the most important organizational theory ever. Contributing to its continuous hegemony are its broad tenets: first, that there is no single way to organize and, second, that not all structures are equally efficient. In fact, the main criticisms of contingency theory are aimed at its broadness and the consequent impediments to falsification (Ellis, Almor, and Shenkar, 2002).

At the beginning of the twenty-first century, these basic contingency ideas may seem to be nothing more than common sense. It should be noted, however, that if a *longue durée* perspective is adopted, the availability of theories that try to capture a society filled with large complex organizations is relatively recent. Contingency ideas were much more novel in the 1950s. The pervasive appeal of contingency theory is also explained by the fact that it often refers to organizational design understood in a sense that is wider than that of formal structures. In a popular definition, Lorsch and Morse (1974) apply the term "organizational design" not only to the planning of the management structure (division of labor, special integrating roles and units, teams and task forces, hierarchy, rules and procedures, plans, and goals), but also to such formal organizational variables as measurement and evaluation practices (performance appraisal practices, control systems, and information systems); reward schemes (compensation schemes, promotion practices, jobs, and assignment practices); and selection and development systems (recruiting and selection practices, training and development practices). Even the term "structure" often carries a meaning broader than that of formal organizational charts. Fombrun (1986) argues, for instance, that structure refers to three distinct realities: repetitive activities, social and political networks, and social interpretations and meanings. Drazin and Sandelands (1992) argue, similarly, that there are three levels of structure: deep (tacit rules), elemental (interactions among actors), and observed (social facts). Although contingent ideas became dominant in regard to formal structures, there is still some research directed at proving the applicability of contingent frameworks in areas such as human resources and leadership, topics for which universalistic or essentialist ideas are difficult to dispel. In fact, in order to distinguish the contingency theory that refers to formal structures from theories based on contingent ideas that refer to other management topics, many authors use the expression "structural contingency theory" (Hickson, Hinings, Lee, Schneck, and Pennings, 1971; Cohen and Lachman, 1988; Galunic and Eisenhardt, 1994; Ellis, Almor, and Shenkar, 2002).

A contingency is defined as a manifestation of the context that an organization must adapt to in order to secure its survival or to achieve satisfactory performance. Luthans and Stewart (1977) emphasize the functionalist nature of contingency approaches: "The contingency approach is defined as identifying and developing functional relationships between environmental, management and performance variables" (p. 183). "Adaptation," in this context, refers to the adoption of a particular structural form to fit a specific context, which is, by definition, more powerful than the organization itself (Donaldson, 2001). In the words of Thompson (1967, p. 24), contingencies are "factors not subject to arbitrary control by the organization." Contingencies are "determinants" (Miller and Dröge, 1986, p. 543). Contingents are drivers of design. It is the organization that adapts to the contingencies and not the other way around.

We now move to a description of the most important contingencies identified in the literature, then to the ones that we believe to be the drivers of corporate power structures.

External contingencies

Contingencies located outside the organizational boundaries and within the so-called external environment were the first to be identified by scholars working on the morphology of organizations. The vocabulary that was employed in naming them, as well as their precise conceptual demarcations, varies. However, we can list the external contingencies on which most authors would agree.

Uncertainty is perhaps the most general contingency. Donaldson (2001) regards it as the most important, and affirms that it underlies most other external contingencies. By "uncertainty" we mean that the results of actions, either by actors in the environment or by the focal organization, are unpredictable because the probability distribution of outcomes is unknown, or is based merely upon a subjective

guess. Uncertainty is problematic because it clouds cause-effect relationships of events and, as a consequence, contributes to the executives' lack of reliable parameters for action. Furthermore, the time-span
of definitive feedback – the speed at which the environment provides
data on the effects of an organization's actions – is either too short
or too long to support decision-making. Specifically, the ability to
cope with external uncertainty, controlling for a number of factors,
including substitutability (availability of alternative sources for coping
with uncertainty), centrality (when important decision-making processes pass through the focal actor), and pervasiveness (the focal actor
is directly linked with many members of the organization), is the key
to internal organizational relevance and, therefore, the key to organizational power (Hambrick, 1981a; Cohen and Lachman, 1988).

Industry dynamism is another classic contingency. It is related to
the complexity and predictability of the business environment. Product life-cycle and intensity of competition are the two most important
qualifiers of industry dynamism. Integral to industry dynamism are
three second-order contingencies: growth, volatility, and research and
development intensity. The growth of the sector in which the organization is playing may force it to increase in size in order to remain competitive and to develop maintenance and governance units. Volatility
is the extent and pace of changeability of the environment. And as for
research and development intensity, industry dynamism is, of course,
the most important factor defining the degree of placidity versus turbulence in the environment.

The contingency *task environment* refers to the players that have
exchanges with the focal organization in any given sector. It includes
competitors, suppliers of materials, capital, and labor, customers, and
even regulatory groups (Thompson, 1967; Daft, Sormunen, and Parks,
1988).

In the early 1980s, authors within the neo-institutional school (e.g.
DiMaggio and Powell, 1983; Meyer and Scott, 1983) began to recognize the importance of the non-economic dimensions of the task
environment. These new dimensions were identified as being social
and political (Pfeffer and Salancik, 1978), institutional (Levitt and
Nass, 1989; Palmer, Jennings, and Zhou, 1993), and symbolic (Meyer
and Rowan, 1977), and have become increasingly crucial to ensuring
the legitimacy of organizations. In fact, in the broad domains of corporate governance and corporate social responsibility these formerly

general and non-operational environments have been transformed into highly relevant and specific non-economic contingencies which are often played out in the judicature or in the media arena. This makes them even less controllable by business executives, who are less accustomed to dealing with contingencies that do not follow a purely economic logic of action, such as public opinion and social movements.

Technology is a contingency that embraces both the processes employed to convert inputs into outputs, and the more-or-less centralized control and integrative devices. That is, this contingency refers to both productive and administrative technologies (Miller and Dröge, 1986).

Internal contingencies

No matter how numerous and heterogeneous the potential external contingencies may be, they are not the only ones to which organizations must adapt. In the early stages of contingency theory, Duncan (1972) identified what he called internal contingencies – those located in the internal environment. The very expression "internal environment" is intriguing. It refers to *intra muros* organizational elements that are more influential and resilient than the object of organizational design – structure – which is assumed to be more adaptable. Thus, what constitutes a contingency cannot be resolved *a priori* – ontologically – but must be resolved on a situational basis.

As a consequence, and as happens in the case of the external contingencies, the list of internal contingencies is long, with a vocabulary not fully shared by all scholars. Furthermore, concepts are not neatly differentiated, although there is considerable consensus on the list described in this section: size, internal task, strategy, knowledge base, culture, and internal political processes.

Size is a classic internal contingency. It refers to the number of organizational members whose labor must be specialized and then coordinated. Through intervening variables, such as frequency of decisions and social control, size exerts an impact on the structuring of activities (task specialization, standard routines, and formal paperwork), concentration of authority (centralization of decision-making and need for a central maintenance unit), and control of workflow (either through personal or impersonal procedures). Size is among the contingencies most studied by the Aston Group, who track its origins back as far as Weber:

Once the number of positions and people grows beyond control by personal interaction, the organization must be more explicitly structured. In so far as structuring includes the concept of bureaucracy, Weber's observation that "the increasing bureaucratic organization of all genuine mass parties offers the most striking example of the role of the sheer quantity as a leverage for the bureaucratization of a social structure" is correct. (Pugh, Hickson, Hinings, and Turner, 1969, p. 112)

Lorsch and Morse (1974) provided numerous examples of internal contingencies – in fact more than twice as many as Lawrence and Lorsch (1967) had identified a few years earlier, and they had their own strict definition of internal environment:

. . . the set of signals available to organizational members about what is expected of them. These signals are shaped by the formal organization and measurement practices in the unit and by expectations of superiors, subordinates and peers . . . The internal environment is, in a sense, a mediator between the individual and the work he must perform (the external environment). Stated another way, the internal environment is man's explicit and implicit invention to help members relate to the work of the organization in dealing with the external environment. (p. 13)

Lorsch and Morse (1974) divided the broad internal contingency of *internal task* into other sub-contingencies such as: the technology used by the organization to accomplish the output required by the environment, the speed versus accuracy trade-off of the processing of throughputs, the sales and diversification of products or services, and acquisitions. Thus, technology may be either an internal or external contingency, depending on the perspective taken: either as a requirement for competitiveness externally imposed, or as the productive process that orders the internal working system.

Strategy is a significant internal contingency because of its epistemological nature: the definition of the sectors or domains relevant to the organization, the aims of the organization within that domain, and the means by which goals will be achieved. Although strategy is not necessarily rigid, it does imply commitment and permanence. Because it cannot be changed overnight or changed radically, it may become a contingency. Hambrick and Lei (1985) agree with this argument:

"another group of variables that denote a firm's strategic positions – and are therefore relatively fixed in the short run – could also be considered as contingency variables. Examples of such variables are market share, vertical integration, and brand image" (p. 768).

Several other internal contingencies are widely recognized in the literature. One is the observability and embeddedness of the organization's *knowledge base*, as it marks the domain of what the organization can do operationally, distinctively, and excellently. Another is *culture* or corporate values, the set of ideals that are permanently and deeply embedded in both procedures and behaviors. Peters and Waterman (1982) spoke of the thickness of culture as one of the causes of performance excellence.

Internal political processes, such as the power of the different units in the firm, could be seen as another contingency. In fact, departmental power and internal politics were preferred research topics for early contingency theory scholars, most of whom were Europeans – the Aston Group and Crozier, for example.

Executive environment contingencies

Along with the internal and external domains, there is yet a third domain of contingencies. Like the domain of internal contingencies, it is located *intra muros*. It refers to the top managers who work in the organization's upper echelons, and we call it the executive environment. Whereas middle managers and employees may also become internal contingencies for some organizations, they are more often considered as being located in the periphery of organizations or even *extra muros*, a variable cost and, therefore, a group to be designed rather than to drive design.

This executive environment contingency has been recognized by Lorsch and Morse (1974), Duncan (1976), Eisenhardt and Schoonhoven (1990), Miller (1991), Lewin and Stephens (1994), Merz and Sauber (1995), Hollenbeck (2002), and Beersma, Hollenbeck, Humphrey, Moon, Conlon, and Ilgen (2003), among others, and Don Hambrick and his colleagues have made it the focus of their study of the upper echelons and strategic leadership theories. There have been many important works based on this theory, such as those by Hambrick, Cho, and Chen (1996), Cannella and Monroe (1997), Hambrick and Cannella (2004), Finkelstein (1992), and Haleblian and Finkelstein

(1993); but its best and most complete presentation is probably that of Finkelstein and Hambrick (1996).

Executives are considered to be a separate internal contingency for a number of reasons: (1) because executives' mind-sets, decision-making habits, logics of action, and managing styles are highly inertial (Lewin and Stephens, 1994); (2) because executives' career success may, in specific ways, prevent self-scrutiny, double-loop learning, and further adaptation to new environments, making executives more rigid (Argyris, 1991); (3) because there is abundant evidence in the upper-echelons literature of executive entrenchment and of their "power motivation" rendering them exceedingly reluctant to surrender power easily or voluntarily; and (4) because executives, like any other organizational actor, are subject to local games for survival and pre-eminence, but the results of their games set the context for the local games of the less powerful actors (Burns, 1977). Among the currencies exclusively exchanged in executive power games are the horizontal and vertical structures of organizations. It is executives who decide the design of the parts of the political corporate structures they occupy that are not subject to compulsory regulation. For these reasons the upper echelons of organizations are also called self-discretionary structures.

As with internal and external contingencies, numerous contingencies have been identified in the executive environment.[2] Perhaps the most studied contingency in this domain is the *top management team composition*, because teams at the top have repeatedly been found to be more influential than CEOs in the definition and implementation of an organization's strategy and in its performance (Finkelstein, 1992). One critical element of team composition is the personality of the team's executives, which is often measured on two of the big five character dimensions – extroversion and agreeableness – considered to be the most important factors for teamwork. Other important elements include the performance level of individual members of the top management team and their functional background, organizational familiarity, industry experience, willingness to take risks, self- versus other-directedness, interpersonal orientation, entrepreneurial orientation, background in finance and law, the tenure of the

---

[2] The reader interested in further discussion of these contingencies can profit from reading Finkelstein and Hambrick (1996).

CEO, and whether or not the CEO is an outsider and has ever been a COO.

Even the feelings of uncertainty with which top managers react to external contingencies are considered in the literature to be contingencies. Duncan posed this argument as early as 1972 and Ellis, Almor, and Shenkar (2002) have elaborated upon it, finding the source of the emotional reaction toward uncertainty in the following characteristics: cognitive complexity, need for cognition, sharpening versus leveling style, and need for cognitive closure. Although high rates of the first three factors increase feelings of uncertainty because of the complexity they uncover, cognitive closure, through seizing or freezing effects, may balance that complexity and bring it within emotionally tolerable limits.

The effects of the management team composition and dynamics on performance are significant. They are, however, unpredictable: within this cause-effect relationship operates the well-known butterfly effect, or a sensitive dependence on initial conditions by which small differences in input (e.g. a new rule on how to discuss strategic decisions) ultimately create large differences in output (e.g. results) (Eisenhardt and Shoonhoven, 1990).

Following Child's strategic-choice arguments in the 1970s, *CEO characteristics* have been proposed as design drivers. The smaller the size of an organization, the greater the impact the top executive will have on its strategy (Miller and Toulouse, 1986a, 1986b). Many of the characteristics are the same dimensions mentioned as being relevant for the members of the top management teams, and will not be repeated here. None the less, some specific aspects of CEO influence in the organization, such as their impact on strategy, have attracted special attention. For example, Gupta (1984) proposed a heterogeneous list of CEO characteristics to account for variance in their influence: organizational familiarity, individual experience, functional background, willingness to take risk, self- versus other-directedness, and interpersonal orientation. CEOs' perceptions and their scanning styles have also been extensively studied (Daft, Sormunen, and Parks, 1988; Garg, Walters, and Priem, 2003). Even the effects of the deep psychological layers of cadres have been noted in the literature, as in the work of Kets de Vries.

Of course, the methodological challenge is how to select from the infinite variations in human traits, the attitudes and styles most relevant for work at the top. The literature has recognized an endless list. Because Lewin and Stephens (1994) explicitly deal with this problem of selection, we also note their choices here: need for achievement, Machiavellianism, egalitarianism, trust in people, locus of control, risk propensity, and moral reasoning. The importance of locus of control has been noted by several scholars (Miller and Dröge, 1986; Miller and Toulouse, 1986a, 1986b).

Thus structures are considered to be more flexible than contingencies in the executive environment and more flexible than those in either the internal or external environments. They therefore represent the organizational element to be adapted, made contingent upon other elements, and designed. Structures are the ultimate tool for organizational adaptation. And herein lies one of the paradoxes of change processes. Because behaviors are more inert than structures, the former become contingencies and the latter objects of design. The assumption and hope of change management is that modifications to structures will exert an impact upon organizational roles and tasks and that these two, in time, as habits develop, will have an impact upon activities and eventually upon behaviors. Change is seldom straightforward, and the use of structures as an organizational transformation level is an unavoidable detour.

Corporate political structures are the adaptive mechanism that deals with the specific environments that affect the pinnacle of organizations. Although specific contingencies of top management teams and boards of directors have been identified, the leap toward proposing criteria for the design of corporate governance or corporate political structures has been made only exceptionally and partially. Finkelstein and Hambrick (1996) is an academic exception, and Strebel (2004) is a practitioner-oriented one. In the following pages we attempt to contribute to the filling of that void.

The contingencies of corporate power structures

Contingency theory is a practical theory-in-use, to use Argyris and Schön's (1974) term. It is a more action-oriented and useful-for-practice theory than others such as the neo-institutional school, network approaches, and population ecology. Contingency theory is even more practical than the strategic leadership or upper echelons theories, which are analytical and descriptive. This is no coincidence: among

the most influential proponents of contingency theory are such distinguished management professors as Harvard's Paul Lawrence and Jay
Lorsch. Furthermore, to the extent that contingency theory is recognized and employed as a theory useful for practice, it feeds self-efficacy
in executives and, as a consequence, improves the chances of precipitat-
ing action and achieving better results (Priem and Rosenstein, 2000).
As recent evaluations of contingency theory acknowledge, its appeal to
practitioners has not diminished over time (Ellis, Almor, and Shenkar,
2002).

A theorist's aspiration toward parsimony fits well with an executive
need to focus upon an economy of variables when taking purposeful
action. Lawrence and Lorsch (1967) say in a revealing paragraph:

> For us as researchers it has seemed important to be economical in using con-
> cepts, because from a methodological standpoint we are only able to deal
> with and understand the relationship among a few variables at once. Simi-
> larly, this conceptual frugality is important for the manager confronted with
> decisions about organizations. Given the nature of man's thinking equip-
> ment, the variables must be few if they are to be mentally manipulated
> simultaneously. This happy coincidence of our needs as researchers and the
> need of the practitioners is one reason that the findings of this study should
> be useful to managers. (p. 5)

In designing contingent structures, top managers need to ascer-
tain the contingencies that should be adapted to, choosing from the
myriad current and future possibilities (Garg, Walters, and Priem,
2003).

It is patently clear that there are a large number of heterogeneous
design drivers. Gresov (1989) speaks of a multiplicity of contingencies,
and Ellis, Almor, and Shenkar (2002) list 145! Such abundance poses a
conceptual challenge for a unified and parsimonious contingency theory. Miller (1991) has said that "the selection of the dimensions needed
to describe environment, structure and strategy is never definitive"
(p. 36) and Miller and Toulouse (1986a) have maintained that "the
thrust of the [contingency] literature is somewhat fragmented, with
different authors concentrating on different variables" (p. 1389). Ellis,
Almor, and Shenkar (2002) have advised that "scholars have been frus-
trated by the fact that numerous research efforts have yielded only
fragmented empirical support for the theory" (p. 41). Moreover, the
evidence of the causality argument – that contingencies determine

structure that predicts performance – which is key for a function-alist theory such as contingency theory, is indirect or indeterminate or contradictory (Tushman and Nadler, 1978). As Miller, Dröge, and Toulouse (1988) have stated, for instance: "Unfortunately, there remains much confusion and contradiction in the literature, and no consensus has emerged concerning the relative ability of these context variables to predict structure" (p. 544). Thus "a more real-istic view is to assume multiple contingencies and multiple struc-tural fits" (Galunic and Eisenhardt, 1994, p. 235). Because of these limitations, Miller (1981) has developed a configurational approach that, while still within the contingency tradition, tries to account for the multiple covariations of environments, contingencies, and organizations.

Furthermore, in selecting the contingencies that are critical for the designing of corporate power structures, there is an added challenge: although work on the impact of contingencies on the design of hor-izontal structures has been extensive, there is a dearth of work on contingencies affecting the design of the formal structures of executive committees, CEO offices, and boards of directors (see, for the latter, the exception of Strebel [2004]). Zelleke (2003), for instance, acknowl-edges that "the original contingency theorists did not focus on corpo-rate governance structures; their emphasis was on the organization of the company's management structures. Nonetheless, contingency theory principles can be readily applied to the corporate governance domain" (p. 15).

In the following pages, we propose a list of basic contingencies rel-evant for the design of corporate political structures. It coincides with several of the contingencies posed by Finkelstein and Hambrick (1996), who made a similar attempt. We have made this preliminary list ten-tative, with categories deliberately broad enough so as not to lose sig-nificant parts of the phenomenon. This selection will be utilized in Chapters 4 to 6 as we analyze more examples of different types of small numbers at the top. And it will be reconsidered in the concluding chapter where we make our final statements. Our entire book demon-strates that Zelleke's assessment of the field, quoted in the previous paragraph, was on target, except for the adverb "readily"!

That the design of corporate power structures should be driven by a distinct set of contingencies is confirmed by a lengthy list of authors ranging from sociologists like Michels, Parsons, Thompson, and

Stinchcombe, to management authors such as Bartlett and Ghoshal. To give just one example, Stinchcombe (1990) says:

It is, then, the factual distribution of information relevant to crucial uncertainties (crucial in particular, in economic organizations, for the net value of the object or service produced by organizations) that determines the actual structure of the problem confronting the functional structure. Structures of organizations, and of parts of organizations, vary according to the sorts of uncertainties they confront, and so according to what sources of information they depend on and to how that information is best got to the decision-making units. The board of directors is organized as a committee, the assembly line as a hierarchy, because the financial and trustworthiness uncertainties faced by the board are different from the labour cost uncertainties faced by the assembly line. (p. 3)

Corporate political structures are organized distinctively because, in response to their special environments, they must do different things. To say it abstractly, *à la* Thompson, they manage both the short- and long-term interfaces between the organization and its environments and they also manage the organization in ways that make the transitions between the short- and long-term interfaces possible.

How, then, is the environment specifically related to corporate political structures? What are the most important contingencies peculiar to them? We begin by selecting the contingencies that belong to the external environment, which have been well recognized and studied by contingency theorists.

The first distinct source of high uncertainty for corporate political structures and one that may influence their design is the competitive environment. By definition, the external environment cannot be controlled by the organization, particularly during periods of turbulence and deep and rapid change. The first and strongest impact of the environment is on strategy formulation (the definition of the ends of the organization) and strategy implementation (the definition of the fundamental means employed to achieve those ends). Both strategic tasks, although often distinguished and sequenced analytically, can seldom be separated and ordered in practice (Quinn, 1980).

The apex of an organization is, according to both literature and practice, in charge of strategy. For instance, the CEO and the executive committee in a large corporation typically initiate the strategy definition process, the board of directors approves it, and the CEO and the CEO's team implement it under the control and monitoring of the board.

The twofold strategic task of choosing an organization's goals and the basic means of achieving them generates the highest possible uncertainty for two reasons. First, goals are problematic, as Herbert Simon, James March, Karl Weick, and others have demonstrated. Their determination is not only an intellectual process, but also a political one, subject to the uncertain dynamics of coalition formation and bargaining. And second, strategy generates uncertainty because the relationship between means/ends and cause/effect, except for the case of placid environments, is also problematic. Thompson (1967, p. 134) classifies strategic decisions as either "judgmental" (when there is agreement regarding goals but uncertainty regarding the appropriate means) or "inspirational" decisions (when there is uncertainty regarding both preferences and means). For Thompson (1967), the intensity of uncertainty at the top is "the greatest" (p. 12).

Thus, strategic uncertainty is the first contingency specific to corporate political structures. It may be defined as the uncertainty implicit in deciding the two main objectives of the strategic process: goals definition and the goals–means equation. These two objectives present decision challenges that are, in several respects, dual in nature: cognitive and political, referring to both inside elements and outside relationships of the organization, and to its short- and long-term horizons.

There is no doubt that corporate governance practices are changing. The reforms affect all the decision-making governance bodies and roles, and aim at creating an actually functioning system – not merely rubber-stamp institutions. Most of these changes have been preceded or accompanied by new social or professional norms (codes of best practice) and legal reforms (both in civil and criminal laws). Although the specifics of these reforms vary with the various business systems (Guillén, 2001; Aguilera and Jackson, 2003), they are occurring in most Western economies and have convergent contents, especially for publicly traded companies. For instance, boards of directors, generally regarded in the post-war years as being passive groups and, properly speaking, not even teams, have, in the 1980s and 1990s become more integrated and proactive in monitoring performance and in evaluating CEOs. Specific reforms in board composition and processes range from the requirement of having three committees (auditing, compensation, and corporate governance or nominations) through suggestions that there be a minimum percentage of independent directors, to recommendations on the content of the information to be received by directors in advance of their meetings. Specific reforms that have been suggested for channeling the initiatives of shareholders and institutional investors and conducting annual shareholders' meetings include the use of new technologies in such aspects as the calling of meetings, the exercising of voting rights, and proxy regulations. But transformations not only affect corporate governance bodies. They also accentuate the individual liability and risk exposure of directors for decisions taken; for information and accounts made public to the market and regulatory bodies; and for the fulfillment of duties of care, loyalty, and candor, among other matters. In summary, the current institutional environment of corporate governance structures emphasizes control and monitoring of, above all, the executive function, by the boards of directors as representatives of shareholders. However, control and monitoring is just one of the two main functions of boards, and can be achieved through the differentiation of roles. Boards are also responsible for making strategic decisions, and the strategic process is not as easily regulated (Pound, 1995). This function demands integration (Forbes and Milliken, 1999; Daily, Dalton, and Cannella, 2003; Sundaramurthy and Lewis, 2003).

Moreover, there is a peculiarity in the status and enforceability of most of these corporate governance reforms. Except for the case of the USA, which has a business system that, like its society at large, is highly regulated (the Sarbanes–Oxley Act being a good example), most of the new rules are not compulsory or obligatory, and only some are inscribed in legal texts. In most countries, they are "comply or explain" rules from which companies are allowed to diverge as long as they do it with transparency and justification (e.g. the Higgs Report in the UK and the Aldama Report in Spain). As a consequence, the enforceability of corporate governance is limited, and is exercised primarily by professional bodies, social groups, and the media – the latter being both a channel and an autonomous actor with regard to the legitimization of business practices (Mazza and Alvarez, 2000). These corporate governance reforms are, then, primarily social rather than legal in their enforcement. They are soft norms or weak structures superimposed on corporate political structures and processes that have already been characterized as being embedded in such weak situations as strategic uncertainty, in which there is a high ambiguity in regard to the relationship between causes and effects. The reforms limit but do not suppress the CEO's and board chair's discretion for designing the differentiation and integration of executive tasks and roles in corporate governance. In terms of role theory, it can be said that role prescriptions in the upper echelons are weak and that optional arrangements such as small numbers of executives at the top levels of the organization are then feasible. Integration in corporate power structures is still very much up to the decision of the executives.

Thus, the second key contingency for the design of corporate political structures is the normative environment for corporate governance. This contingency is characterized by both legal accountability and social and ethical scrutiny, imposed not only on corporations as artificial entities and on teams such as boards, but also on executives, on top managers, and on directors as individual professionals. Although these norms are, in most cases, designed to control, they are weak measures, often merely recommendations of voluntary compliance and limited enforceability.

We have just discussed the two basic external contingencies. In the following pages we introduce two basic internal drivers, which appeared in one of the foundational books of the contingency tradition: Burns and Stalker's *The Management of Innovation* (1961). Such pioneer works have the advantage that, in the absence of previous research posing numerous variables to be refined or disconfirmed in a scholarly fashion, they must be as parsimonious as executives would be in the enactment of action. We believe that Burns and Stalker's arguments about relevant contingencies, although proposed for the organization as a whole, serve as a particularly good fit for the organization's upper echelons.

The contingencies that these two authors conceive of as belonging to the internal environment are not independent of external contingencies. On the contrary, internal contingencies are often the organizational mechanisms used for adaptation to the external environment that have in time become rigid, unchangeable, and therefore contingencies in and of themselves. The first internal contingency that we import from Burns and Stalker is what they call the working system – the way in which a corporation defines the behaviors that are expected of its members. These behaviors are grouped into activities aimed at the accomplishment of tasks that are assigned to roles. In the most common terminology, the working system is the division and coordination of labor – the structure.

The roles at the top defined by the vertical structure (e.g. members of the executive committee, CEOs, external directors on boards, and their coordination) present specific challenges. What differentiates the coordination of roles at the top from collaboration at lower levels of the organization is "reciprocal" interdependence (Thompson, 1967, p. 54). This is different from "pooled" (e.g. among the divisions in a multidivisional corporation) and from "sequential" (e.g. in a production line) types of coordination. It is reciprocal interdependence because strategic decision-making, the specific task of corporate governance responding to the distinct contingency of strategic uncertainty, is the most difficult, complex, unpredictable, and ambiguous executive task possible. It requires the cooperation of all the actors involved, satisfaction with the team governing the corporation, with its other members, and positive levels of team integration. Revealingly, in many legal systems, directors share the responsibility for the decisions taken by the board, even when they may have disagreed with them individually, so long as they remain on the board or have not filed a written, reasoned disagreement. Put another way, at the top, more than in any other place, decision-making bodies should be teams, not merely groups, because they should have "high task interdependence, high role differentiation, high task differentiation, and distributed expertise" (Neumann and Wright, 1999, p. 377).

Thompson calls cooperation at the top "coordination by mutual adjustment" (p. 62) because continuous, self-regulated, reciprocal feedback is needed during the course of strategic decision-making and implementation. And this type of coordination cannot be planned or regulated.

A variety of mechanisms are available for the coordination of roles in horizontal structures (Galbraith, 1974), but these mechanisms do not apply to vertical structures. The first of these mechanisms consists of rules or programs, eliminating the need for interdepartmental communication. However, as we have just argued, this is not possible for the mutually adjusted decision-making processes germane to vertical structures. Hierarchy, the second tool, does not operate at the top because there is, strictly speaking, no hierarchy between the chair of the board and the CEO. They belong to different legitimacies – the CEO to managerial, and the chair to institutional ones. The third level for coordination is targets or goals, which are useful to increase the amount of discretion at lower levels, but do not apply well to layers such as upper echelons, characterized precisely for being the decision-makers setting those objectives. Two more mechanisms, slack resources and self-contained tasks, also go against the specificities of the job at the top. They apply to pooled and sequential tasks, but not to reciprocal tasks. Investing in vertical information systems, the sixth mechanism, works better when the information is formalized and quantifiable, but not when it is qualitative and ambiguous, the distinctive characteristic of the strategic data to be processed at the top. The seventh type is a matrix organization, one of the basic types of horizontal structure. Finally, the eighth integration device, lateral mechanisms, such as direct contact (e.g. between a CEO and a chair of the board of directors), liaison roles (e.g. lead director), task forces (e.g. for the search of a new CEO), and teams (auditing, nomination, and compensation committees), are the very ways in which corporate governance is structured. The challenge is precisely how these lateral mechanisms can be properly designed for corporate governance. Our central thesis is that small numbers at the top is one of the structural solutions available for integration of corporate political structures.

There is another characteristic of executive tasks that makes integration at the top challenging. As we have argued, the differentiation of roles at the apex is becoming institutionalized significantly but not fully, either by law or by professional norms aimed at guaranteeing transparency and control. The institutionalization of corporate governance is occurring under an ideology of distrust of the executive power. It is also done under one metaphor – that of checks and balances – imported from the design of democratic political systems. For instance, it is generally recommended that the roles of the CEO and the chair of the board be independent, a separation analogous to that of the executive and the legislative powers of government.

In stark contrast, the integration of top management and governance roles is institutionalized to an even lesser degree. This integration is less relevant for the functioning of democratic polities than for corporations where, contrary to "political polities," there are primary objectives or goals, and therefore coordination is a *sine qua non* for the functioning of the system. For instance, in current governance reforms there are no generalized and obligatory prescriptions on, for example, decision-making processes for executive committees or boards of directors (e.g. on the use of consensus versus dialectic methods for decision-making), on the handling of information for strategy decisions (e.g. what strategy information is received, when, and with what level of detail and analysis), on due processes for structural or strategic overhauls, or on the heterogeneity of professional backgrounds and industry knowledge of their members. Prescriptions for role differentiation are much stronger than those for role integration. Legislation and social norms in corporate governance still leave ample space for "structural latitude," to use Gresov and Drazin's expression (1997), especially in the design of integration.

The asymmetry between an increasingly regulated differentiation aimed at control and a poorly prescribed integration is what makes the phenomenon of small numbers at the top possible. This arrangement provides more and better integration and, as a consequence, a better balance between differentiation and integration at the top. More integration is needed precisely because, as already stated, vertical structures should be more than a mere control system. They are also, perhaps even primarily, a set of roles for the process of making key strategic decisions. And for the task of strategic decision-making at the top requires talented executives collaborating competently, intensely, reciprocally, and with high levels of trust.

Thus, the third contingency of vertical structures is the decision-making tasks that executives must perform through continuous, non-programmable mutual adjustments. These tasks require high levels of integration, which is much less regulated and much more open to design latitude than is the more prescribed differentiation of corporate governance roles.

Burns and Stalker (1961) suggest two other internal contingencies, grouped under the heading of career systems, which we use in our selection of key contingencies for the design of corporate political structures. The first is the political system of a firm, which grows directly out of the previous internal contingency, the tasks of executives at the top. The second, the career status system, we pose as our first executive environment contingency.

All the scholars in the contingency tradition, from Hickson on, as well as the authors working on the topic of power and influence in organizations, such as Kotter, Mintzberg, and Pfeffer, recognize that the more interdependencies exist among organizational actors, whether units or individuals, the more internal contingencies will appear and, in turn, the more political will be behavior in the organization. As Thompson noted, integration at the corporate top adopts the form of "mutual adjustment" (p. 57), whereby what is coordinated and exchanged (information, knowledge, expertise, and styles, for example) cannot be specified *a priori*; this explains why high-intensity politics are a contingency specific to the top. Nowhere in the organization are there more task interdependencies.

The logic of human action prompts social actors to free themselves from the contingencies that limit agency – that is, to gain freedom from control over themselves by others (Emerson, 1962). This impetus for freedom from contingencies is the origin of politics. In corporate settings, executives hold the control and decision rights over the most valuable materials over which politics are played in corporations – what Cohen and Bradford (1989) call "currencies" – such as task resources, social relationships, inspirational values, political cover, career advice, and rewards and punishments. Managers must possess these currencies in order to be effective at their roles. In fact, as Donaldson and Lorsch found in their 1983 review of decision-making at the top, executives tend not to see their careers and the politics they play separately from the welfare of the organizations they lead, and genuinely want their organizations to survive and thrive (see, against this position, Luthans [1988]). Top managers are agents of the survival *élan* that Thompson postulated for organizations. And they play politics and crave for power as means to attain the resources needed to be efficient.

As Burns and Stalker (1961) say in their definition of organizational politics:

The product of the various demands, either actually or potentially conflicting, which are made of the total resources of the concern . . . political activity has to do with the amount of say which individuals or groups have in the destiny of the firm as a whole . . . the matter of conflict includes the degree one may exercise over the firm's resources, the direction of the activities of other people, and patronage (promotion and the distribution of privileges and rewards). (p. 144)

Thus, politics are an inescapable fact of organizational life at the top because they are embedded in executive tasks. In a way, it could be said that politics are one of the executives' technologies for organizational action. Therefore, it should be selected as one of the most important contingencies in the design of corporate political structures.

Thus, the fourth contingency is the political dynamics of upper echelons, which arise from the objective interdependences present in the reciprocal coordination of the performance of strategic tasks. Political dynamics are fueled by executives' need for control over the resources they require for accomplishing their tasks. They are those resources over which organizational politics are played.

Burns and Stalker's final contingency, the status career system, also arises from our third contingency, executive tasks, but because of the individual dynamics it prompts, we classify it as our first human or executive environment contingency.

Careers are the point of intersection between the corporation's professional categories and social classes – that is, between the professional and the private world of the executives. Hierarchical ranks confirm or disconfirm the advancement or stagnation of the professional careers of executives. In an organizational society, professional status defines social status, and the social self-identity that managers try to protect and enhance. The behavior aimed at protecting careers and status becomes another key contingency at the top. As Uyterhoeven, Ackerman and Rosenblum (1973) say:

The next step in organizational diagnosis is to identify the people. This task should not be confined to listing their names, titles, and job histories. Just as each function has its own goals, ambitions, and plans so does each individual. Thus, an organization not only represents a group of people, it consists of a set of personal strategies. (p. 74)

In the same way that structures at the top require behaviors, activities, tasks, and roles from their incumbents that are clearly differentiated from those of lower organizational layers, the human materials of top managers – their needs, wants, and motivations – are also combined in unique ways. And the design of corporate political structures has to adapt to that executive environment, which is, like the external and internal contingencies, less changeable than formal structures. Notwithstanding its importance, however, this critical contingency "has not been developed sufficiently" (Lewin and Stephens, 1994, p. 183).

Because the number of slots decreases at the top of the hierarchical pyramid and because of the high potential rewards and losses, competition is intense and career advancement is hazardous. Advancement is also difficult because senior managers with long careers and experiences tend to be consummate political players (Luthans, 1988). Career competition is also intense, because of the energy drawn from their typical power orientation (McClelland, 1961). And it is lonely because, as Burns and Stalker (1961) have emphasized: "in advancing or protecting his status a man may act alone" (p. 149). Ocasio (1994), Ocasio and Kim (1999), Cannella and Shen (2001), and Shen and Cannella (2002) have demonstrated that institutional constraints and corporate governance regulations do not eliminate organizational in-fighting by executives and that CEOs in troubled firms have more to fear from the competition of the members of their own executive committees – from their own appointees – than from external candidates to their succession. The pinnacles of organizations are truly Shakespearean contexts.

This solitary struggle for status and career advancement becomes a source of feelings of anxiety, to be added to objective difficulties of task uncertainty at the top (Jackall, 1988). It is also contrary to the reciprocal collaboration needed for decision-making at the top, making the necessary integration of roles at the top more difficult.

Thus, the fifth driver of design rises from the hierarchical ordering of roles at the pinnacle of organizations and its consequences for the careers and social prestige of managers. The protection of careers and status fuels a highly individualistic, competitive dynamic that is contrary to the collegiality demanded by interdependent work at the top and adds to the professional and psychological challenges of executives.

The previous contingencies are based upon the available literature; there is abundant research on external contingencies and a rapidly growing body of works on the tasks of top executive roles, occasioned by corporate governance reforms. However, as Lewin and Stephens (1994) rightly point out, there is a scarcity of work done on the executive environment, a situation that has not improved much since their assessment over a decade ago. Furthermore, although there still are some references available on the competitive and individualistic aspects of the human environment at the top, there is much less emphasis on another aspect of the executive environment, one that we came to consider critically relevant after our first forays into the phenomenon of small numbers at the top: the emotions, feelings, commitments, and styles of interpersonal relationships among executives at the top. These relationships may balance the personal and professional separation among top executives demanded by the institutional environment and often compensate for the interpersonal distance brought about by the ego demands and career ambitions of executives at the top. In Chapters 4 to 6, we define, describe, analyze, and discuss examples of small numbers at work and the interpersonal relationships in which they are engaged. We now advance our notion of it.

Thus, the sixth contingency is the consequence and the reverse of the previous one. The pinnacle of the organization is a shared ambience for the few, and a place of challenge, visibility, responsibility, and anxiety. The psychological tension, which the apex creates, needs to be balanced with intense interpersonal relationships among the small numbers of incumbents.

We began this chapter by visiting the literature on the political theories of organizations and organizational design. We argued that the most influential design school, the contingency tradition, has not been fully applied to the design of corporate governance instances, such as executive committees, chief executive offices, and boards of directors. We have also maintained, agreeing with Davis and Thompson (1994), that the failure of organizational theories to account for the theoretical and practical challenges of corporate governance has facilitated the dominance of this field, which boomed academically and in business practices in the 1990s through agency theory. In the last pages of the chapter we have attempted to help fill that void by tentatively advancing the six broad areas of contingencies that we believe are more relevant for the design of corporate power structures.

Corporate political architecture not only differs from that of horizontal structures, but is also more challenging. Some of the proposed contingencies incorporate tensions, paradoxes, and dilemmas that make adapting to them puzzling, problematic, and, often, a balancing act and a dual task. For example, there will be dualities in solving the first contingency, strategic uncertainty, because it affects both strategy formulation and implementation, both the internal and external alignments of the organization, and the short- and long-run horizons – all of this in the context of executives usually being good at only one of any two dimensions, a limitation emphasized in the next chapter.

The second contingency, the institutional environment, carries within itself the asymmetry between, on the one hand, strong norms about control and differentiation, and, on the other hand, weaker norms on decision-making and integration. Similarly, in the third contingency, strategic tasks, there is an in-built tension between the necessary inter-dependency of governance tasks and the latitude for action managers need to prepare the organization for would-be environments.

But there also are contradictions and cross-pressures among the contingencies themselves, adding to the challenges of corporate political design. There is, for example, a contradiction between the need for flexibility to react to strategic uncertainties (first contingency) and the inertia and constraints contained in the current governance reforms (second contingency). There is also a paradox between the mutually adjusted collaboration at the top (third contingency) and the politics that top managers play in order to accumulate as many resources and as much discretion as possible, in order to manage current and would-be alignments simultaneously (fourth contingency). And there is a contradiction between the contingency of executive tasks (third contingency) that requires mutual adjustments and the contingency of individual competition aimed at career advancement (fifth contingency). Similarly, the contingency of interpersonal relationships at the top (sixth contingency), where the objective of closeness with others in the executive tasks prompts affective needs, contradicts the detachment required for pursuing individual careers and for professional non-particularistic decision-making (fifth contingency). We revisit these six contingencies in the concluding chapter of the book, after presenting an in-depth analysis of duos, trios, and foursomes in the middle chapters. In particular, we consider whether these contingencies are useful or need to be modified, added to or deleted from.

Perhaps of all the dualities and tensions mentioned, the one that most makes small numbers at the top an interesting option for the design of highly discretionary structures capable of responding to the contingencies specific to the corporate apex, is the asymmetry between an increasingly institutionalized differentiation of corporate governance, focused on control, and the much more poorly defined integration required for decision-making. Small numbers at the top offer a good balance between differentiation and integration because, in the absence of superordinate formal structures, they provide better and tighter integration through interpersonal means. In turn, the integration requirement makes the executive contingency the most critical and distinctive in the design of corporate political structures. And it is critical at the two poles of the design process: the subject or the designers, and the object or the designed. As Learned, Ulrich, and Booz (quoted in Glover and Hower, 1963) say: "The executive who must work with the human materials around him must also work with the human materials in himself" (p. 4).

However, given the existence of dualities and contradictions and the impossibility of satisfying all contingencies simultaneously, the answer to political design may lie in configurations or *Gestalten* (Miller, 1981; Gresov, 1989) that privilege the adaptation to some of the contingencies and postpone the satisfaction of others – a decision that will have to do with the perceptions executives, the designers of corporate political structures, hold of themselves as political actors and their preferences.

In the hope of better understanding the contingency executive environment, the next chapter is devoted to examining the roles, actions, and politics of executives. We expect that the executives' answers to the challenges of managing solo are revealing of themselves in action, of their political personae, and of this most human contingency.

2 | Performing the "infinite job" solo: executive dilemmas, roles, and actions

> Managers need to be ambidextrous.
> Juggling provides a metaphor. It is only
> when the juggler can handle multiple balls
> at one time that his or her skill is respected.
>
> Tushman and O'Reilly, 1996, p. 8

> Without the "superb politician" complex
> organizations would be immobilized.
>
> Thompson, 1967, p. 143

IN THIS CHAPTER we focus on one of the arguments for the existence of small numbers at the top of organizations: the numerous and demanding challenges to be faced and multiple and varying roles to be played by executives at the apex of complex organizations.

The ideal might be that jugglers and superb politicians manage and govern organizations, as the authors of the quotations heading this chapter wish, but such people are rare in the general population and even not common in the managerial class. Corporate political structures have to be designed for executives with average professional talent and motivations. We contend that the solo management of complex organizations requires above-average competencies. By solo, we mean the occupancy of an executive leadership position without role-sharing or without the support of a tightly knit constellation of executives – without any of the small-numbers schemes. Small numbers at the top, we suggest, should not be considered as a rare and unusual arrangement, but as a normal option for corporate political design.

This chapter is sequenced in the following way. First, we argue that organizations are essentially dual, and that contradictory tensions and paradoxes that cut across their structures, processes, and decision-making efforts produce some unavoidable dualities in executive work.

Next, we review and comment upon the numerous and varied executive roles, emphasizing the difficulties associated with the solo performance of those roles. Finally, we discuss how theories of action recognize wide latitude in the enactment of executive work, especially with regard to the behaviors needed to muster the political capital required to break organizational routines. In doing so, we rely on earlier work by Alvarez (2000). Chapter 2 has an added aim. By detailing and assessing the dilemmas, roles, and actions of executives, we hope to better understand the phenomenon that we called executive contingencies in the previous chapter: individualistic status, career competition, and the interpersonal relationships among executives derived from the emotional intensity at the organization's apex.

In Chapter 3, we examine the executive's job again, from the perspective of role theory to provide further arguments that executives' roles and their integration are building blocks for the design of corporate political structures.

Dualities in organizations and in top executive roles

In Chapter 1, following Thompson's lead, we proposed the basic contingencies to be addressed in designing corporate political structures. We again refer to Thompson (1967) in starting our argument in this chapter: that dualities in structures, processes, and decision-making criteria lie at the heart of organizations and of executive work. In Chapter 11 of *Organizations in Action*, Thompson identifies a fundamental organizational dilemma that he calls the "paradox of administration": the tension between, on the one hand, the search for tight alignment between the organization and the environment in order to reduce uncertainty, and, on the other hand, the search for decoupling from that same extant environment in order to retain flexibility for responding to various possible future contingencies. As Thompson (1967) says: "For the organization as a totality, the important question is not what it has accomplished but its fitness for future action" (p. 88).

The paradox of administration poses the challenge of designing the structure of organizations to deal with both short- and long-term horizons. As Penrose (1972) claimed, organizations should make the function of maintenance compatible with the function of growth, the former to be conducted by managerial services and the latter by entrepreneurial units. Similarly, Duncan (1976) believed that organizations must be ambidextrous in order to play to the short term and the long term simultaneously. Organizational structures must make departments that are intended for routine tasks and specific environments compatible with departments that are focused on non-routine tasks and uncertain environments (McDonough and Leifer, 1983). And as Tushman and O'Reilly (1996) maintain, organizations should have units specializing in mature markets and evolutionary change and other units that are capable of innovation and revolutionary change.

Therefore, dualities in structures and, as a result, dualities in executive jobs are natural occurrences in complex organizations. Although already recognized by Dalton in 1959, it is perhaps Uyterhoeven's (1972) piece on "managers in the middle" that first directly explained how structural dualities produce cross-pressures in managerial jobs: multi-divisional business organizations or M-Forms, with several layers, create simultaneous cross-pressures on general managers of divisions, cross-pressures that originate in their superordinates at the corporate level and in their subordinates. This predicament forces general managers of divisions to be what Uyterhoeven calls "bilingual" (p. 4). Among the dualities they must balance are coaching for subordinates and being a player with superiors; giving operative instructions downward and providing results with corporate impact upward; being both strategic and tactical; being a delegator and a doer. In concluding his article, Uyterhoeven states that consistent and cumulative learning by executives is what enables them to survive and contribute in their essentially dual roles. Evans (1999) also recognizes these tensions: "opposite forces create paradoxes, seemingly contradictory statements that are more or less true. You cannot make these paradoxes disappear, you cannot resolve them, they do not go away" (p. 67).

Lewis (2000) argues that tensions and dilemmas in organizations are reinforced by the strongly polarizing, either/or ways of an individual's cognitive process. For human cognition works best with simple taxonomies and neatly differentiated categories that allow, for instance, for quick categorization and reaction in case of danger (Walsh, 1988; Nicholson, 2000). When reality is fuzzy, humans tend to impose clear-cut categories to simplify it, for the sake of a quick understanding and as a basis for rapid action. We learn, for example, to exhibit a defensive cognitive reaction called splitting: the creation of artificial distinctions between people or ideas in order to obscure the relatedness of opposites – in order to make decisive action easier and more justifiable. Furthermore, this dichotomizing, built into human psychology, is embedded in human physiology as well, as evidenced by the well-known differentiation between the right and left sides of the brain and the corresponding differences in thinking, the right side of the brain being responsible for creative thinking, and the left side for the more logical and analytical functions. Interestingly, as Agor (1986) reports, executives are more likely than middle- and lower-level managers to use intuition – a cognitive style that facilitates integration more than do analytical styles, which are more applicable for differentiation.

But it is not merely dualities that puzzle executives, for there could be "polychotomous" management (Senger, 1971, p. 81), the same way that there could be three or even more dimensions in a matrix structure. Probably the best and most inspiring treatment of the multidimensionality of top managers' jobs is found in the work of Coffey, Athos, and Raynolds (1968). These authors recognize that the key dimensions of managerial work are not only objective or structural, but also subjective, derived from the cumulative levels of experiences that executives go through as they meet increasingly complex domains of action and roles. To complicate matters, each level of executive experience carries with it a number of dimensions and dilemmas:

(1) The "social dimension" refers to what managers must do in specific settings or roles and leads to the tension between conformity and autonomy.

(2) The "psychological dimension" points to what managers have had to do to become what they are presently and what they will have to do to reach their full potential in the future, and presents the tensions between an identity true to oneself or to the identity demands of others.

(3) "Ideals" represent what leaders ought to do in all settings and roles, and pose a dilemma between dogmatism and accommodation to local pressures.

(4) "Purpose" is closest to role-performance, and refers to what executives must do in order to accomplish tasks. Its dilemma is between efficiency and effectiveness.

(5) "Learning" is a function that top-level managers must undertake in order to better understand themselves and the world. This final dimension presents a dichotomy between, to use Argyris' terms (1991), single-loop learning and double-loop learning, and it is the latter that is difficult, challenging, and unsettling for executives, and involves a decision on personal stability versus unconformity.

Working through these dimensions and dilemmas demands personal maturity while actually facilitating the maturing process. Coffey, Athos, and Raynolds (1968) do not distinguish between personal and executive maturity. Both require the acceptance of imperfection (the consequences of our limited competencies); of ambiguity (the lack of clarity about what the data available on the environment really mean); and of uncertainty (the impossibility of accurately predicting the consequences of our actions). And maturity brings with it the flexibility to balance and optimize over time the five dimensions mentioned in the previous paragraph.

Lewis (2000) also expects that managers' self-reflection and personal maturity will help them to work productively through all these objective and subjective cross-pressures. Gibson and Birkinshaw (2004) build optimistically on the idea that the solution to conflicting organizational demands is not in the structural ambidexterity recommended by Duncan, Tushman, and others (Gibson and Birkinshaw argue that formal systems cannot account for all the unpredictable demands of alignment processes), but in the behavioral capacity of the executives in charge for balancing alignment and adaptability. These two authors would like executives to be "Renaissance company men," quoting Hedlund and Ridderstrale (1997, p. 211). A tall order indeed! Mature managers, like mature people, are as rare as superb politicians and jugglers. In fact, there are a number of authors who are skeptical of the ability of executives to balance the often opposing aspects of their myriad demands. It is worth quoting at length from Richard Pascale's book *Managing on the Edge* (1990) in which he addresses in detail the issues of contradictions and paradoxes in management. Pascale says:

The point here is not that American executives aren't smart and analytical. Rather, our minds aren't accustomed to dealing with paradoxical relationships. Compounding the problem, a great deal of what has been written for managers recently is wrong-minded in so far as it demands *less*, rather than more, of our thought processes. For example, the thrust of some recent literature has called upon managers to be more "passionate" and "obsessive" with respect to customers, quality, and so forth. It seems difficult to quarrel with such aims. Indeed, if such terminology only heightens managerial intensity and commitment, there can be no argument, but passionate and obsessive behavior is often single-minded behavior – seeing the world in either/or terms, and going after the "either" or the "or" with a vengeance. Passion and obsession frequently degenerate into simplistic formulae . . . this book advocates wisdom and coolness at a higher level of complexity. (p. 34)

Ghoshal and Bartlett (1997) clearly state that the challenges facing CEOs in their performance of complex roles originate in a generalized limitation, inherent in the human species, to scan, receive, process, and decide upon large amounts of complex information:

The problem is rarely one of the CEO's personal inadequacy but rather the assumption that the CEO should be the corporation's chief strategist, assuming full control of setting the company's objectives and determining its priorities. In an operating environment where the fast-changing knowledge and expertise required to make such decisions are usually found on the front lines of each business, this assumption is untenable. Strategic information cannot be relayed to the top without becoming severely diluted, distorted, and delayed. And even when it does survive the journey in some useful form, top level executives rarely have the current knowledge, the specialized expertise, or the fine-grained insight needed to make the sophisticated judgments implied by the strategic proposals. (p. 304)

Ghoshal and Bartlett agree with Jay R. Galbraith that information-processing is the key challenge to organizational design. The puzzling, often impossible, requirements placed on managers are well expressed by Gosling and Mintzberg (2003):

The problem, of course, is that plain old management is complicated and confusing. Be global, managers are told, and be local. Collaborate and compete. Change, perpetually, and maintain order. Make the numbers while nurturing your people. How is anyone supposed to reconcile all this? The fact is no one can. (p. 55)

Even single, specialized roles can be highly demanding. Hambrick (2003) provides the example of the dilemmas of managers serving in the role of analyzers, following Miles and Snow's well-known terminology:

[Managers] are walking a tight rope; trying to be innovative at the same time they are trying to be efficient and reliable. They can easily be seen as vacillating and unsure of themselves. They don't have the same clear North Stars to guide them, as Defender or Prospector managers do. Should they have some subunits that look and behave like Defenders, while others look like Prospectors? Should they engage in temporary campaigns to make the organization Prospector-like, then swing back in the Defender direction, then move in Prospector direction, and so on? (p. 118)

With regard to corporate governance, the current debate on combination or independence of the roles of CEO and chair of the board provides good examples of arguments for the difficulties of properly balancing dualities. Lord Cadbury, the champion of corporate governance reform in the UK, favors role independence because the time horizons and the purpose differ for the chair and the CEO: the latter turns decisions into action; the former stands back and adopts a standpoint of strategic purpose. In this context, Cadbury (2002) quotes from Anthony Jay (1972):

The difference is so profound that it is practically impossible to discharge both duties properly at the same time. The present and the future do not run in harness: their demands and emphases move at a different pace and sometimes pull in opposite directions, and it is rarely satisfactory if the conflict takes place in a single man's mind. If one man tries to do both jobs, one of them is likely to go by default. (p. 108)

Distinguished sociologists also appreciate the incompatibility between the tasks of governance and management for a single performer. Parsons (1960) says:

This is because it is not possible to perform the functions of focusing legitimation and community support for the organization and at the same time act as the active management of it – that is, when the differentiation of function in the structure has gone far enough. The "board," or whatever structural form it takes, is a mediating structure between the affaires of the organization at the managerial level and its "public." It can become absorbed in the managerial structure only at the expense of its primary function. (p. 93)

It is not only extremely difficult to discharge the roles of CEO and chair of the board simultaneously with excellence; merely performing one of these roles constitutes a considerable endeavor. As Cadbury (2002) says, there are many dualities inherent in the role of board chair: individuality and collegiality, continuity and change, managing and coaching the board, and winning the agreement of board members while maintaining their independence of judgment.

Argyris (1991) warns that smart and successful executives are especially prone to falling into learning traps. Their capability for balancing the variety of organizational tensions and plurality of executive dimensions through decision-making and for acquiring professional flexibility by learning from these experiences, he argues, is even rarer than it is in the general, non-executive or non-successful population. This is so, he explains, because executives tend to stick to the cognitive protocols that led them to success without adapting them to new and different environments and because they tend to have a win–lose approach to conflict, a necessity for being and looking as though they are in control, and a rejection of double-loop learning – of the questioning of the basic modes of their development.

All these arguments should make it easy to agree that the multi-dimensional executive that Coffey, Athos, and Raynolds (1968) describe is not a common phenomenon. A well-balanced combination of traits and attitudes is not widespread, even among top executives.

Some studies have empirically demonstrated the rarity of the psychologically mature executive. Pucik, Judge, and Welbourne (1995), for example, looked at the executive temperaments and career paths that were better suited than others to managing change – the only process that can solve the paradox of administration by transitioning the organization from the short run to the long run.

Pucik and his colleagues studied six traits of managers that are similar to the characteristics selected by Cannella and Monroe (1997) in their review of strategic leadership theories that are critical for the understanding of executive psychology:

(1) *tolerance of ambiguity*, or the acceptance and enjoyment of new and uncertain environments;

(2) *tolerance of risk*, or the capability for working in unstable, unsafe, and unpredictable environments;

(3) *internal locus of control*, or the belief in one's ability to influence and control events and outcomes in one's life (as opposed to believing that life is controlled by chance, fate, or powerful others);

(4) *self-efficacy*, or the belief that one's efforts will result in goal attainment;

(5) *affective disposition*, or the tendency to respond positively to the environment; and,

(6) *openness to experience*, defined in terms of curiosity, adaptability, originality, and broad-mindedness.

They hypothesized that possession of the six characteristics would have a positive impact on managers' abilities to lead change efforts, by viewing change in a positive manner and thereby freeing themselves from the high levels of stress typically generated by transformational processes. These characteristics were also expected to have a positive effect on successful coping, career adjustment, stability, and organizational commitment.

Pucik, Judge, and Welbourne found three of the listed six psychological characteristics of managerial character to be predictive of successful change management: high tolerance for ambiguity, positive affectivity, and low risk aversion. However, only a quarter of the managers studied exhibited these characteristics, which supports our argument that capabilities for enacting change – a dual activity essential to executives' jobs – are not widespread in the managerial population. Jugglers and superb politicians are indeed uncommon.

Nutt (1993) presents another study pointing to the relative scarcity of executives who possess the flexible decision-making styles required for adequately managing the paradox of administration in environments of high uncertainty and ambiguity. The key aspect of executives' cognitive processes, Nutt argues, is their decision-making styles, such as Myers-Briggs' sensing, intuition, thinking, and feeling. He found that flexibility – defined as the access to each of Myers-Briggs' four modes of understanding – is observed infrequently among the managerial ranks. When it does exist among managers, it is found primarily among CEOs and members of executive committees. However, the frequency is low: only 8 percent of the executives and 3.5 percent of all managers in his study possessed that degree of cognitive flexibility. This result led Nutt to propose that duos or small teams with complementary styles at the top is what works best for executive leadership positions; such thinking is in line with our overall argument.

Macro studies support cognitive psychology in arguing that managers with the traits and styles appropriate for equivocal environments are a rarity. For example, Norburn (1989) finds that the sociological profile of British CEOs is significantly different from that of the members of their top management teams – that CEOs are indeed "a breed apart" (p. 12), characterized by exposure to cosmopolitan experiences and multiple functional and company backgrounds, which lead them to be self-reliant, with an interventionist style. Norburn recognizes that it is difficult, if not impossible, to instill these qualities in wide sectors of the population – even in members of the executive class. Similarly, Cox and Cooper (1989) argue, in another study of British CEOs, that personal experiences generating feelings of loneliness or detachment constitute the peculiar background for occupying top positions. Such people are pushed to become more responsible than their peers, thereby developing a pattern of independence, self-reliance, and assertiveness. Individualism is then a trait of current top managers, fueling what we posed in Chapter 1 as the first contingency of the executive environment: competition for status and careers at the top.

Executive roles: heterogeneity and challenges

Scholarly work on roles at the top has been abundant, with several studies deeply influencing typologies of roles. In this section we summarize the work of a few of them: Mintzberg (1973), Belbin (1981, 2000), Bartlett and Ghoshal (1998a), and Rivero and Spencer (1998). This review is not intended to be exhaustive,[1] but to provide some examples of the research underlining the large number of roles at the top, their heterogeneity, and their intrinsic task challenges; and to highlight the difficulties of transitioning among them.

An early and influential acknowledgment of the plurality of roles played at the top is Mintzberg's (1973) study of the chief executives of five organizations that differed in size and nature of activities. He identified ten basic managerial roles, grouping them into three categories: interpersonal roles (figurehead, leader, and liaison), information-processing roles (monitor, disseminator, and spokesperson) and decision-making roles (entrepreneur, disturbance handler, resource-allocator, and negotiator). Indeed, a large number of roles!

Other authors, such as Pearson (1989), compiled their own catalogs of basic top executive activities, such as creating distinctive work environments, spearheading innovative strategic thinking, managing company resources productively, directing people development and deployment processes, building dynamic organizations, and overseeing day-to-day operations. Pearson's catalog of six activities essentially combines Kotter's (1982) management tasks (planning and budgeting, organizing and staffing, controlling and problem solving) with Kotter's (1990, 1996) leadership tasks oriented toward corporate renewal.

In a chapter on the design of the CEO and COO roles, Rivero and Spencer (1998) identified a set of eleven roles and behaviors essential to the executive leadership of a large complex organization: strategist, architect, ambassador, corporate image-keeper, policy manager,

---

[1] For the interested reader, Hales (1986) presents a splendid summary and evaluation of the early literature on management roles.

performance manager, operations manager, functional manager, process manager, people manager, and information manager.

Farkas and Wetlaufer (1996) found five basic leadership approaches or role clusters:

(1) *strategy approach*: the CEO is primarily focused on the future and on external matters;

(2) *human-assets approach*: the CEO is concerned with the development of employees;

(3) *expertise approach*: the CEO's intent is on fostering learning around a distinctive competitive advantage;

(4) *box approach*: the CEO focuses on the activities Kotter (1982) calls "management" – planning, organizing, controlling, and problem-solving;

(5) *change approach*: the CEO focuses on the transition from current to future congruencies between the organization and the environment.

It is revealing of the institutionalization of individualistic assumptions of top management positions that even when authors recognize the difficulties and heterogeneity of executive roles they continue to emphasize the need for top managers to become flexible – as if this were easy! Farkas and Wetlaufer (1996), for instance, after underlining the differences among their five approaches, indicate that a CEO "can and should change over the course of his or her tenure" and should perform the different roles "decisively and boldly" (p. 112). Another significantly over-optimistic example is Gosling and Mintzberg (2003):

> To be effective, managers need to face the juxtapositions in order to arrive at a deep integration of these seemingly contradictory concerns. That means they must focus not only on what they have to accomplish but also on how they have to think. Managers need various mind-sets. (p. 55)

In a paper that begins with a highly skeptical view of the feasibility of managing all the managerial paradoxes, Gosling and Mintzberg (2003) soon switch to an optimistic tone, asking managers to develop five mind-sets: (1) managing the self, or the reflective mind-set; (2) managing organizations, or the analytical mind-set; (3) managing context, or the worldly mind-set; (4) managing relationships, or the collaborative mind-set; and (5) managing change, or the action mind-set.

As Mintzberg (1994) recognizes, these roles or approaches or mind-sets or role clusters or competences – all of these terms refer to a collection of related activities or behaviors aimed at the execution of tasks for the attainment of goals – are analytically separable, yet they are intertwined in practice, forming an integrated whole, a behavioral *Gestalt*. Given our purpose of promoting a contingency perspective of corporate power structures, it is worth noting yet another argument advanced by Mintzberg – namely, that chief executives will decide on a particular role configuration comprising the whole of their work. These configurations are based on the optimization of two criteria. First, they select different roles following a contingent logic, depending on the constraints posed by their external, internal, and human environments. Second, as Hodgson, Levinson, and Zaleznik (1965) found, executives tend to adopt some roles at the expense of others, depending on their own psychological predispositions toward particular roles. Similarly, Belbin (1981, 2000) distinguished between primary roles, to which the team-member manager has a natural affinity and predisposition, and secondary roles, demanded by the manager's position in the hierarchy and the corresponding contingencies. The primary roles, those roles preferred psychologically, belong to what we call the executive contingency.

Since the early 1990s, managerial roles have been undergoing a transformation that is probably without parallel since the generalization in the 1960s of the multi-divisional structure and the establishment of a basic set of top managerial tasks and careers. Ghoshal and Bartlett (1997) maintained that this model was applicable when economic capital was the scarce resource and executives were absorbed in the capital-allocation processes. Bartlett and Ghoshal (1998a) proposed a new model of management roles congruent with the way in which companies at the turn of the century were abandoning the M-form structure and transforming themselves in order to cope with new competitive imperatives. Bartlett and Ghoshal found, however, that many top-level managers still played roles that were relevant to the old model such as "the formulators of strategy, the builders of structure, and the controllers of systems" (p. 81), and yet their description of new managerial tasks in leading corporations revealed a highly differentiated role repertoire. (1) The entrepreneurial process is led by front-line managers such as the heads of strategic business units, who are focused on innovation and results and dominated by an external orientation. (2) The integrative function is focused primarily on co-ordination and people development and is carried out by managers working in trimmed-down headquarters. These integrators are structurally equivalent to the former middle management, although with fewer control responsibilities. (3) Institutional work is aimed at holding the corporation together through integrative mechanisms such as values, distinctive competencies, and basic strategic priorities, and is conducted at the apex of the corporation. These three basic managerial tasks demand competencies that cannot easily be carried out by the same manager, even sequentially.

In summary, executives perform various roles, analytically separable, but played in conjunction, as a *Gestalt*. The specific configuration and content of these roles depends on the three groups of contingencies discussed in the previous chapter: external, internal, and executive. As argued above, most of today's organizations have no stringent requirements about how roles should be played; executives have strong powers of enactment with regard to their roles. Whitley's (1989) conceptualization of managerial tasks helps one to understand that these tasks can be performed in several ways:

At least five major characteristics of managerial tasks which differentiate them from other sorts of work can be readily identified: (1) they are highly interdependent, contextual and systemic; (2) they are relatively nonstandardized; (3) they are changeable and developing; (4) they combine both the maintenance of administrative structures and their change; and lastly (5) they rarely generate visible and separate outputs which can be directly linked to individual inputs. (p. 212)

As Hales (1986) said, jobs at the apex have "fluid boundaries" (p. 95) that "seem, in general, to be sufficiently loosely defined to be highly negotiable and susceptible to choice of both style and content . . . the work of managers is the management of their work" (p. 101). As Drucker (2004) has recently noted regarding the executive style of the numerous executives he has encountered in his prolonged career: "CEOs were all over the map in terms of their personalities, attitudes, values, strengths, and weaknesses. They ranged from extroverted to nearly reclusive, from easygoing to controlling, from generous to parsimonious". (p. 59)

To assume that executives will enact role configurations with which they feel psychologically comfortable and which guarantees them the greatest leverage in local games and the widest possible room for action is in line with the logic of contingency and resource dependency theories, a theme we now address.

A theory of action

Current developments in structures, whereby formal structures and systems are less influential, makes executive action even more eventful. As Burt (1997) says:

The shift away from bureaucracy means that managers cannot rely as much on directives from the firm. They are more than ever the authors of their own work. Firms gain by being able to identify, and adapt more readily to, needed production changes and market shifts. There are new opportunities for managers, but there are also new costs . . . a corresponding increase in uncertainty, stress, and potentially disruptive conflict. (p. 359)

Theories of action are conceptualizations of the specific features of the social action performed by executives in organizational settings. They are concerned with the basic motives, purposes, and skills behind executive behaviors with regard to the construction or maintenance of organizations. A theory of action would consider, among other things, the following essential dimensions of management: content versus context, long term versus short term, people versus roles, stability versus change, present versus future, control versus flexibility, cohesion versus autonomy, exploration versus exploitation, innovation versus predictability, disclosure versus opacity, social versus technical, and what versus how.

In addition to being useful for understanding practical executive predicaments, an approach based on a theory of action appears to be academically timely, as corroborated by scholars from diverse academic fields. Bartlett and Ghoshal (1993) identify the need for a managerial theory of the firm, arguing that approaches to management are too structurally dominated and divert attention away from important elements in executive roles such as "purpose" and "stretch," elements that they find in leading organizations. As Parsons (1968) had pointed out, "purpose" is the key element of any action theory. Similarly, Kanter (1997) suggests that focusing on action and process is one of the pending challenges of the field of management studies, precisely because weak structures, rules, and roles increasingly proliferate. A similar message is coming from fields which are more discipline-based. In organizational theory, for example, Hirsch and Lounsbury (1997) underline the overly powerful role of the normative environment in the neo-institutional school. To counterbalance that influence, they also ask for a more purposeful notion of organizational actors. Fligstein (1997) also emphasizes the need for a reformulation of theories of action, which he believes should allow more room for social construc-tionist hypotheses and for political entrepreneurship.

Fortunately, in the last several years, there have been some efforts to conceptualize organizational action that, in turn, can help in the design of corporate political structures and in the understanding of corporate political action. In part, these attempts have been in reac-tion to the overflow into management education during the 1980s and 1990s of business fads and fashions that have obscured the essentials of common-sense management, and have thrown executives into a frantic search for the latest how-to prescriptions. It has been argued (Eccles and Nohria, 1992; Alvarez, 1997; Green, 2004) that executives easily become gluttons for formulae because of their over-emphasis on short-term results, a factor that stimulates the desire for easy, simple, and determined explanations. Theories of action could be an antidote to those simplifications.

As described in Chapter 1, authors in the cognitive tradition were the first to link managerial action to organizational politics. The first orga-nizational setting they referred to was educational institutions, which were probably more similar to today's business organizations than to the corporations existing at the time of their analysis in the 1960s and early 1970s. Representative of these pioneer studies on management action is March and Cohen's *Leadership and Ambiguity* (1974). In their now-famous analysis, the authors characterize educational insti-tutions as organized anarchies for three reasons: (1) their preferences are problematic because they do not have clear or consistent notions about what they are trying to do; (2) the technology or methodology they need to use is unclear, because they often do not know how they are supposed to accomplish their goals; (3) the number, influence, and par-ticipation of decision-making actors is fluid, as there are doubts about who should make the decisions. March and Cohen offer eight prescrip-tions for executive leadership in these highly complex organizations:

(1) Be prepared to spend time and energy, because investing time in and of itself becomes a claim on the decision-making system, signals commitment, and demonstrates a willingness to invest political capital in a particular action.

(2) Be persistent, because having more patience than other managers facilitates the acceptance of one's plan.

(3) Exchange status for substance; make concessions to reduce resistance and win allies.

(4) Facilitate the opposition's participation in the change effort, so as to foster commitment and realism.

(5) Overload the system with as many initiatives as possible, in order to increase the number of projects that get through the openings of inertia. In any system there are always cracks, corridors of indifference, and windows of opportunity.

(6) For the same reason, detach problems from solutions by providing garbage cans; simultaneously present many issues up for discussion.

(7) Try to influence the organization imperceptibly, managing unobtrusively; call as little attention as possible to the most important actions, as the most important events are often the least apparent.

(8) Be the one in charge of recording or interpreting the events of your organization, so that people see facts as you prefer them to be seen. At the end of the day, the meaning of reality is socially constructed.

In 1980, Padgett adapted March and Cohen's prescriptions to organizations that are more hierarchical and business-like than the loosely structured educational institutions. Yet Padgett's set of recommendations is consistent with the set provided by March and Cohen:

(1) Old, conservative, and secure businesses should be run by rigid and pro-status-quo executives, because adaptation is not required in such organizations. New and innovative businesses, on the other hand, should be run by uncertain and insecure executives, in order to facilitate doubt, inquiry, and, hopefully, learning.

(2) Organizations should be structured so that high-visibility and low-visibility businesses are segregated, thereby allowing differentiated management styles to be deployed.

(3) Only the leaders of the low-saliency units should be more tolerant and experimental than the corporate executive, in order to lower risks.

(4) Top executives should never make any decisions; they do so only at their own risk.[2]

(5) Top executives should concentrate instead on manipulating rules of discretion (i.e. centralization policy) in order to counterbalance conflicting units and their business heads. In other words, executives should manage context instead of content.

(6) Corporate executives should not fight against subunit biases and internal conflict; instead they should use them to force inertial organizations to keep pace with changing environments.

A revealing similar set of recommendations for action can be found in Wrapp's (1984) classic, *Good Managers Don't Make Policy Decisions*. Wrapp's recommendations to general managers – which go against the grain of popular belief and general management textbooks that portray executives primarily as decision-makers and communicators of precise goals and objectives – converge on an already familiar set of themes: (1) develop a network of information sources; (2) concentrate energies and time on priorities; (3) play the power game; (4) cultivate a sense of timing; (5) press cautiously; (6) appear imprecise; (7) maintain visibility; (8) avoid policy straitjackets; (9) muddle with purpose; (10) exploit change.

Wrapp does, in fact, deliver *avant la lettre* the basics of robust action, which was the key focus of the work of Eccles and Nohria (1992) on the essence of the managerial job. They define robust action as the arranging of organizational elements (from systems and formal structures to shared values and styles) in ways that facilitate the accomplishment of short-term objectives while preserving long-term flexibility. This conception is similar to Neustadt's (1990) fundamental recommendation to US presidents to protect political capital in the short run in order to make it available in the long run for potentially important future policies or decisions. According to Eccles and Nohria, the characteristics of robust action include: (1) acting without certitude; (2) constantly

---

[2] A quote in Quinn (1980), from an interview with Sir Alastair Pilkington, chair of Pilkington Brothers Ltd., exemplifies this point: "I don't set goals for other people. That is one of their key jobs – to define their goals, to define success. I set goals for myself, but not for other people. I set the company goals in my own mind, and they come out in discussions. But I don't sort of lay them down . . . I've never taken a major decision without consulting my colleagues. It would be unimaginable to me, unimaginable. First, they help me make a better decision in most cases. Second, if they know about it and agree with it, they'll back it. Otherwise, they might challenge it, not openly, but subconsciously" (p. 65).

preserving flexibility; (3) being politically savvy; (4) having a keen sense of timing; (5) judging the situation at hand; (6) using rhetoric effectively; and (7) working multiple agendas.[3]

Robust action thrives in what Burns (1961) and Leifer (1988, 1991) called local games: the jockeying by executives to improve their positions in the social structure of the organization, or the perceived value attached to them, with the final aim of increasing their degrees of autonomy for action. These local games are, in turn, favored by the previously mentioned diffusion of practices of organizing based upon weak structures which is leading to high levels of diversification and fragmentation in the tasks and careers of executives. Diversification occurs because templates for organizational tasks and roles are plural and more heterogeneous than the old dominant model, which was not only bureaucratic, but unique (Kanter, 1989; Cockerill, Hunt, and Schroder, 1995; Leicht and Fennell, 1997). Fragmentation occurs because, even in single organizations, as Ghoshal and Bartlett (1997) describe, managerial roles, tasks, and behaviors, are highly differentiated, and, consequently, role transitions are difficult. Moreover, fragmentation adds to the characterization of managerial actions as highly political. As the popular saying goes: all politics are local.

White's (1992) *Identity and Control: A Structural Theory of Social Action* is perhaps the most self-conscious attempt at developing a theory of organizational action. White argues that organizations are contrary to "action," because structure, social order, stability, routines, and responsibilities arise out of efforts to control. Thus organizations serve to block fresh action. Action is the reverse social phenomenon to organizations, as it is based in the breaking of routines and structures. White's book contains an entire section on general managers, the decouplers *par excellence* in an organizational society. In White's view, the job of the executive is to cut through the rigidities of social organization, to dilute the inertia of social forms, and to break the codification brought by rules – and, we might add, to break from fixed roles.

Another attempt at advancing a theory of action was made by Fligstein (1997), who, with the concurrence of such authors as Selznick, DiMaggio, and Hirsch, criticized the neo-institutional school

---

[3] The best empirical illustration of robust action is probably Padgett and Ansell's (1993) piece on Cosimo de Medici's political style.

of organizational theory for its overly deterministic notions of social action. Fligstein also criticized the school for its lack of political dimensions, a point supported by Alvarez (1997). Like Eccles and Nohria, Fligstein proposed that such a theory of action should conceptualize organizational actors as specialists in empathy who are able to relate to the interests and world views of the constituencies playing in local situations, and can align the interests and world views of those constituencies with the organization's strategy. Organizational actors have a large repertoire of action tactics available to them, including:

(1) using direct authority, i.e. formal power;
(2) setting the agenda for other actors;
(3) understanding and using the ambiguities and uncertainties of organizational settings, and taking and using the resources available at any given moment;
(4) framing action by linking broader interpretations of reality to groups' existing conceptions of interests;
(5) shaking up settled situations and hoping that the new configuration is better than the original one;[4]
(6) brokering or being highly active at networking;[5]
(7) asking for more and accepting less;
(8) appearing hard to read (goallessness) and without values oriented to personal gain (selflessness);
(9) maintaining ambiguity, in order to impede others in developing strategies;
(10) building alliances and coalitions through the aggregation of interests;
(11) initiating several courses of action with the hope that some will succeed;
(12) displaying more power than one really has, with the belief that the appearance of power is power;[6]
(13) inducing others to act by making them think they are in charge;
(14) bringing outsiders into a coalition, then becoming central to the coalition, and isolating competitors; and
(15) using deterrents as sources of power.

This list of tactics confirms the notion that executive tasks are highly political as well as enormously psychologically and cognitively difficult.

---

[4] This is what White (1992) calls "wheeling and annealing."
[5] Ron Burt (1992) would call this "bridging structural holes."
[6] The practice of social construction of reality.

We may assume that the capabilities for performing them do not abound in the general population or even in the managerial class. The list also provides evidence that taking proper robust action springs from a set of skills which is not dependent on formalized knowledge. As a consequence, executive leadership cannot be standardized, and is therefore resistant to professionalization (Whitley, 1989). To receive an education for executive positions does not guarantee performance or career success.

It is important to emphasize that the political notion of the functions of executives just developed fits particularly well with today's corporate governance realities. Increasingly, shareholders and other stakeholders are taking offensive action against what agency theory presents as executive prerogatives and are pushing top managers to be more responsive to a variety of external and internal constituencies, thus forcing them to perform an even more complex political balancing act. Because the careers of executives and those of politicians rely on robust action, a kinship is developing between them (Kanter, 1989).

This brings to the fore the difficulty of playing robust action solo.

Farkas and Wetlaufer (1996) reported that between 35 and 50 percent of CEOs are replaced within five years. By 2001 this percentage had grown to the point where two-thirds of CEOs were being replaced within five years (Skapinker, 2001). This should not be a surprising finding, given the challenges of managing at the top to which we have called attention in this chapter. These challenges are created by the tensions of structural and role dichotomies (when the psychological make-up of successful executives tends to be highly individualistic and not conducive to balancing multi-dimensional pressures); by the high number and intrinsic difficulty of executive roles (when executives prefer configurations with which they feel psychologically at ease); and by the political savvy required for robust action in contexts, such as business organizations, that are prone to the unexpected consequences of action. What is really surprising is that such little attention has been paid to plural arrangements in top executives' offices, structures such as small numbers at the top that may alleviate the burdens of the job.

Kanter (1989) found that executives enjoy "unprecedented freedom" (p. 90) in designing their own jobs. They are the architects of their organizations and of their political structures (Howard, 1992). But they still have individualistic instincts that they invest in their careers and affective needs in a context politically and emotionally overcharged – the two main contingencies constituting the executive environment. Ultimately it is within the domain of executives to decide whether or not to have small-numbers structures to respond to these contingencies, and thereby achieve better performance in what Farkas and Wetlaufer (1996) aptly call "the infinite job."

3 | Roles and relationships as parameters of corporate power structures

Roles are used to achieve political ends.

Callero, 1994, p. 240

Neither love nor the division of labor,
neither the common attitude of two toward
a third nor friendship, neither party
affiliation nor superordination of
subordination is likely by itself alone to
produce or permanently sustain an actual
group . . . the process which is given one
name actually contains several
distinguishable forms of relation.

Simmel, 1964, p. 21

SIR ADRIAN CADBURY is the former chair of Cadbury Ltd., UK, and author of the famous 1992 Cadbury Report and Code of Best Practice in Governance. In his recent book, *Corporate Governance and Chairmanship: A Personal View* (Cadbury, 2002), he emphasized the freedom and choice that managers have in the design of corporate power structures and governance:

In the end, those at the top of a company have certain duties to discharge and there are an endless number of ways in which those duties can be divided. The posts of chairman, deputy chairman, chief executive, and senior independent director can be held in different combinations by four, three, or even two people. The objectives remain the same: to provide clear leadership, to ensure that the board is effective and the business is well managed, and to represent the company to the outside world. The aim is to see that as many as possible of the qualities required for these different tasks are present among the members of the top team. How the tasks are allocated is less crucial than that there should be trust between the members of the team and no confusion about who does what. (p. 127)

As the above quote maintains, and as discussed in Chapter 1, small numbers at the top are highly discretional structures. In this chapter we examine the opportunities for the design of vertical structures provided by such freedom and choice. We scrutinize the ways in which top managers shape and play their *roles* and analyze the nature of the *relationships* that bind them together in pairs or larger constellations. In the previous chapters we remarked on the rising demands placed upon women and men at the helm of large corporations and smaller businesses; in the solitude at the corporate apex, executives can experience difficulties in fulfilling the demands of a widening range of stakeholders. The need for a broader span of competencies – or minds, to use Gosling and Mintzberg's (2003) term – as well as the costs of moving among multiple roles in the course of a working day (Ashforth, Kreiner, and Fugate, 2000), have led to an increase in solutions for the design of the executive suite. Among these designs is what we referred to in previous chapters as "small numbers at the top."

In the Introduction and in Chapter 1, we set the stage for a contingency perspective and advanced groups of contingencies from the external, internal, and executive environment, and argued that they must be considered in the design of corporate power structures. In a contingency theory of the management function, role theory is expected to provide a useful theoretical framework (Losada, 2003). But despite the centrality of roles in the understanding of working behavior and the preponderance of studies on the top manager's job, the full potential of role theory has yet to be realized in the field of corporate governance. It is our goal in this chapter to complement our contingency theory perspective by introducing scholarly work on roles and relationships and linking it to the study of corporate governance. Although the discussion on separate versus combined CEO–chair positions is bringing the literature on roles and relationships closer to the area of corporate governance, there is still a great deal of work to be done.

To advance our contingency theory perspective, we need to unravel the parameters of corporate power structures and examine their fit with the key contingencies introduced in Chapter 1. In an attempt to furnish significant yet comprehensible parameters of corporate power structures, we focus on two parameters – roles and relationships – which help explain the differentiation and integration of vertical structures. From a contingency theory stance, roles can be seen as vehicles of differentiation, whereas relationships of differing nature and strength can be seen as integration mechanisms.

We begin by reviewing pertinent work on roles, which we believe can enhance an understanding of the design and dynamics of small-numbers power structures. Then we discuss the resource view of roles and suggest that roles can be a useful governance resource and a means of creativity in the design of vertical structures. Next, we illuminate essential differentiation processes, such as creation, consolidation, sharing, and separation of roles. Finally, we scrutinize relationships as the mechanisms that assist in role integration – a critical but under-developed area in corporate governance – delving into three essential types of relationships that serve as integrators: shared cognition, trust, and affection.

On the nature of roles

In his presidential address in the *American Sociological Review*, Blau (1974) defined social structure as "a system of social relations among differentiated parts of a society or group" (p. 615). He argued that an analytical dissection of the social structure is needed before any attempts at synthesis are made. Blau suggested that "to speak of social structure is to speak of differentiation among people, since social structure is defined by the distinctions people make, explicitly or implicitly, in their role relations" (p. 616). This is of particular relevance for working relationships. Small-numbers power structures, as a specific manifestation of working relationships at the corporate pinnacle, can be envisaged as arrangements that consist of roles and relationships. As Gabarro (1987) pointed out, "Roles and role expectations are part of the context of all social interaction, but they are even more pervasive and are more explicitly defined in working relationships, particularly when they occur within or across organizational hierarchies" (p. 180). Below, we connect the general discussion on roles with the specifics of vertical structures.

It is widely agreed that role is a notion linking social structure and personality and is therefore central to organization theory (Hickson, 1966). Role is a set of activities or expected behavior (Katz and Kahn, 1978). The expectations can range from specific role prescriptions to loosely defined boundaries of legitimate discretion (Hickson, 1966). A person who occupies an office – that is a position, a status, a point in the organizational space – performs a role. The organizational space in turn is "a structure of interrelated offices and the pattern of activities associated with them" (Katz and Kahn, 1978, p. 188). It is believed that executives and board members, being positioned at the apex of the organization, enjoy legitimate discretion and, as "hierarchical super-ordinates (bosses)," to use Hickson's (1966, p. 225) term, are among the few prescribers of role specificity to roles in organizations.

Subject to much less role prescription than are people at the lower levels of organizations, those in the top layer are expected to exercise their legitimate discretion within certain boundaries. These boundaries are socially constructed by influential parties, such as shareholders, media, institutional investors, and analysts; and shape what is expected from the professionals at the top of a company. The social construction of these boundaries affects the fluidity of the roles of top management. According to Robert Rubin, former co-CEO of Goldman Sachs and ex-Secretary of the Treasury of the USA, this fluidity of roles is greater in the world of politics:

At Goldman Sachs, Citigroup, or any other company, you have a job and a role. Whatever your title may be, whether CEO or clerk/typist, you have an idea where you fit into the organization. Positions may have some fluidity, but they also have fairly clear definitions. For someone working in a senior position at the White House or one of the cabinet agencies, by contrast, it was never entirely clear what your role – or anybody else's – was. (Rubin and Weisberg, 2003, p. 138)

The CEO's role is associated with certain responsibilities and priv-ileges. As Rubin concluded, continuing the comparison of his experi-ences as the head of a private company with those as a government official, "A private-sector CEO has the power to hire and fire based on performance, to pay top managers large bonuses, and to promote capa-ble people aggressively" (Rubin and Weisberg, 2003, p. 178). Further-more, as discussed at length in Chapter 1, there is a range of behavioral expectations for the individuals who run corporations. Some of these expectations are implicit; others are stated explicitly in codes of good governance. These expectations change over time, as revealed in a study of the selection processes of the CEOs of 850 firms over the period 1980 to 1996 (Khurana, 2002). The current conception revolves around the chief executive's ability to motivate and inspire both external and inter-nal stakeholders and, as Khurana's study reveals, the external market for CEOs is based on characteristics as intangible and as difficult to measure as charisma.

Role is a classification across social structures. For example, the chief executive role across the Fortune 500 corporations exhibits certain common behavioral expectations from such bodies as shareholders, investors, and the media. Position, in turn, is specific to a particular social structure and therefore indicates a given location (Baker and Faulkner, 1991). Role specificity differs with the type of organization (Hickson, 1966). Both Weber's (1978) bureaucracy and Burns and Stalker's (1961) mechanistic structures are contexts of higher specificity. Weber's charismatic structure and Burns and Stalker's organic structure, on the other hand, are contexts of lower specificity, whereby "role definitions are more general and continually change with interaction" (Hickson, 1966, p. 226). In this sense, being the CEO of British Petroleum can present certain peculiarities that cannot be found in the executive suite of Exxon Mobil because of the differences between these two organizations.

Finally, one or more individuals, depending on their personal competencies, predispositions, and convictions, enact a position in one way or another. Executives have certain predispositions and antipathies, which to some extent determine the role specialization they can undertake successfully (Hodgson, Levinson, and Zaleznik, 1965). To return to our example, the CEO of British Petroleum, Lord John Browne, has a different style from Exxon Mobil Corporation's Lee Raymond.

The individual who plays the role of the chief executive is usually credited with the company's successes and failures. The 2004 Global 500 issue of *Fortune* carried a profile of John Browne, who, as the editorial introduction argued, "built BP into the largest oil company in the world, taking over the spot long held by Exxon Mobil" (Friedman, 2004, p. 10). Another article in this issue credited Browne with quadrupling British Petroleum's revenues in the nine years since he had become CEO, and claimed that "Browne is the dominant, public face of British Petroleum" (Schwartz, 2004, p. 61). Similarly, Carlos Ghosn's magnetic smile on the cover of a recent issue of *Business Week* was accompanied by an article pronouncing him the savior of Japan's No. 2 car maker, Nissan (Bremner *et al.*, 2004, p. 40).

Enacted in one company or another, executive roles are not homogeneous and monolithic units. They have different elements, such as sub-roles or bundles, which in turn consist of activities, tasks, responsibilities, and obligations, which, taken together, shape the behaviors of the executives. The line between roles and sub-roles is fine and context-specific. What in one organization may be considered a single role with particular components (sub-roles) to be performed by one person, could be broken down into elements in another organization, with each element assigned as a separate role to a different individual. An example of an unusual innovation in vertical design is the consolidation of the CEO roles at Nissan and Renault, a position to be held by Carlos Ghosn from April 2005 (Bremner, 2004, p. 41). Thus it appears that separable roles can be played in conjunction, as a *Gestalt* (Mintzberg, 1973); yet it usually goes against the grain of good governance to have one person playing two separate roles. For example, consolidation of the CEO and the chair roles in the hands of one executive is subjected to criticism. The move is often approached with suspicion by proponents of corporate governance reforms who aim to distance the executives at the top in order to strengthen the control over executive actions.

In some large corporations, where the top executive position demands greatly differing skills, competencies, and styles and the management of a wide range of tasks and relationships, these activities have been structurally separated. The CEO focuses on external issues and a COO is in charge of internal affairs, i.e. having "a bold visionary type seconded by a discreet nuts-and-bolts operator" (Murray, 2000, p. 2). Although Hambrick and Cannella (2004) have concluded that the use of COOs is on the decline and that it constitutes a high financial cost to the firm, some corporations continue appointing an executive in that second place.

The notion of role as a resource

In bringing contributions from role theory into our discussion of corporate power structures, we adopt the theoretical concept of role as a resource (Baker and Faulkner, 1991). This notion builds on traditional perspectives of roles, in that it conceives of a "role as a bundle of norms and expectations" (Baker and Faulkner, 1991, p. 280). However, it also departs from such approaches inasmuch as a role is not enacted from a position (Biddle, 1986). Rather, the relationship between role and position is reversed: individuals use roles to enact positions and the relationships among these positions (Baker and Faulkner, 1991). Another important distinction of the notion of role as a resource is the implicit assumption that combinatorial patterns of roles into positions are not fixed. In that way it differs from conventional role theory, which considers the configuration of positions to be invariant. Hence the notion of role as a resource provides conceptual ground for discussing patterns and processes of role differentiation, whereby each role could be enacted into a distinct position (e.g. separate CEO and chair of a company) or, alternatively, two or more roles could be consolidated in a single position (e.g. a CEO who is also a chair).

From Baker and Faulkner's (1991) perspective, a role is a resource in two senses: as a means to claim, bargain for, and gain citizenship and acceptance in a social community; and as a key to, or nexus of, social, cultural, and material resources in the pursuit of the interests of incumbents and claimants of a role. The role of the chief executive, for example, serves as a resource when enacted into a position in a particular firm, inasmuch as it enables its incumbent to claim authority and gain membership within an elite layer of professionals and provides the incumbent with the discretionary power to define the strategic direction and organization of the firm's activities. Furthermore, in most cases it allows the executive access to more resources, higher remuneration, and greater perks than any other member of the organization. There is an important clarification here: "attempts to claim and exploit roles as resources may be disputed, contested, or simply ignored" (Baker and Faulkner, 1991, p. 285). Such contests are particularly likely to occur in the executive suite when, for example, there are a number of heirs apparent to an incumbent CEO.

Roles are enacted into positions by individuals. However, roles are also context-dependent; major transformations in the external environment could lead to their growth or decline. Baker and Faulkner (1991) have illustrated the theoretical concept of role as a resource in their example of the transformation of the Hollywood cinema industry, brought about by the introduction of the blockbuster movie. The rise of the blockbuster changed the relative efficacy of different role combinations, leading to the decline of some combinations and to the rise of others. The specialization of film producers increased and was combined with the separation of the artistic and business domains. Moreover, there was a trend, the outcome of both adaptation and imitation, toward the increasing fusion of such artistic roles as writer and director in a single position. Those individuals who used role separation and role consolidation to solve technical and organizational problems adapted. Those who copied the combinations because they thought it would make them legitimate players in the new blockbuster era simply imitated. In both ways, however, roles were enacted into positions and served as the sources of legitimacy and access to other resources.

Transferring Baker and Faulkner's (1991) insight to the domain of vertical power structures, the story of the creation and propagation of the chief financial officer (CFO) role is revealing. In a study of the rise of the CFO in the American firm, Zorn (2004) concluded that the surge in the promulgation and popularity of the CFO precept was fueled by profound changes in the external environment of companies: "CFOs became popular in tandem with firms' increased attention to the whims of the financial markets" (p. 345), as "part and parcel of the shareholder-value movement" (p. 346).

The notion of role as a resource allows the duality of agency and structure to be addressed by viewing roles as vehicles that actors use to seek independence in their work (Callero, 1994). The greater autonomy in roles at the top of the company (compared to those of line or middle managers) is conducive to a greater number of role configurations, which are usually open to design, negotiation, and proactivity in their enactment (Baker and Faulkner, 1991; Callero, 1994; Alvarez, 2000; Cadbury, 2002). Although corporate governance consists of highly regulated and institutionalized functions, as exemplified by an increasing number of legal and social codes and practices, it still allows for different combinations of division of labor and decision rights. Thus a CEO may or may not be chair of the board and may or may not have a COO as a lieutenant dealing with the day-to-day issues of running the business.

Combinations of roles may differ in efficiency. Depending on how well they match the relevant contingencies, some role combinations may be more efficient than others in addressing these contingencies. A combined CEO-chair position, for example, could be considered as going against the grain of recent governance codes demanding a separation of these roles and a relational distance between the individuals who play them. However, in conditions threatening the firm's competitiveness and survival, decision-making is enhanced and unity of action enforced when both roles are played by the same executive. Chapters 4 and 5 of the book deal in detail with a range of options for small numbers at the top.

Further developing Baker and Faulkner's (1991) notion of role as a resource, Callero (1994) suggested that individuals employ roles as platforms for exercising control and power and as a means for achieving political ends. In his view, one of the most important strategies for gaining influence and exercising power is the use of roles as a resource for changing the social structure. A manifestation of this strategy in the area of corporate governance occurs when "chief executives or presidents of formal organizations can use their roles to restructure a bureaucracy by creating new roles and eliminating others" (Callero, 1994, p. 240). It is in this political opportunity of role activism that the notion of role as a resource for action could serve the purposes of this book and enrich the development of a contingency theory perspective of small numbers at the top. Placing the emphasis on some roles at the expense of others requires attention to the design of roles and responsibilities at the corporate pinnacle in terms of creating, separating, sharing, or combining roles to address critical contingencies. Having clarified the differentiation of roles and responsibilities, the top executives also need to agree on ways to integrate their inputs. In the next section we provide a discussion of these issues.

Role as a resource for action

In Chapter 1 we drew attention to the asymmetry between the increasingly regulated differentiation of executive roles and the poorly prescribed integration of the roles at the top of the company. Here we attempt to provide a more balanced view of the differentiation and integration processes at the top, suggesting that roles can be considered as useful governance resources. As discussed in Chapter 1, the notion of role as a governance resource acknowledges the ability of executives to differentiate and integrate their roles into positions in a way that fits into the external, internal, and executive contingencies. In examining small-numbers structures of duos, trios, and larger constellations at the corporate pinnacle, we unraveled essential differentiation processes, such as the creation, separation, consolidation, and sharing of roles, along with core integration processes such as shared cognition, trust, and affection. As Figure 1 reveals, reciprocal role interdependence demands role integration at the top.

In Chapter 1 we defined reciprocal role interdependence as coordination by mutual adjustment, which is based on continuous,

**Role
differentiation**

**Role
integration**

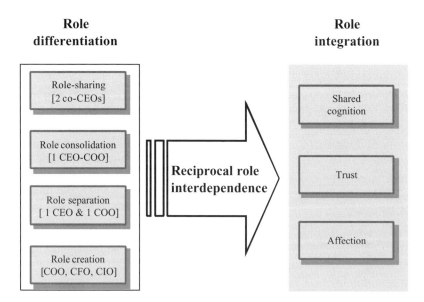

Figure 1. Using role as a resource for action: role differentiation and role integration.

self-regulated, reciprocal feedback among a group of executives during strategic decision-making and implementation. Mutual adjustment is essential for both general and upper-echelon managers because of the nature of the task and the fact that limitations in the cognitions and abilities of executives require them to rely on their peers and subordinates (Gabarro, 1987). Below, we discuss in detail the mechanisms for role differentiation and integration.

Role differentiation

It can be argued that role differentiation at the top of a company takes place through four essential mechanisms: the creation, separation, consolidation, and sharing of roles, each of which is now defined and illustrated.

Role creation
This refers to the *de novo* introduction of roles and their formalization into positions in vertical power structures. It may also denote the return to roles and positions that have already existed in the corporate power

structures but have been abandoned because of the lack of fit with the relevant contingencies.

Roles at the top have been evolving as the firm evolves toward an increasing differentiation; this is exhibited in the wide range of executive roles that can be currently found at the top of a company. Identifying the timing of the *de novo* creation of a particular executive role, however, is not easy. There are different accounts in the academic literature and the business press seeking to explain the timing and reasons for the rise and fall of specific executive roles. The studies by Dobbin, Dierkes, Kwok and Zorn (2001) and Hambrick and Cannella (2004) of the COO role are examples, as is Zorn's (2004) account of the CFO role.

The CEO designation was created for executives with overall responsibility for the actions and performance of an organization (Finkelstein and Hambrick, 1996). To manage the internal operations of the firm, the figure of the COO was added. The COO, sometimes referred to as the Inside Boss, holds responsibilities for the execution of strategy and for the day-to-day operation of the business. The role is complementary to that of the CEO, the Outside Boss, who is responsible for the development and maintenance of relations with the relevant external stakeholders.

COOs were generally viewed as a perk for the CEOs of growing, profitable, diversified firms, or as positions denoting the heir apparent chosen by the top person (Dobbin, Dierkes, Kwok, and Zorn, 2001). Hambrick and Cannella (2004), for example, date the creation of the COO role to a 1954 book by Peter Drucker – *The Practice of Management* – in which he argued that the top job is too big for a single power holder (Drucker, 1954). In their study of the top jobs at 433 large American corporations during the period 1964–1994, Dobbin, Dierkes, Kwok, and Zorn (2001) identified the COO position in vertical structures as being introduced in the mid-1960s, initially by growing and diversified companies. With the declining popularity of the COO role, the role of the CFO gained importance. Dobbin, Dierkes, Kwok, and Zorn (2001) suggest that the role shift was related to a change in the view of the firm – from an investment portfolio to a bundle of core competencies. This shift in perspective led to a change in expectations for the CEO. The former view had called for a chief executive with a financial background and a second-in-command responsible for operations; whereas the latter view demanded a visionary CEO, with a CFO to deal with the financial issues which arose. As a result, Zorn (2004) argued, "the CEO–CFO was bound to become the dynamic duo of the late-1980s and 1990s," with the CFO managing "relations with shareholders, market expectations, and the firm's stock price" (p. 352).

In acknowledgment of the increased strategic importance of information technology (IT), another executive office, that of the chief information officer (CIO), was developed, and by 1989, 40 percent of Business Week 1000 companies had a CIO (Gupta, 1991).[1] Venture capitalist Vinod Khosla, a co-founder of Sun Microsystems in the early 1980s, argued the importance of the CIO:

An obvious consequence is that the CIO has suddenly become the second most important executive in a company. For a long time, the number two strategic person tended to be the top marketing executive; now it's the technologist. A visionary CIO – not the old model of the CIO – is the key to a company's success. Some big companies understand that – I'm thinking of Cisco, Schwab, Wells Fargo, Federal Express, Wal-Mart – but most don't. (Khosla, quoted in Champion and Carr, 2000, p. 99)

Recently, with the outsourcing of the information technology function by some companies, the CIO role could maintain its importance, as a strong and hierarchically powerful leader is needed to manage the outsourcing arrangement.

In the 1980s and 1990s other chief officer roles were created, generally referred to using the generic term "CxO," or similar labels such as the "C-suite," "C-level executives," or simply, "C" titles. CxO titles include chief technology officer (CTO), chief marketing officer (CMO), and even chief administrative officer (CAO), to denote a professional in charge of all staff functions (Delmar, 2003). Recently, yet another label has been included in the CxO list: chief strategy officer (CSO), to denote the position with ultimate responsibility for strategy. The CSO title is much more common in technology and Internet companies, and in some cases has been given to co-founders (Delmar, 2003). The creation and termination of a specific C-role reflects and signals the strategic importance of a given function for the enterprise.

It is essential when designing the small-numbers corporate power structure to decide which CxO roles should be included in the corporate

---

[1] Gupta quotes Synnott (1987) as having coined the term chief information officer in 1981.

inner sanctum. This decision usually depends on the nature of the business, the key factors for its success, and the availability of top talent in the internal and external labor markets. While new CxO roles and positions are being created, others are being eliminated. Furthermore, there are various options for the subordination and superordination of the CxO roles. In businesses in which IT is of critical importance, for example, the CIO can report directly to the CEO; whereas in businesses in which IT is considered less than crucial, the CIO can report to either the COO or the CFO. Such variance once again affirms the latitude available in the design of vertical structures.

Role separation

This mechanism is employed in order to split a role previously performed by an individual into parts that can be assigned to two or more individuals. The nature of role separation at the corporate apex could be mechanistic or organic (Figure 2), following Burns and Stalker's (1961) distinction. Mechanistic systems are characterized by problems and tasks that are broken down into specializations, and mechanistic role separation splits roles at the top in the same way – into such specializations as CEO, COO, CFO, and CIO.

In organic systems, individuals perform their specialized tasks with an awareness of the tasks of the firm as a whole. Organic role separation is a situation in which roles maintain their separation, with either a certain sharing or a shared awareness of tasks that can be performed jointly. Organic role separation is present in top offices where certain tasks are shared, even though the roles are distinct (e.g. one individual is the CEO and another is the COO; see the example in Figure 2). So although the CEO and COO can play separate roles, they can, as Rivero and Spencer (1998) explain, be played symbiotically, with certain activities being shared. Michael Dell, the chair of Dell, and Kevin Rollins, its CEO, are a case in point. Asked about his relationship with Michael Dell, Kevin Rollins says:

Michael and I, to a great extent, share the office. While we both have areas we work on – and we try to define those quite closely – we share a lot of responsibilities, and whoever is available does those things. We collaborate on our ideas of what we want the company to do. But I think that in terms of the day-to-day business, I run the company. He runs technology. We share the strategy stuff. (Spooner, 2003)

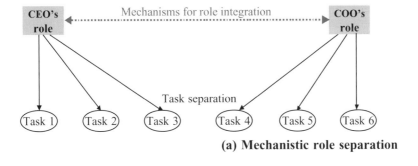

(a) Mechanistic role separation

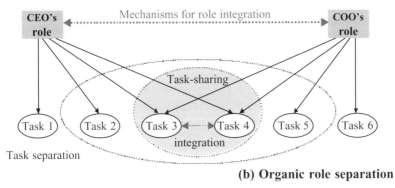

(b) Organic role separation

Figure 2. Examples of mechanistic and organic role separation.

Mechanistic role separation is observed in cases in which each of the two top managers performs a separate role and a separate set of tasks. The distinction between mechanistic role separation and organic role separation is an important one, as the two types require different integration mechanisms. In the case of mechanistic role separation, the integration comes primarily through superordination and communication. The organic role separation requires more complex integrating mechanisms, such as shared cognition, trust, and affection. We discuss the different role integration mechanisms in the following section.

The separation of roles has governance implications, and the importance of the CEO-chair combination or separation is a critical element in the debate over what constitutes good corporate governance. Role separation is characteristic of companies in the United Kingdom (95 percent of all Financial Times Stock Exchange 350 firms) and of German and Dutch two-tier board structures, in which the chair runs a supervisory board of non-executives and the CEO leads a management board comprising only executives (Coombes and Wong, 2004). In the UK, the separation of these two top roles, which is considered to reinforce the board's independence, is triggered by explicit recommendations in such well-respected policy documents as the Cadbury Code of Best Practice in Governance. That code not only recommends compliance with role separation but also advocates that firms that do not comply with it provide a public explanation of the reason for consolidating these positions.

Role consolidation

When two or more roles are enacted in a single position and performed by a single executive, we can call it role consolidation. The CEO-chair role consolidation, known as a CEO duality (Stewart, 1991; Finkelstein and Hambrick, 1996), has caused a great deal of controversy in recent discussions on good corporate governance. The consolidation of these two roles is typical of US companies; 80 percent of Standard and Poor's 500 companies combine the two positions (Coombes and Wong, 2004). Such consolidation, however, is far from universally applied. Harrison, Torres, and Kukalis (1988) explored the nature and relationship of the CEO and chair positions in a sample of 671 large US manufacturing firms for the period 1978–1980, and found that a consolidation of the two roles occurred in cases of strong external threats, when the survival of the business demanded power centralization and tightened control.

Another manifestation of role consolidation in the domain of vertical power structures is the case of a CEO who has assumed responsibility for the day-to-day coordination of the business, thereby enacting the CEO and the COO roles in a single position. Or one executive may play the CEO role in two companies simultaneously, as exemplified by Carlos Ghosn, who became the CEO of both Nissan and Renault on April 1, 2005. As reported in the press, "Ghosn will remain CEO of Nissan, becoming chief executive of two car companies with headquarters on two continents" (Fonda, 2003).

The common metaphor of simultaneously wearing several hats is a useful one for describing role consolidation. As Robert Rubin (Rubin and Weisberg, 2003) describes his former work as US Secretary of the Treasury, "you wear two hats at the same time," one as a head of an agency, and another as part of an administration "in which everything revolves around the President" (p. 178).

Role-sharing

Role-sharing assembles the competencies, attitudes, styles, and networks that are necessary for performance of a job but are unlikely to be possessed by a single individual. Of particular interest to this volume is the case of shared roles – when more than one individual occupy a particular executive position as co-CEOs, co-COOs, co-chairs, or co-CIOs. Goldman Sachs has been known for decades for its co-CEO, co-COO, and co-department-head arrangements. At Intel there is a "two-in-a-box" approach to key management positions. In the world's largest chipmaker, the job of the CIO is so important that two people share the title. Their jobs, however, are different – one is focused on external information technology issues, while the other deals with internal issues (Foremski, 2003).

Role-sharing involves the formal claim of "cohabitation." At the activity level, it can involve either shared or separate responsibilities. A husband-wife first-generation family firm explained their success in the following way: "As co-CEOs there must be absolute clarity in and outside the company concerning how roles are divided. And we do not allow anything to fester between us for more than 4–12 hours" (Lank, 2000, p. 197). Ironically, what is essential for role-sharing is precisely the manner in which role elements are divided. It is also important that they are integrated through mechanisms such as trust, affection, and shared cognition. Understanding how a particular role-sharing operates is essential in order to bring clarity to all internal and external stakeholders who relate to the co-chiefs. The difficulties that can occur in such cases tend to arise from the lack of an authority line defining a direction of orders, reporting, and responsibilities. To avoid giving confusing messages to the organization and the outside world, it is important for the joint office holders to share the same views of the future of the organization and to speak with a single voice.

Harvard Business School's Linda Hill wrote about leadership as a collective genius and argued that role-sharing often occurs when a new product or project is started, requiring a broad range of skills and styles (Hill, 2000). It is also valuable when the role has clearly identifiable sub-roles such as inside and outside focuses that can be performed by two individuals. Of particular relevance to understanding role-sharing are those cases in which top executives decide to share the executive suite as a response to the work overload and the widening range of stakeholders with whom the person at the corporate apex must deal.

To embark upon role-sharing is a brave move, because it requires the solo professional to admit to an inability to fulfill all the demands of the top job and a preference for relying on the competencies and viewpoints of a colleague.

There are other forms of sharing at the top; power-sharing and advisory relationships are two such examples. Power-sharing is a type of role-sharing in which there is an agreement that the power is shared, even though the job titles may differ. The board of directors of Ford Motor Company initiated such an arrangement in July 2001. As the press at the time reported:

In July the Board formalized a power-sharing arrangement between the two men. It created a new office of the chairman and chief executive that makes Bill Ford an equal partner with Nasser in running the company day to day. Instead of relying solely on informal conversations, Ford and Nasser hold formal meetings twice a month at which they discuss a prepared agenda. Sounds good, except that the new office has been seen as an erosion of Nasser's authority . . . It is clear that both men are redefining their roles. (Taylor, 2001, p. 105)

The governance structure established at Ford Motor Company was depicted by the media as a source of confusion. In his *Fortune* article, Taylor (2001) argues that it establishes Bill Ford "as a separate power center and creates an agenda that seems to conflict with Nasser's mandate to improve shareholder value" (p. 108). He further defines the move as a dubious success because the power is shared between Nasser, who "fought his way up through the company" and Ford, who "seems to owe his position to birth."

When top managers feel the need for complementary competencies but do not want to share a position, they can use advisory relations. Trust-based advisory relationships between senior managers operate at the "subterranean level of anonymity," as the professionals at the corporate pinnacle are usually unwilling to reveal incompetence or vulnerabilities (Joni, 2004). In some cases and under particular circumstances these confidants could become successors of the CEOs whom they have advised. For example, Sharon Patrick, long-time friend and confidante of Martha Stewart, took the reins of her business empire, Martha Stewart Living Omnimedia (MSLO), following Stewart's indictment in mid-2003. It is worth noting that role-sharing and role separation can occur at two different levels: (1) the level of the role itself, and

(2) the level of its components – the sub-roles or tasks. Whatever the level of differentiation, however, it will require integration. Furthermore, the balance between shared and unique responsibilities changes over time with the development of the relationship, the performance, and the changes in the managers' comfort levels (Finkelstein and Hambrick, 1996; Nadler, Spencer, and associates, 1998).

Role integration

The integration of horizontally differentiated structures along activities of the value chain refers to "the quality of the state of collaboration that exists among departments that are required to achieve unity of effort by the demands of the environment" (Lawrence and Lorsch, 1967, p. 11). Lawrence and Lorsch used integration to refer to both the state of collaborative relations and the process through which that state is achieved. In our examination of vertical power structures, we refer to integration as the relationships and associated processes that secure collaboration among reciprocally interdependent individuals who occupy top offices. Relationships are used to integrate the roles and tasks. Hence, relationships constitute the other core lever, along with roles, in the design of small-numbers structures.

When exploring the relationships that serve as integrating mechanisms of differentiated roles at the top, it is important to note that they can be multiplex, whereby multiplexity requires "a specification of tie as overall pair relation" (White, 1992, p. 79). To understand how integration occurs in small-numbers power structures, it is important to unravel this multiplicity and explore a range of available relational strings that can pull the individuals together in a coordinated fashion. When the scope of the relationship gradually expands with repeated satisfactory exchanges, formal working relations become socially embedded in personal bonds and the individuals develop a special attachment to the relationship itself (Lawler, 2001). For example, the tie between a CEO and a COO in the same company can be considered multiplex if it involves professional as well as affective exchanges. Multiplexity also implies that trust thickens as additional layers, dimensions, and relational content are added to a relationship (McEvily, Perrone, and Zaheer, 2003b).

Hence, on the one hand, we must examine integration mechanisms in their totality because "In the relation as it actually exists, the total personality of the one party works upon that of the other" (Simmel, 1903, p. 496). On the other hand, we have to depict the range and nature of different threads that bind individuals together and the implications that each thread may have on the integration of the roles of two, three, or more executives in constellations at the top. In the section that follows, we introduce and discuss three different "threads" (relations) that we believe serve as integrators of small-numbers corporate power structures: shared cognition, trust, and affection.

Relationships as mechanisms of role and task integration

Roles are grounded in interactions that occur in the course of daily working life and are "intimately bound to a matrix of social relations" (Barley, 1990, p. 68). They cannot be understood independently from relationships, as it is the others who set expectations and pose (sometimes conflicting) demands on role-playing. The need to examine roles in conjunction with relationships was suggested by Merton's (1957a) article on role-sets. Merton defined the role-set as the set of relations in which one becomes involved by the virtue of the social status one occupies. That is, the role-set of the occupant of the CEO position in a large corporation will involve relationships with various groups, such as employees, unions, investors, shareholders, and the media who would have expectations of the CEO's behavior.

A social status or position may consist of an array of roles, not merely one single, associated role. As Mintzberg (1973) revealed, CEOs play ten different roles when interacting with different audiences. Merton explicitly distinguished his notion of the role-set from another core sociological concept, that of multiple roles, which denotes the different roles associated with the various social statuses in differing institutional spheres. For example, a teacher who is a father, a musician in an amateur band, the president of a community club, and the coach of a junior football team partakes in and has specific relationships in all these spheres. Katz and Kahn (1978) further refined Merton's notion of role-set by limiting the set of relationships to a relatively small number of other professionals who usually occupy offices that are adjacent to the individual's office in terms of workflow or power hierarchy. In this sense, their definition is much narrower than Merton's original notion and perhaps closer to what our book has set out to accomplish.

Derived from the role-set idea is the notion of executive constellation. Finkelstein and Hambrick (1996) argued that "there is much to gain from focusing on the constellation of executives at the top of organizations" (p. 116). In general terms, a total constellation of specialists is "the one that allows or aids the system to establish a full orbit in its dimensions of necessary movement" (Bales, 1955, quoted in Hodgson, Levinson, and Zaleznik, 1965, p. 78). In this regard, a total constellation of top managers should be expected to exhibit the necessary role differentiation and sufficient integration to facilitate the achievement of the organization's goals. Hodgson, Levinson, and Zaleznik (1965), for example, studied the "executive role constellation" at the top level of a highly innovative mental hospital, and defined it as "a matrix of interpersonal relations, with its specialization, differentiation, and complementarity of roles" (p. 12). In another domain, the examination of the executive role constellations of three Oscar-winning Spanish film directors revealed that depending on their style and the additional roles they were willing and able to claim and perform (e.g. writer, producer, art director), they maintained larger or smaller constellations, which followed distinctive paths of evolution (Svejenova, 2002). Such findings allow for the speculation that organizational actors are able to shape the vertical power structures to suit their interests and predispositions (Alvarez, 2000).

Relationships of a specific kind and nature are the mechanisms for the integration of top roles. Recent corporate codes suggest that close relationships at the top should be avoided, as they may lead to misconduct for personal benefit at the expense of the company's interests and those of its shareholders. A rift between two top executives can cause at least as much damage to a company, however, as illustrated by the widely publicized feuding in the press between Viacom's chair and CEO, Sumner Redstone, and its now-former COO, Mel Karmazin, and by the rift between Ford's chair, Bill Ford, and its CEO, Jacques Nasser (Taylor, 2001, p. 105). Productive relations at the top exist, however, and can be beneficial for the company. Dell's founder, Michael Dell, has become a chair of the company after promoting Kevin Rollins to CEO. Recent accounts of their relationship affirm that they are "so close they often finish each other's sentences. The duo collaborates on the day-to-day management and strategy vision" (*Fortune*, August 9, 2004, p. 53). They are said to share the office and "conspire" (*Fortune*, August 9, 2004, p. 52) on the company's strategy. Asked about how

their relationship works, Michael Dell explains: "We're very collaborative. We share all the issues and opportunities. It's not at all a typical
hierarchy," and Kevin Rollins adds: "The nuance is not what we each
do, but where our expertise lies. Michael's expertise lies more in technology. My expertise lies more in the institutionalization of running a
big company. But we both do strategy, we both meet customers, we
both manage the P&L" (Dell, Rollins, Stewart, and O'Brien, 2005,
pp. 107–108). Rollins comments that while they are both opinionated,
they "have a lot of trust in each other's judgment" (p. 107).

In this section we seek to unravel such beneficial ties that bind small
numbers at the top and provide integration in the executive and governance suite. We begin with shared cognition and then discuss the role
of trust and affection in integrating the roles and tasks at the top.

Shared cognition

The repetitive satisfactory exchanges among executives in small-
number structures influence the integration of roles at the corporate
apex. In many of the cases of successful small numbers we encountered,
top executives talked about a shared intuition they have developed,
allowing them to think and act as a unit rather than as two individuals
with different views and agendas. This shared intuition is reminiscent
of what Becker and Useem (1942) labeled "limited meaning" (p. 16).

Members of a dyad, triad, or a larger executive constellation develop
such "limited meaning" over time and with repeated exchanges. Joint
experiences "result in concepts, ideas, habits, and shared memories,
which to the members are symbolic of the pair. These limited meanings
tend to establish norms of action and reaction and to have directive
influence on the behavior of the pair both when they are together and
when they are separated" (Becker and Useem, 1942, pp. 16–17). In this
regard, limited meaning is a source of time- and attention-economizing
communication.

The notion of limited meaning has certain common features with
what is called "shared cognition," a more recent concept that has been
used by strategy scholars to understand processes of strategy-making.
The extent to which the executive team members' mental models for
strategy are shared, overlap, or agree is defined as shared cognition
(Ensley and Pearce, 2001, p. 146). It could be a useful way of understanding how executive dyads or larger constellations make decisions.

Through his work with close relationships in collaborative circles of creative individuals, Farrell (2001) has developed yet another way of conceptualizing shared cognition and intuition at the top – the concept of instrumental intimacy. His definition provides useful information about the way in which pairs operate:

Creative innovations are most likely to occur after a pair of collaborators has gone through a series of exchanges of ideas that each views as relatively equal in value. As the level of risk in the exchanges escalates, as they begin to exchange less finished work, they set the stage for instrumental intimacy. Instrumental intimacy occurs when each begins to use the mind of the other as if it were an extension of its own . . . The boundaries between the self and other diminish until the members are able to think out loud together as if they were one person. During the stage of greatest instrumental intimacy, when merger is at its highest point, in their dialogues with one another it is common for the participants to find their ideas emerging in a cascading flow, such that neither one knows or cares who thought of the ideas first. (pp. 157–158)

The relationship between Sony's co-founders and top executives, Masaru Ibuka and Akio Morita, which extended over several decades, is reminiscent of Farrell's depiction of instrumental intimacy: "They were bound together by a tie so tight it was more like love than friendship. The connection was so deep that not even their wives could break into it when they were together . . . [at an old age] when they're both sick . . . they sit together in silence, holding hands . . . communicating without words" (Nathan, 1999, p. 2).

For over forty years, Masaru Ibuka and Akio Morita grew Sony together, from adjoining offices, reveling in each other's company. Their personal secretaries . . . like to remember them facing each other on the rug, playing with a prototype . . . That's the kind of friendship they always shared . . . they managed for such a long time, right up against each other, matching perfectly in their work lives and their personal lives. They were incredibly lucky to have found each other. (Nathan, 1999, pp. 1–3)

One way to integrate tasks and roles at the top, then, is through the development of a shared cognition between the individuals involved in small-number structures. It's a development that requires time and repeated, satisfactory exchanges, gradually leading to a more open dialog and, for the fortunate few, a friendship that extends far beyond the workplace.

Trust

Agency theorists have argued that executive contracts and incentive systems can, to some extent, regulate the behaviors of top executives and limit their self-interest. However, executive contracts alone cannot guarantee the integration and alignment necessary for the stability of small-numbers power structures. Malhotra and Murnighan (2002) suggest that cooperation could be achieved without contracts on the basis of informal mechanisms such as trust. Building and maintaining trust relationships is essential for managers and professionals, given that their work involves an important amount of mutual accommodation (McAllister, 1995). One of the most serious causes of destabilization of a professional pair is a violation of trust by one of the parties (Gabarro, 1979).

Joni (2004) has recently argued that "Personal trust develops in the workplace through shared experiences and knowledge of colleagues' character. Hence similarly to shared cognition, trust requires repeated exchanges so that individuals can decide on each other's trustworthiness. From such crucibles as impossibly tight deadlines or shop-floor emergencies, we quickly learn on whom we can rely" (p. 84). Whereas shared experiences increase the chances of trust developing, the use of contracts for the purpose of binding executives at the top may have the reverse effect. After studying the effects of contracts on interpersonal trust, Malhotra and Murnighan (2002) concluded that the use of binding contracts reduces the likelihood of the development of trust. Executive contracts are "routinised solutions to problems of agency, control, and uncertainty" (p. 534).

Trust can have an affective foundation, as when we trust people because we like them; or trust can have a cognitive base, as when we trust people because of their professional competency and expertise (McAllister, 1995). Cognition-based trust is founded in the reliability, dependability, responsibility, and competence of each partner (Barber, 1983; McAllister, 1995). This is especially important under conditions of uncertainty and complexity, where mutual adjustment and coordinated action is imperative (Thompson, in McAllister, 1995). Cognition-based trust is strengthened by reliable role performance, cultural or ethnical similarities, and professional credentials (McAllister, 1995).

Unlike the foundation of competence and reliability provided by cognition-based trust, affect-based trust stems from an insight into

the motives of the members of a professional duo or a larger constellation, and is manifested in high sensitivity to the personal and
work-related needs of one's associates (McAllister, 1995). According
to Parkhe (1998), trust is a *Gestalt*, "a complex integration of the psychological, sociological, and economic dimensions in an irreducible
whole experience" (p. 227); it is manifested as a totality of experience.

Both pathways to trust – the affective and the cognitive – require time
and a history of mutually satisfactory interactions over an extended
period of time (Gabarro, 1987; Krackhardt, 1992). Affective trust is
the glue of a duo or a constellation of individuals with reciprocated
affection that can be observed in siblings, spouses, romantic couples,
and friends who embark upon task collaboration (Marshack, 1998).
The presence of both cognition- and affect-based trust in a relationship
leads to thick trust (Gambetta, 1988; Putnam, 2000) and allows the
members to unite their careers, a phenomenon of extremely tight and
durable coupling at the top, which we discuss in Chapter 6.

Trust influences organizing through two main causal pathways:
structuring and mobilizing (McEvily, Perrone, and Zaheer, 2003b,
p. 93). Of special relevance for the design of corporate power structures are the mobilizing implications of trust, whereby it can motivate
top office holders to contribute, combine, and coordinate their competencies, skills, and styles in a collective endeavor (McEvily, Perrone,
and Zaheer, 2003b, pp. 93–94).

Affection

Affection as a mechanism of role integration can be understood with
the help of two recent and related strands of social exchange theory –
relational cohesion (Lawler and Yoon, 1993, 1996; Lawler and Thye,
1999) and the affect theory of social exchange (Lawler, 2001). The first
strand, relational cohesion, depicts "the effects of repeated or frequent
exchanges on actors' definition of their relationship as a unifying force
or an object of attachment in its own right" (Lawler and Yoon, 1996,
p. 89). Emotional processes in conjunction with instrumental ones generate commitment to the relationship – i.e. staying in the relationship,
contributing to the joint undertaking – even when other good options
may exist (Lawler and Yoon, 1996, p. 91). In this view, "the exchange
relation becomes an expressive object of intrinsic value to the actors"
(p. 104). The second strand, the affect theory of social exchange, goes

to a deeper layer of integration, as it focuses on how and when emotions that have been generated in the social exchange process produce stronger or weaker ties among the individuals involved (Lawler, 2001). Lawler accounts for the effect of positive emotions (e.g. excitement, pleasure, pride, gratitude) and negative emotions (e.g. sadness, shame, anger) on the strength of that relationship. The emotional level of role integration is perhaps the most difficult to achieve in corporate power structures, especially given that it must address executive contingency, such as the intensity of relationships at the top.

A role and relationship design of small numbers at the top

The gist of this chapter is the notion that executives can exercise discretion in designing vertical power structures to address critical external, internal, and executive contingencies. In order to accomplish this goal, they can evoke essential mechanisms, such as role differentiation and role integration. The former mechanisms are related to the creation, separation, consolidation, and sharing of roles; whereas the latter refers to the nature and depth of relationships, such as shared cognition, trust, and affection, in addition to others that bind together the incumbents of differentiated roles in the top office. In the chapters that follow we discuss the specificity and dynamics of small-number structures at the top – professional duos, trios, and larger executive constellations – focusing on the way in which they handle differentiation and integration in response to critical contingencies.

PART II

Small numbers at the top

4 | *Professional duos*

Two are thus able to accomplish what one
might never have accomplished alone.

Farrell, 2001, p. 158

At the end of 1990 . . . Steve [Friedman]
and I were named co-chairmen . . . We told
everyone to assume that either of us could
speak for both and that touching base with
one was sufficient. This worked because we
shared the same fundamental views about
the firm, trusted each other totally, kept in
close touch, and were both analytically
minded in our approach to problems.

Robert Rubin, former co-chairman of
Goldman Sachs, in Rubin and Weisberg,
2003, p. 101

THE DOCUMENTARY *Startup.com*, by co-directors Chris Hegedus and Jehane Noujaim (2001), brings to light the rise and fall
(out) of the professional duo of high-school buddies Tom Herman and Kaleil Isaza Tuzman, the founders of the e-venture govWorks.
This classic buddy story, set amidst the dotcom frenzy and its subsequent crash on April 14, 2000, reveals the personal and professional
struggles of the two childhood friends and partners in this start-up company who sought to develop a site that facilitates transactions between
local government and citizens. The story is a realistic account of the
nature and dynamics of professional duos, two issues at the heart of
this chapter.

There were several professional partnerships associated with the documentary, which was made by the tight, two-person crew, co-directors
Hegedus and Noujaim. Hegedus is the wife and creative partner of the

documentary's producer D. A. Pennebaker, one of the pioneers of the *cinéma vérité* genre. Finally, and most importantly, the protagonists of the story are the pair Tom and Kaleil. Through a laborious process of film editing, the co-directors condensed the 400 hours of video footage they had taken while following the two co-founders of govWorks eighteen hours a day for the better part of a year. As the production notes reveal, "the film examines the collision of friendship and business," and illuminates the answer to a difficult question: "With so much pressure and money at stake, can you be a good business person and a good friend at the same time?" (Hegedus and Noujaim, 2001).

Halfway through the movie we see Kaleil upset with Tom after a meeting with a venture capital firm; he was upset because Tom had expressed an opinion about the company strategy that differed from his own. Kaleil feels strongly about the importance of communicating consistent messages and said that they risked damaging the company's future if they contradicted one another in public. Kaleil is firm: "We should never be in this space" (Hegedus and Noujaim, 2001); and "this space" is the space of disagreement between the company's top two in front of employees or external constituents.

The division of labor among the founders becomes essential, as an increasing number of demands are placed on their time and energy: "We can't do everything," acknowledges Tom, and proposes that he and Kaleil differentiate their roles. However, it is not easy to decide who will do what. Kaleil refuses to be simply Mr. Outside, to narrow his role and involvement to talking to venture capitalists and securing financing for the business. He wants a share in strategic decision making. It is hard to compromise egos, even though their friendship dates back to their high-school years. By the end of the movie, we have heard about Tom's bitterness and failed aspirations as he acknowledges he has always viewed himself as being a co-CEO – a position that the strong-minded Kaleil is now unwilling to share. And it is apparent from viewing and hearing the experiences and thoughts of the central characters that there are major difficulties and dilemmas inherent in job-sharing in the executive suite.

When ambition, power, and money come into play, especially in situations involving enormous pressure, the inherent instabilities of professional duos come to the fore. Dealing with them is a question of professionalism and relational maturity, and of providing enough space for the other – something the breed of single-minded CEOs finds difficult to do. Throughout the movie we frequently hear Kaleil and Tom use the word "love" when talking about their relationship, even at times when it is breaking down and the business is deteriorating. Eventually the business does sink. The partners had raised almost USD 60 million and signed forty-five cities, including the New York City parking system. However in the post-dotcom-crash months (after April 14, 2000), unable to find additional investment capital, govWorks is forced to file for corporate bankruptcy protection under Chapter 11 of the US bankruptcy legislation, and the technological platform of the company is sold to a multi-national company. However the spectator is left feeling hopeful for the professional duo. Despite the rough ride, they are still friends and have linked their careers for yet another endeavor. This career unity is a stronger commitment than mere professional collaboration, a topic we discuss at length in Chapter 6.

Startup.com is a great introduction to the issues we address in this chapter: the genesis and functioning of a particular small-numbers structure at the top, the professional duo. Having two instead of one professional at the corporate apex is an alternative that can potentially match the contingencies we advanced in Chapter 1. To gain insight into the nature and dynamics of professional duos, we delved into the sociological and social-psychological literature on dyads. Furthermore, as we prepared to write this book, we collected a vast number of press releases, interviews, and articles on professional duos from a wide array of professions and businesses. Some of our duos dissolved before the book was completed, and with their dissolution provided useful clues to the instabilities of executive pairs and the mechanisms by which they can terminate.

Many duos born out of mergers and acquisitions have a fleeting life; they terminate within two years of their formation. Such has been the fortune of pairs like Reed and Weill at Citigroup, Schrempp and Eaten at DaimlerChrylser and Redstone and Karmazin at Viacom. Others, however, showed long-term resilience and fruitful collaboration, sustaining their partnership at the helm of one or more companies over several decades: Honda and Fujisawa at Honda; Morita and Ibuka at Sony; and Weinberg and Whitehead and later Rubin and Friedman, at Goldman Sachs.

The pairing of individuals at the top of organizations is not a contemporary phenomenon. Historical annals record such early examples as those of the co-consuls in Republican Rome who entered, shared, and left office together (Sally, 2002). Similar manifestations of co-rule were unveiled in third- to fourth-century Japan as a result of the application of the "pair rule" known in Japanese as *himehikosei*, "princess-and-prince system" or "sister-brother pairs." Pair rule has been associated with a clear division of labor: a shamaness at the helm of spiritual affairs and her brother in charge of pragmatic matters, and later, also, of military action (Allen, 2003). More recent historical duos include Marx and Engels, the co-authors of *The Communist Manifesto*. Within the span of their four-decade partnership, Engels sustained Marx not only emotionally through their friendship but also financially. Professional duos can also be found in the history of science. In a study of Nobel Prize laureates, for example, Zuckerman (1967) discovered eight co-working pairs who shared the prestigious prize. Some of them were father-son partnerships, like the Braggs (Sir William Henry Bragg and William Lawrence Bragg) or the Thomsons (Joseph J. Thomson and George P. Thomson), while others, like Pierre and Marie Curie, were husband and wife.

In recent years, medical practices have increasingly adopted what has become known in their circles as "a job-share model," which requires "two or more physicians to link their skills, energies, and time to provide comprehensive care to patients. For the arrangement to work best, the physicians should also share similar competencies and a common patient care philosophy" (Worzniak and Chadwell, 2002, p. 29). Because the job-sharing physicians provide cross-coverage for their patients they must establish effective communications with patients to inform them that the two doctors are interchangeable. Practices such as co-rulership, co-work, or job-sharing provide the basis for professional duos to emerge.

It is impossible for us to cite here all the examples of duos that we encountered in the course of our study. A representative list of the pairs with some background information on the companies in which they have been involved appears in the Appendix. However, all these cases have contributed – in one way or another – to our understanding of professional duos: the forms they take; their genesis, development, and termination; and some factors that might increase or diminish their odds of success.

In this chapter we examine the nature and types of professional duos, setting them apart from the relatively broad and general sociological concept of the dyad. We explore the importance of complementary background, experience, and style of the individual members that constitute a professional duo. A distinction is made between hierarchical professional duos and partnerships. Then we examine the process that can transform a dyad (a basic unit of two individuals) into a professional duo (a dyad with committed working relationships over a given period). Professional duos can either dissolve or become stronger over time, culminating in "united careers" – a less common type of pairing that is explored in greater depth in Chapter 6. In this chapter we analyze the formation, functioning, transformation, and termination of professional duos and discuss the inherent instabilities of duos as a vertical structure and the range of decoupling and exit strategies that the partners in the duo can experience or employ.

The nature of pairs at the top

The professional duo is one of several small-numbers arrangements available for implementation at the discretion of a company's executives or governance boards when considering the design of corporate power structures. It consists of two executives who, over time, perform the top job together in a coordinated fashion and are held jointly accountable for the company or unit's results. The press has been rife with creative labels for such arrangements: two-headed offices, professional duets, professional marriages, co-stewardship, and job-sharing are a few examples.

Professional duos are dyads in the traditional sociological sense, in which the two individuals enact professional roles and have a working relationship. In the formal language of social network theorists, "A dyad is an unordered pair of actors and the arcs that exist between the two actors in the pair" (Wasserman and Faust, 1994, p. 510). This apparently dry or schematic definition refers to two essential characteristics of a dyad – the individual actors that form it, and their relationships. The relationships, in turn, determine and are determined by the nature of the exchange. They can be simple: a professional relationship, or multiplex whereby the bond between the individual members of the duo is multi-layered, consisting, for example, of both friendship and professional collaboration.

More than a century ago, the eminent German sociologist Georg Simmel wrote a series of essays (Simmel, 1902a, 1902b) on the role of small numbers such as dyads and triads in shaping behavior. Simmel (1950) was the first to formalize the idea of "the bearing, which the mere number of associated individuals has upon these forms of social life" (p. 87). His pioneering claim was that dyads represent different structural arrangements than do individuals, triads, or larger constellations, merely because of the number of individuals that form them. Simmel distinguished dyads from other small-numbers associations, such as triads and quartets, by emphasizing their greater unity, co-responsibility, and interdependence; and the unique opportunity they provide for preserving the individuality of their members (Simmel, 1950).

Scholars have used a variety of terms and definitions when writing about dyadic phenomena such as dyads, pairs, and couples. In this chapter, following Becker and Useem (1942), we use such terms as "dyad," "duo," "group of two," and "pair" interchangeably.

As we have seen, Simmel perceived dyads to be a unique small-numbers structure. He acknowledged that the pattern of interaction in a dyad does not lead to the creation of a superstructure in the minds of the two members, and hence does not yield a depersonalized pattern. In the words of Simmel (1950):

the decisive characteristic of the dyad is that each of the two must actually accomplish something, and that in the case of failure only the other remains – not a super-individual force, as prevails in a group even of three. The significance of this characteristic . . . also makes for a close and highly specific coloration of the dyadic relationship. Precisely the fact that each of the two knows that he can depend only upon the other and on nobody else, gives the dyad a special consecration – as seen in marriage and friendship, but also in more external associations, including political ones, that consist of two groups . . . the dyad element is much more frequently confronted with All or Nothing than is the member of the larger group. (pp. 134–135)

Operating as they do in the absence of a superstructure such as the one that exists in a group, duos find that "it is impossible to shift blame, obligations, and responsibilities upon an impersonal structure when a crisis occurs, action is called for, or a decision is to be made" (Becker and Useem, 1942, p. 14). Furthermore, the dyad is the only social structure that allows the preservation of the individuality of its elements. In the cases of professional duos of executives, as shown in Chapters 1 and 2, these "elements" are usually highly distinctive individuals with a strong need for autonomy (Lee and Tiedens, 2001), status, and accomplishment. Other structures, such as the triumvirates or larger constellations discussed in Chapter 5, demand conformity to the whole (i.e. to the team as a superstructure) and provide far less room for the deployment of individuality.

For a dyad to become a professional duo, a history of escalating task-related exchanges over an extended period is required (Gabarro, 1987; Krackhardt, 1992). The escalating exchanges of two individuals lead to an improved awareness of their respective competencies, styles, and reliabilities. Furthermore, it is essential that the members of the dyad perform jointly and are held jointly responsible for a set of activities. The majority of examples of professional duos that we encountered have arisen either from an existing affective relationship such as kin or from a working dyad in which the two individuals have exhibited important complementarities in their competencies and temperaments. Both commonality and complementarity are important for the operation of professional duos.

Commonality. Jarvis (1999) argued that "commonality is the necessary element which brings the partners together in the first place, provides the set of common ground rules, and helps smooth differences which begin to surface later in the relationship and organization" (p. 137). In their analysis of the politics of strategic decision-making in high-velocity environments, Eisenhardt and Bourgeois (1988) encountered "stable coalitions" or "stable alliances" of top management members, such as a pair of vice-presidents, a chair and a president, and a software director with a marketing director, all of which revealed demographic similarities in age, office location, and history (Eisenhardt and Bourgeois, 1988). Several of them had previously been co-founders of other firms. To make the partnership work, however, the members of a professional duo need to have not only common background, values, and experiences, but also essential complementarities of skill, style, and social capital.

Complementarity. In general terms, there can be material and emotional role complementarity, the former associated with administrative functions and tasks (Hodgson, Levinson, and Zaleznik, 1965; Gronn, 2002; Seers, Keller, and Wilkerson, 2003) and the latter with the division of emotional labor (cf. Rafaeli and Sutton [1991] on emotional contrast strategies of the "good cop, bad cop" type).

Gronn (1999), for example, detailed the case of a complementary lifetime association, which he called a "leadership couple": the founder and institutional leader of Timbertop, a nationally famous Australian school with innovative teaching methods, and his second-in-charge of operations. Gronn (1999) argued that "odd," "unlike" couples, or "opposites," had higher productivity and longevity. He followed Hodgson, Levinson, and Zaleznik's (1965) early work on the executive role constellation in emphasizing the importance of specialization, differentiation, and complementarities of tasks in establishing and maintaining professional duos. We discussed some of the issues related to role specialization and consolidation in Chapter 3.

For example, an illustration of complementarity can be seen in the case of the co-CEOs of the Canadian firm, Research in Motion (RIM), the company behind BlackBerry. As written in a recent *Business Week* article:

Those who know RIM attribute much of its success to the complementary relationship of its co-CEOs. Without Lazaridis, the silver-haired science buff who once won a special award from his public school for checking every science and math book out of the library, RIM would have no technology. And without Balsillie, the business maven who as a young father mortgaged his house and poured much of his net worth into Lazaridis' fledgling operation in 1992, it would have far less commercial success. (Brady, 2004)

Balsillie is "the corporate strategist, the financial wizard, the negotiator, and the face of the company on Wall Street." Lazaridis, in turn, is "the science mastermind, the production guru, the dreamer, and the one who solves customers' problems" (Brady, 2004).

The case of Soichiro Honda and Takeo Fujisawa is another example that reveals a top pair's complementarity:

Any account of Honda's success must grasp at the outset the unusual character of its founder, Soichiro Honda, and his partner, Takeo Fujisawa. Honda was an inventive genius with a large ego and mercurial temperament . . . It was not until he teamed up with Fujisawa in 1949 that the elements of a successful enterprise began to take shape. Fujisawa provided money, as well as financial and marketing strengths. (Pascale, 1996, p. 84)

Odd couples abound in the business world, especially in those enterprises that demand a range of core competencies, which are difficult to encounter in a single individual. These are only a few of the many examples:

- Lazaridis (the "science buff") and Balsillie (the "business maven") at RIM;
- Honda (the engineering mind) and Fujisawa (the manager) in the early days of Honda Motor Corporation;
- Yves Saint Laurent (fashion designer) and his long-time friend and business partner Pierre Bergé;
- Steve Friedman (the trader) and Robert Rubin (the investment banker) at Goldman Sachs;
- Antony Burgmans (with a marketing background) and his now for-mer co-chair Niall FitzGerald (with financial experience) at Unilever;
- Jerry Greenberg (Sales, Marketing, Finance, Operations) and Stuart Moore (Vision, Values, People Growth, Methodology) at Sapient.

Complementarity is fostered by different backgrounds and beliefs. As Whitford (2000) pointed out, for example, Greenberg is a Democrat and Moore is a Republican. In this way, the members of the pair are able to provide different perspectives and are better able to deal with cognitive complexity at the top.

Professional duos constitute small-numbers vertical structures that satisfy specific contingencies at the top. They can be highly resilient arrangements in several ways. (1) By having two members rather than one in the corner office, professional duets are better able to satisfy the fundamental dualities of executive work, a topic we dis-cussed in Chapter 2: internal versus external duties, controlling ver-sus entrepreneurial orientations, and management versus governance tasks. (2) As dyads are often complementary structures, they allow for the full deployment of achievement and power motivations of both executives in their own domains. (3) Both the making and the break-ing of dyads are highly visible acts. Such visibility makes executives extremely cautious about being or appearing to be responsible for the cessation of their pairing.

Types of professional duos: hierarchical pairs and partnerships

Although complementarity is a common feature of well-functioning professional duos, they can differ in other respects. Hodgson, Levinson, and Zaleznik (1965) differentiated between two types of pairings. In one the roles at the top are related to each other at the same level of power. In the other they could encompass two different levels of power or, in the case of family businesses for example, two generations. Focus-ing on the CEO–COO pair, Rivero and Spencer (1998) also discussed two basic models of structuring leadership at the top of the organization. In one, a hierarchical pattern was characterized by clear role differentiation, whereby an externally oriented CEO engaged in overall corporate governance and strategic issues and an internally focused COO ran the company operations. In the other, a partnership structure was embodied in the idea of a corporate office, in which there was an increased emphasis on shared responsibility.

Following the above distinction, professional duos can be "partnerships" or "hierarchical pairs," and in partnership dyads, both members have equal power, at least by design. Partnerships consist of individuals such as co-CEOs, co-presidents, or co-chairs, who share a position (e.g. cases detailed by O'Toole, Galbraith, and Lawler [2002] and Sally [2002]). Hierarchical dyads are those pairwise relationships in which there is a clear authority line of superordination and subordination. Among "hierarchical pairs," the executives occupy complementary positions with a difference in power – a board chair and a CEO (Stewart, 1991), a CEO and a COO (Nadler, Spencer, and associates, 1998; Heenan and Bennis, 1999; Hambrick and Cannella, 2004), or a CEO and a CFO (Zorn, 2004).

In business organizations, hierarchical dyads are a relatively well-institutionalized structural form, one which is more common than partnership duos. The leadership literature has shown an increasing interest in understanding these cases of role- and position-sharing using terms such as conjoint agency (Gronn, 2002), co-leadership (Heenan and Bennis, 1999), or shared leadership (Pearce and Conger, 2003), to list but a few labels. However, accounts in the business press and other media generally continue to be skeptical and critical of the efficiency of power-sharing at the top (Pellet, 1999; Raso, 2000; Osterland, 2001). As explained by Harrison, Torres, and Kukalis (1988), "normative prescriptions and other factors militate against the creation of multiple holders" (p. 225) of the CEO and board chair positions. Figure 3 provides several illustrations of corporate power duos that are of partnership or hierarchical design, and these are discussed below.

Hierarchical professional duos
The two most frequently studied pair structures in corporate political design are the vertical arrangements of chair and CEO, and CEO and COO. It is worth noting that the scope and power of the CEO role are

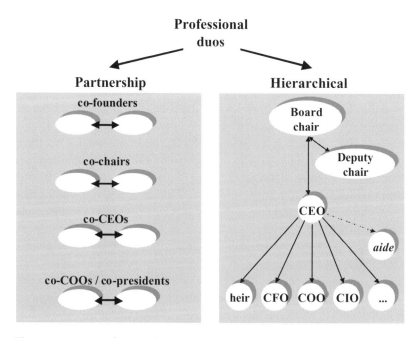

Figure 3. Structural examples of partnership and hierarchical professional duos. (It is assumed that, as is customary in Europe, but different in the United States, the chair is hierarchically superior to the CEO. Such depiction coincides with the trends of corporate governance reforms.)

not the same in the United States as in Europe. Therefore, the nature of interdependencies and relationships at the top in the two contexts differ. In the United States, the CEO is usually the chair of the board and the COO is the president of the company. In Europe, "president" is the title generally used to denote the chair of the board, and the CEO assumes more of the executive responsibilities.

CEO–chair. Zelleke (2003) provides an analysis of the ways in which the UK and US governance systems differ: in the UK model, the chair and CEO positions are almost invariably separate whereas in the US model, they are more likely to be combined into one position. In an earlier study of a sample of 671 large American manufacturing firms for the period 1978–1980, Harrison, Torres, and Kukalis (1988) examined the nature and relationship of the positions of CEO and chair of the board of directors, focusing on the consolidations and separations in these two positions. The results highlighted the dominance of the consolidated structure (with 72 percent of the firms having consolidated positions) and a tendency among firms with separate positions to consolidate the two top positions under the CEO. Cadbury (2002) argued that the roles of the chair and chief executive can be separated or combined, depending on what will "make it as easy as possible for the holders of office to do what is expected of them" (p. 113).

CEO–COO. Hambrick and Cannella (2004) examined the incidence and effectiveness of CEOs who operate with COOs and concluded that the decision to have a COO represented a major structural choice – one that divided between two people a set of top-level responsibilities that could have been fulfilled by a solo manager. Hambrick and Cannella (2004) concluded that having a COO is best viewed as a form of perk for the CEO. In fact, their data suggested not only that the price of a COO could not be justified on the grounds of performance, but that having a COO had a negative impact on performance. Further skepticism about the rationality of introducing an additional structural layer below the CEO is offered by Dobbin, Dierkes, Kwok, and Zorn (2001), who note that in some cases imitation rather than rationality has been the basis for adopting that structure. Depending on the background of the CEO (an executive contingency) and the nature of the business (both its strategic uncertainty and its decision-making requirements), the hierarchical dyad may not necessarily be in the form of a CEO–COO pairing. Rather, as Zorn (2004) suggests, it could be a CEO–CFO dyad, for example – a structural form that is suited to firms in which CEOs without financial backgrounds must run a diversified business. Alternatively it could be a hierarchical CEO–CIO duo, one that is suited to firms in which information technology plays a strategic role.

CEO–heir apparent. Another variation in hierarchical professional duos is that of an incumbent CEO and an heir apparent to the CEO who work together over a transition period (Cannella and Shen, 2001). After the resignation of Karmazin as COO of Viacom, the chair and CEO of the company, Sumner Redstone, appointed two co-presidents and co-COOs to replace him. He acknowledged that both COOs were candidates for succession to the CEO role. It could be argued that sharing the job of president with the awareness that it is a race for the top job creates rivalry between the two members of the newly appointed professional duo and could endanger the stability of their partnership. This example of the dynamics in executive trios (a CEO and two co-COOs) is further analyzed in Chapter 5.

A particular instance of a succession pair comes from the first succession event in an organization, when its founder-CEO is replaced by a "professional CEO" (Wasserman, 2003). Contingency theory, the perspective adopted in this book may help us to understand why founders get replaced. Wasserman (2003) suggests that "the 'changing contingencies' perspective . . . gives us strong forward-looking reasons . . . why founder-CEOs might be replaced after achieving critical milestones" (p. 165). In some cases, the founder remains in the company and must create and sustain an effective working relationship with the professional CEO who has the final say on the company's future; Google, a company in which the co-founders Larry Page and Sergey Brin maintain a productive working relationship with Eric Schmidt, the professional CEO, is one example.

CEO–aide. Yet another variation of the vertical professional duo is that of a senior executive and a personal assistant, also known in the literature as an "assistant-to" or an "aide" (Whisler, 1960). The corporate role of assistant-to-the-president could be traced back to the military model of an aide-de-camp to the general officer. Usually, there is a highly personal relationship between the aide and the officer. In the words of General Washington to the Congress, "Aides-de-camp are persons in whom entire confidence must be placed" (Whisler, 1960, p. 193).

The creation of the aide role as part of the corporate office design has a tremendous impact on communication and power relations in the management hierarchy (Whisler, 1960, p. 183). The aide not only provides additional competencies to an executive office but also acts as a shield, managing access to the chief executive and collaborating on a range of issues. As the legendary Jack Welch reveals in his foreword to the book *Managing Up*, written by his executive assistant Rosanne Badowski:

any successful collaboration between a boss and an assistant is a lot less hierarchical than it looks from the outside. For fourteen fantastic years, Rosanne and I were nothing less than partners . . . most of the time we were both managing sideways, the way teammates do. We passed the ball back and forth, blocked for each other, shouted directives and encouragement (and occasional expletives), suffered together after losses, and, perhaps most of all, shared in the victories. (Welch, quoted in Badowski, 2003, pp. ix–x)

To summarize, the main differences between a vertical pair and a partnership is that in a vertical pair the two individuals occupy separate positions or offices, and, formally, there is a power differential between them. However, in examining well-functioning vertical pairs in detail, what comes to the fore are elements of shared cognition (as they must combine their competencies to address the complexities at the top) and manifestations of trust and affection. For example, in certain cases of CEO–chair duos, the relationship can be approached and operationalized as a partnership even though the two individuals operate at two different levels or in two domains (Stewart, 1991). Also, in the cases of CEO–aide pairs, personal bonding is essential. In other cases, manifestations of rivalry can be observed, particularly in CEO–COO and CEO–heir apparent pairings in which there is a certain overlap of domains of operation and ambitions.

Partnership professional duos

In his book, *The Last Partnerships: Inside the Great Wall Street Dynasties*, Charles Geisst (2001) tells the stories that helped shape Wall Street. In their early years, in the nineteenth century, most partnerships did not have formal management structures, and partners oversaw the areas they knew best. Many of the securities firms are still remembered for their partners, Geisst argues. Here we use partnership to refer to a form of collaboration at the top whereby two executives decide to share office and power.

Co-founders. Co-founders, at least in the initial stages of enterprise creation, can be viewed as horizontal duos, or larger constellations, at the top of the organizations they create. Referring again to the example of Tom Herman and Kaleil Isaza Tuzman, when a confused employee asked them to explain who really calls the shots at their company govWorks, Tom acknowledged: "We are not really co-CEOs but in some ways we really are because at the end of the day we have an agreement that decisions regarding the company are made by the two of us together" (Hegedus and Noujaim, 2001). Recalling the case of these two high-school buddies is appropriate here because, as Nicholson (2000) explains, "Male buddydom is probably the single most common platform for the origination of business" (p. 180). Start-ups thrive on friendships, as can be seen in examples such as Hewlett and Packard, Procter and Gamble, Marks and Spencer, Ibuka and Morita, and Harley and Davidson. The paired executives are usually individuals with complementary abilities and styles that, when combined, provide strength for the newly established enterprise.

However, as illustrated by the case of Kaleil Isaza Tuzman and Tom Herman, what usually starts out as an egalitarian relationship based on trust and affection, can later turn sour when difficulties arise and business complexities increase, and equal partners may start making unequal claims and require more power. In such cases the role of the board of directors is crucial in seeking to consolidate leadership under one CEO.

Co-chairs. Sharing the chair position is another type of partnership without power differential. In this case, the two individuals share a governance rather than an executive position. This duality is illustrated, for example, by Antony Burgmans, whose marketing background until recently complemented the financial acumen of the (now former) co-chair of Unilever, Niall FitzGerald (Ball, 2004).

A case quoted at the outset of this chapter warrants repetition and elaboration. In his memoirs *In an Uncertain World*, Robert Rubin (Rubin and Weisberg, 2003) recollects his years in a co-chair role with Steve Friedman at Goldman Sachs, and provides an instructive account of what constitutes a successful role-sharing and power-sharing arrangement:

At the end of 1990, John Weinberg stepped down, and Steve and I were named co-chairmen. Following the Weinberg–Whitehead example, we didn't try to divide up responsibilities or subject areas. We told everyone to assume that either of us could speak for both and that touching base with one was sufficient. This worked because we shared the same fundamental views about the firm, trusted each other totally, kept in close touch, and were both analytically minded in our approach to problems. When this structure does work – and that is a rarity – the advantages are substantial: there are two senior partners to call on clients and two people who can work together on issues with no hierarchical baggage, and who can reinforce each other in discussions with the rest of the organization. Also, when difficulties arise, having a partner reduces the feeling of loneliness at the top. (p. 101)

This quote is revealing of some of the "ingredients" necessary for professional duos to jell at the board level: (1) there is good human material out of which the duo is "made" – that is, the members share values, share a vision for the company, and have healthy egos that allow for power to be shared rather than contested; (2) the relationship that binds the two individuals is based on trust and good communication;

and (3) the pair speaks with a single voice to the internal and external constituents. We believe these requirements could be extended to other executive pairs.

Co-CEOs. Another specific manifestation of partnership professional duos is that of co-CEOs who share a title and sometimes an office. Sapient's Jerry Greenberg and Stuart Moore acknowledged that "Neither makes an important decision without consulting the other" (Whitford, 2000). Despite the fact these two men share titles, it is important to note they have a clear division of labor, which allows for their individual differences or contingencies. That arrangement may, in fact, be typical of the hierarchical professional CEO–COO duos in which one member is the Inside Boss and the other the Outside Boss. However, unlike CEO–COO pairs, Greenberg and Moore have equal power. As revealed by Sapient's co-CEOs, "Another quality of successful co-CEOs is trusting each other, deeply" (Whitford, 2000).

In some organizations, role-sharing has almost become an institutional practice. For example, departments have been co-run at Goldman Sachs since the naming of the company's first co-CEOs, the self-appointed duo of Weinberg and Whitehead. At Intel, the "two-in-a-box" approach has paired professionals with different skills and styles. For the Riu Hotel chain, headquartered in Mallorca, Spain, the co-CEO form of duo structure is used in each hotel of the chain.

To summarize, it is important to acknowledge that complementarity is necessary in order for hierarchical and partnership duos to function effectively as small-numbers structures at the top. The nature of the complementarity can be in either or both the task and emotional domains. Hence, for both hierarchial duos and partnerships, we observe a certain division of labor, manifested in role differentiation. Moreover, we can find the sharing of particular responsibilities. What differs in the two types of duos, however, is the nature of the relationship that serves as an integrator of the divided labor. In the case of hierarchical professional duos, the default integration mechanism is power. In the case of the partnerships, as power is shared and cannot be used in the resolution of disputes, trust, shared cognition, and joint decision-making and sense-making prevail. This leads to a dynamic process, in which professional duos function and either transform over time, or terminate. In the next section, we examine these dynamics.

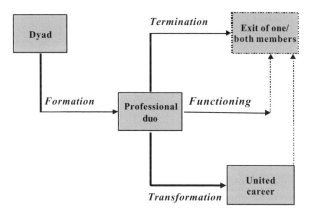

Figure 4. Dynamics of professional duos.

The dynamics of professional duos

Both hierarchical professional duos and partnerships are shaped over time and can follow various trajectories. Figure 4 outlines several such potential trajectories. Their theoretical foundations are drawn from the sociological literature on social and affective exchange and trust and from the social-psychological literature on instrumental and intimate relationships. Based on ideas from these fields, and from insights we gained from the wealth of examples included in our study, we detail four stages in the evolutionary dynamics of professional duos: (1) the formation, (2) the functioning, (3) the transformation, and (4) the termination of a professional relationship. The discovery of complementarities and the development of trust and relational cohesion influence the evolution. In this chapter we focus on the genesis of the dyad and its becoming, and functioning as, a professional duo. The transformation from a professional duo into a united career is addressed in Chapter 6.

Formation: from a dyad to a professional duo

In an attempt to grasp the essence of professional duos, several pertinent questions need to be addressed.
- What is the genesis of a professional duo?
- How, why, when, and where does it form?
- What problems does a duo, as a small-numbers structure, resolve?

- Who would want to share power and position, and why? When does this structural arrangement work and when does it fail?
- Which of the contingencies we advanced in Chapter 1 does it fit?

Below we address some of these questions.

Genesis of the relationship

The professional duo, as a form of committed partnership, can arise in two principal ways: from a social relationship (an affective dyad) or in the course of a task-based interaction (a working dyad). Two individuals can initially share a strong and binding social relationship and use it as a foundation on which to shape their professional partnership. From an evolutionary perspective, given that for much of human evolution most individuals would have lived their lives within a clan system of extended kinship groups, our psychology seems suited for a social universe that is known and finite (Nicholson, 2000). Hence, there is a tendency toward kin selection in ventures that involve high uncertainty, like new venture creation (Ruef, Aldrich, and Carter, 2003). Affective dyads such as siblings, spouses, romantically involved couples, or close friends are usually grounded in reciprocated affection (Marshack, 1998). In task-based interaction, two people may interact in work through role-specified surface encounters (Gabarro, 1987), i.e. solely in terms of their technical briefing (Belbin, 2000). Task-based ties differ from affective relationships because they are influenced by different situational and contextual forces (Gabarro, 1987) and are subject to different social controls (Marwell and Hage, 1970).

Professional duos arise at work, usually through work proximity or repeated task-based interactions. Propinquity, the state of being near in space and time, has been considered to be one of the most important factors in building stable coalitions between top managers. One example of propinquity leading professionals to decide to share power is that provided by John Whitehead, former co-CEO, along with John Weinberg, at Goldman Sachs. The pair initiated their relationship at the company's offices. In an interview, Whitehead (2002) recollected:

John Weinberg joined the firm about three years after I had, because he was three years younger. He also graduated from the Harvard Business School. I was assigned by John's father, who was then the senior partner and my boss, to take John under my wing and teach him the ropes. So, being a three-year veteran, I did that, and we had desks that faced each other starting in 1950 when he joined. We became partners eight or nine years later and we rose up the ladder together, every step of the way. Each of us had the same percentage of interest in the firm. Eventually, we decided to be joint co-managing partners when our predecessor, Gus Levy, suddenly passed away and we had to take over the management of the firm. (p. 5)

Furthermore, a professional duo can be conceived through two employees who work together in the same company finding the opportunity to join another business or establish their own business. This case is illustrated by Sapient's co-CEOs and co-chairs who met as consultants employed by what is now Cambridge Technology Partners (Whitford, 2000). What brought the two together was a shared belief that the existing consulting paradigm was flawed. Today, the two executives have succeeded in redefining what it means to deliver client success, leading their industry in on-time, on-budget project delivery.

In addition to work proximity, magnet places (Farrell, 2001) serve the function of putting like minds together. A magnet place can be an art studio, a laboratory, a university – in general, any place that attracts individuals with shared values and aspirations. Universities have long been meeting points for like-minded people, so it is not surprising that so many co-founders of growth-intensive businesses meet and "click" there. Harvard, Stanford, and Cambridge are some well-known examples of cradles for the Hewletts and Packards of the world.

In recent times, business schools have focused on promoting business incubators and stimulating entrepreneurship. As a result, an increasing number of new ventures are undertaken by two or more high-school buddies. Jerry Yang and David Filo co-founded Yahoo while studying at Stanford University, as did Google co-founders Sergey Brin and Larry Page. In the words of Nicholson (2000), "one could say that the whole of Silicon Valley stems from gangs of young men who carried on playing together beyond their college years" (p. 179).

The family is also a natural environment for breeding professional duos. In families, exchanges among members begin at an early age, and by the time professional collaboration between two family members is contemplated, a strong basis of insight on respective abilities and character exists and facilitates the entry into and success of joint undertakings between a child and a parent or between siblings (e.g. the brothers who co-founded and run Miramax: Harvey and Robert Weinstein).

Formation of professional duos

There are three main origins of professional duos: they can be appointed by a higher authority; they can be introduced and brought together by match-makers; or they can be the result of self-appointment.

In the majority of cases, professional duos come into being through an appointment from the board or an executive committee. For example, the Frenchman Philippe Camus and the German Rainer Hertrich were appointed as inaugural co-chief executives of the Franco-German aerospace giant European Aeronautic Defence and Space Company (EADS). When they joined forces, they hardly knew one another. As a *Financial Times* article entitled "Arranged Marriage Has Grown into Model Match," reveals, "The secret merger discussions, which brought the French and German predecessors together, were handled by Jean-Luc Lagardère, Mr Camus's mentor, and Jürgen Schrempp, Daimler-Chrysler boss" (Spiegel, 2003, p. 36). In this sense, their appointment is also illustrative of the "match-making" of professional duos, especially relevant for the Far East. One of the most famous executive professional duos, that of Honda and Fujisawa, was born in Japan, a society where introductions are of particular importance and value. Takeo Fujisawa, a management expert, and Soichiro Honda, a technology expert, met in 1949 through Fujisawa's old friend Hiroshi Takeshima, who put him in contact with the young inventor, Honda, who was looking for someone to invest in his business. Finally, professional duos can be self-appointed, as revealed by the case of John Weinberg and John Whitehead at Goldman Sachs or that of Stuart Moore and Jerry Greenberg, the co-CEOs and co-chairs of Sapient.

Professional duos are formed for different reasons. They can be necessary in order to provide a range of competencies and relationships to businesses which demand very different mind-sets that are difficult to find in a single executive (e.g. in the fashion industry where creative people team up with business people, or in the art world where the artist pairs with a producer). In defining the dyad as a particular case of the executive role constellation, Hodgson, Levinson, and Zaleznik (1965) explained: "The pairing may provide the basis of a very effective means of coping with the inside-outside problems of the organization. One of the pair looks after the boundary processes of the organization, while the other looks after its internal dynamics" (p. 486).

Professional duos can also arise from the need to economize on cognitive processes in fast-paced environments or in contexts that require
a range of complex competencies. Moreover, having two people at the
top can allow them to be at two different places at the same time, to
address different stakeholder groups simultaneously (as acknowledged
recently by Nike's co-presidents).

Beyond formation: the functioning and termination of professional duos

In this subsection we examine some of the processes and mechanisms
related to the functioning and termination of professional duos. Their
transformation into united careers is discussed at length in Chapter 6.

Functioning

How do professional duos operate, especially those of the partnership
type that have to share responsibilities and power? In the first place, the
genesis and the formation stage are critical in choosing the right mix of
individual competencies, capabilities, styles, and attitudes. The members of successful duos usually have different cultural backgrounds
and personalities and distinct skill and relational sets. Although it is
not possible to be normative about the most beneficial combination of
characteristics for a duo, there is wide agreement in the literature that
the traits of the two members of a duo should blend well. This blending,
cemented with shared values and interests, as well as with shared vision
for the business, provides a strong foundation on which cooperation
can thrive. With this foundation in place, there are different mechanisms that could help the duo "tick." As discussed in Chapter 3, the
design of roles as a resource for action is one such mechanism. In order
for the professional partnership to achieve success, it is important to
articulate the division of labor (Gronn, 2002) – to specify which tasks
are to be performed separately and which are to be carried out jointly.
It is also necessary in structuring the relationship to secure sufficient
space for each partner to exercise personal responsibilities (Gronn,
2002) and to provide mechanisms that integrate these contributions
back into a single voice and action program of the duo.

Another design element that would help to ensure the smooth operation of a duo is a shared awareness of the critical interdependencies
of the two members and the ways in which coordination and mutual

adjustment can take place. A well-rehearsed working relationship with a strong level of commitment and interaction is required for such a conjoint agency (Gronn, 2002) to occur. Gronn (2002) suggests that "Conjoint agency means that agents synchronize their actions by having regard to their own plans, those of their peers, and their sense of unit membership" (p. 431). As revealed in a recent article, Robert Rubin and Steve Friedman worked well as co-COOs and then as co-CEOs of Goldman Sachs because they learned how to resolve their disagreements and to "listen and entertain" views contrary to their own (Loomis, 2003, p. 120). Also, as Rubin has acknowledged, their effectiveness as a pairing arose because they "fell easily into a process for working out differences" (Rubin and Weisberg, 2003, p. 311). Stuart Moore, Sapient's co-CEO and co-chair, has a similar story of how he and Jerry Greenberg resolve their disagreements: "If one of us feels very passionate about it, more so than the other one, we'll say, 'Fine, you want to do it that way, I'll go along'" (Whitford, 2000). In general, however, such yielding is uncharacteristic of the personalities that occupy the executive suite: "very rarely will the kind of people who are likely to become CEOs be able to function this way" (Rubin and Weisberg, 2003, p. 311). Perhaps it is precisely because of the peculiarity of the professionals who occupy the top office that professional duos are unstable arrangements and end up, sooner or later, in a dissolved partnership.

Termination

Just as there are many different ways for a professional duo to form, there are many ways for it to end. The end may occur with the voluntary resignation of one member who chooses to embark on an individual professional challenge, in the same organization or elsewhere (e.g. the exit of Rubin as Friedman's co-CEO at Goldman Sachs in order to go into politics; Zander's resignation as a COO of McNeally at Sun Microsystems to later become the top man at Motorola).

Termination can also be forced, as exhibited in a series of ousting maneuvers at the corporate helm, some of them in organizations that were suffering through the difficulties of post-merger integration (e.g. the ousting of Eaton at DaimlerChrysler) or the uncertainties of a forthcoming Initial Public Offering (e.g. the case of Corzine's ousting from the role of co-CEO at Goldman Sachs). Another way out of a professional duo is through a board decision to move back to a sole CEO structure (e.g. the case of Betsy Holden at Kraft Foods, demoted from her co-CEO position with Roger Deromedi on the occasion of the latter being appointed by the board as the solo occupant of the executive suite). The board can also decide on a staged succession in a co-chair structure, as illustrated in Unilever: co-chair Niall FitzGerald was replaced by Patrick Cescau, whereas co-chair Antony Burgmans saw his mandate extended for another four years. Following pressures to streamline its power-sharing arrangement, on February 10, 2005 Unilever announced that, effective from April 2005, the co-chair structure was to be abandoned. Antony Burgmans was appointed a single non-executive chairman of NV and PLC with Patrick Cescau as a single group chief executive.

In some of these cases of termination, the press associated the departures with a "difficult year" or with interpersonal frictions between the members of the professional duo. For example, the recent departure of Mel Karmazin as a second-in-command to Sumner Redstone at Viacom can be read as a combination of both performance and personal issues. It was captured revealingly in the title of an article in the *Guardian*: "Karmazin Quits Viacom After Years of Rivalry" (Teather, 2004, p. 19). Teather not only discusses the disagreements over potential acquisitions and advertising strategies and the "simmering tensions" between the two men, but also mentions the problems with the radio business, to which Mel Karmazin had aligned his fate and which hampered the performance levels of the firm's TV and cable networks. Finally, the members of a professional duo can exit simultaneously, as was demonstrated in 2004 by the joint departure from Gucci of leading designer Tom Ford and managing partner Domenico de Sole.

The exit of one member from a dyad leads, by definition, to its break-up. Furthermore, in dyadic associations, the departure of one member not only puts an end to the small-numbers structure, but it also could change the two executives who constituted the dyad (Becker and Useem, 1942, p. 16). This change may occur because the intimate association afforded by the dyad serves to constitute a fusion of the individualities into a common whole (Cooley, quoted in Becker and Useem, 1942, p. 16) reminiscent of a phenomenon Farrell (2001) called "instrumental intimacy" – a high-level connection between the thought processes of two or more individuals. Becker and Useem (1942) presented different reasons for the termination of duos: "pairs based on economic structures may be discontinued because of horizontal or vertical mobility of one or both members, termination of employment, destruction of the economic pattern upon which their association depends, and personality clashes" (p. 16).

In the next subsection, in order to gain a better grasp of the lifecycle of a professional duo, we use, as an illustration, the case of Scott McNealy and Edward Zander who worked for several years as a hierarchical professional duo at Sun Microsystems. The duo was formed from a working relationship, and went through the stages of functioning and termination.

An illustration[1]

Sun Microsystems' duo of McNealy and Zander is an example of a professional duo with a working genesis, complementary roles (CEO and COO, respectively), and a hierarchical relationship. It was created in 1998 and disintegrated in 2002. Hence, we can explore issues in the genesis and functioning of the pair that may have hampered its consolidation and led to its demise.

The McNealy–Zander tandem developed in the late 1990s at Sun Microsystems. Sun, originally an acronym for the Stanford University Network, was co-founded in 1982 by Vinod Khosla (visionary and entrepreneur of the start-up, and its first CEO), "Andy" Bechtolsheim (hardware), Bill Joy (software), and Scott McNealy (manufacturing and personal skills). It soon positioned itself in the high-tech industry as a challenger to Microsoft and developer of its own standard. The company has become the leading global supplier of network computing solutions.

Genesis and formation
Scott McNealy became Sun's CEO in 1984 after having joined the company as Vice-President for Manufacturing in 1982. Edward Zander joined Sun in 1987 as Vice-President of Corporate Marketing and, from the outset, had access and exposure to McNealy. Between 1991

---

[1] The primary source for much of the background information on Sun Microsystems is Karen Southwick's *High Noon: The Inside Story of Scott McNealy and the Rise of Sun Microsystems* (New York: Wiley, 1999).

and 1995, Zander was president of Sun's software subsidiary SunSoft, and between 1995 and 1998, president of Sun Microsystems Computer Company (SMCC). The tandem was formally announced in 1998 with Zander's appointment as COO of the company. In 1999 he was also given the title of President. Although Scott McNealy was characterized by the press as preferring single-headed control, he formed the tandem structure because of the increased complexity facing top managers with multi-faceted, insurmountable roles: "the job of being CEO, chairman, president, and COO, which Scott was, is an unwinnable job. Scott doesn't have the bandwidth to handle everything" (Raduchel, quoted in Southwick, 1999, p. 199).

The professional tandem of CEO–COO was a governance innovation at Sun, embedded in a series of other important structural changes that coincided with or followed Zander's appointment as COO. A new executive management committee was formed with responsibility for running Sun's day-to-day operations and long-term strategy planning efforts, with Zander being one of the committee members. A few months after Zander's promotion to COO, Sun announced changes in the organization structure, eliminating individual operating companies and moving to a set of divisions focused on products, technologies, and services under the direction of Zander. McNealy's favorite "planet structure," whereby each division kept its autonomy and at times pursued competing aims, was no longer viable for the highly interrelated client solutions that required the integrated effort of several divisions (Southwick, 1999, p. 194).

As Moore (2001) revealed, the tandem was born from the need for a close task collaboration that was expected to provide McNealy with a much-needed strong organizational hand. Various company executives described McNealy and Zander as complementary in styles and competencies. Whereas Ed Zander was characterized as clear and systematic, McNealy was portrayed as being "unpredictable in his approach to an issue" (Southwick, 1999, p. 198).

The following description further emphasizes their differences:

Zander is quite a contrast to McNealy both physically and psychologically. Relatively short, slender, and balding, his competent business-like image is far from the jock facade that McNealy cultivates. Zander always wears a suit (usually Armani) and tie, while McNealy rarely dons formal attire. Almost a decade older than McNealy, Zander spent 14 years at button-down hierarchical companies . . . before joining Sun in 1987. Zander provides a much-needed balance to the capricious CEO: he is more attuned to everyday business requirements than religious campaigns. Were he to leave Sun, it would be a serious blow to the company's effort to shore up relationships with important customers and partners. (Southwick, 1999, p. 198)

Although Zander and McNealy did not socialize together, they did have great respect for one another and appreciation for each other's competencies and contribution to Sun. However, they lacked the strong affective bonding that secures commitment and cohesion. Their commitment was to the future of Sun, not to each other's careers.

The coupling was a complementary one, as McNealy mainly focused externally and on vision development, whereas Zander was expected to enhance the connectivity among Sun's businesses. In addition, the roles were hierarchical, as McNealy was holding the CEO role, while Zander was performing the role of a COO. McNealy's personal account of his role at Sun reveals:

I'm on the bully pulpit . . . Fundamentally, the CEO's job is to figure out what the vision is, not necessarily create it. Develop a plan that uses company resources to best take advantage of that plan. Get it approved by the board, then go on and execute on it, deliver the numbers to the shareholders, and get yourself re-elected another year. That's my job. I decide who's on my staff, I charter them, and I approve the plan, and away we go. Then I spend the rest of my time evangelizing where we're headed and why it's the right answer. (Brockman, 1996)

Zander was aware of his inward, coordinating role – differing from McNealy's outward orientation and visionary role – in the alignment of Sun's many interrelated businesses: "Scott is Sun. He is the soul and inspiration of the company. Clearly my function right now is to make sure things work out around here: We hit our numbers, deliver on our products, meet on our goals and commitments" (Southwick, 1999, p. 199).

As Gronn (1999) suggests, tandems jell when odd couples form them. However, in this odd couple both members competed for careers, as both of them aspired to a CEO seat. Zander was fourteen years older than McNealy and therefore unlikely to benefit from a future CEO succession at Sun. Being an experienced, ambitious, and charismatic leader, Zander had for a long time been attracted to CEO responsibility. Long before he decided to retire as a COO of Sun, he mentioned that:

"People in my capacity always get calls. Personally, I'd love to be the top guy, to run my own thing . . . On the other hand, Scott gives me a lot of leeway. We have a good relationship and it has been a good ride" (Southwick, 1999, p. 198).

Termination

Before initiating the tandem, both McNealy and Zander had long independent careers at the corporate apex. McNealy had held the CEO position at Sun since 1984 and Zander came to Sun in 1987 from an extensive high-tech background in companies like Data General and Apollo. The moves made by McNealy in 1998–99 seemed to be the initiation of a joint career path with Zander. An important demonstration of McNealy's commitment to Zander's ideas was his adoption of Zander's reorganization, putting an end to his planet structure (Southwick, 1999, p. 197). Furthermore, speculation by many observers emphasized the fact that the publicly visible organizational change also fulfilled McNealy's private agenda of preventing Zander from leaving Sun; he was being courted by such top companies as Apple and Silicon Graphics. The coupling was further strengthened when Zander was given the additional title of Sun's President at the time when Compaq and HP started well-publicized searches for new CEOs and put Zander on their shortlists. As Southwick (1999) affirms, McNealy was determined to keep Zander at Sun, signaling his intentions through this promotion. Furthermore, the career move of Zander was "coupled" with McNealy's relinquishing a title he had held for years. Former executives at Sun had acknowledged that Zander was indispensable for Sun's competitiveness because he was the strong lieutenant that McNealy needed to keep operations focused.

In the last year of business difficulties, however, the press reported that the frictions between the professional duo had increased, and Zander announced his retirement as of July 1, 2002. On the day of the announcement, McNealy said to analysts and reporters, "What can I say but thanks to just an awesome effort by Eddie over all these years." McNealy took over the presidential title from Zander and commented that he did not plan to look for a replacement. As the *San Francisco Chronicle* commented at the time of the announcement, Zander had been so instrumental in Sun's success in all those years that Morgan Stanley's report on the day of the announcement called him irreplaceable. As the source claimed, Zander had been postponing his planned departure to see Sun out of the dotcom slump. Revealing the difficulties in their collaboration, McNealy acknowledged, "It's a rare person that can work with me as a COO." On December 16, 2003, it was announced that the board of directors of Motorola had "unanimously elected" Edward Zander chairman and CEO of the company, effective on January 5, 2004.[2]

In summary, we believe that the primary reasons for the dissolution of the McNealy–Zander professional duo are to be found in the confluence of three factors. (1) The duo's genesis from a working relationship, lasting more than ten years, that had been based on close task collaboration at the apex, extending to mutual professional respect and appreciation, but not to deep affection. (2) The hierarchical structuring of their relationship as CEO and COO despite the fact that both members had clear CEO career aspirations. (3) Sun's difficulties in 2001, which sharpened the frictions in the duo and increased McNealy's tendency to intervene in day-to-day management aspects.

Sustainability of professional duos

Studies that focus on personal and business cycles and how they influence the evolution of professional duos could provide insight for understanding the making and breaking of close professional partnerships. In the case of personal cycles, it may be useful to examine the effects of important life-cycle characteristics and events such as age gaps on professional duos and linked careers. For instance, Zander was much older than McNealy, and it is only natural that he should have had aspirations to a CEO position. Goldman Sachs' co-CEO Whitehead felt that time was running out for him to explore his dream, so he decided to join US politics. Business cycles could also have an influence on a duo's evolution and survival. Poor performance results tend to strain even the strongest relationships and to easily break the weaker ones, as the pressure from multiple stakeholders increases.

As emphasized in previous chapters, corporate power structures and governance require highly capable and strong-willed individuals to deal with the complexities of the task and political uncertainties. These can become stronger by joining forces in small-numbers arrangements, such as professional duos. The very tension between strong

---

[2] http://www.motorola.com/mediacenter/news/detail/0,,3683/_3076/_23,00.html

individualities reinforces the robustness of dyads because of members' mutual dependence and the visibility of the possible attempts to break the dyad. Two are needed to succeed and one is sufficient to fail.

In his *Nicomachean Ethics*, Aristotle wrote that "equality is felt to be an essential element of friendship" (quoted in Blau, 1969, p. 195). The lack of power distance between the members of a professional duo is believed to be conducive to its sustainability. It removes one potential source of conflict – power motivation – and makes it easier for conflicts to be resolved amicably. The power aspirations of one member of a dyad at the expense of the other prevent it from jelling, and usually lead to its dissolution. This situation could, of course, be exacerbated by the absence of strong affective ties.

Depending on how the individuals in small-number structures deal with conflict, these structures could be a productive or a counter-productive force. For example, Simmel distinguishes the victory of one party as a radical way of ending a conflict. Other ways include compromise and conciliation. As mentioned by some of the successful pairs at the top that we interviewed, the ability and willingness to reach a compromise in cases of diverging views is the glue that sustains the partnership. As Luis Valls, former co-chair of Spain's Banco Popular, acknowledged when we interviewed him on the success of his decades-long professional relationship with his brother and co-chair Javier Valls, "If there is a difference of opinions, one of us gives way."

In spite of the success of such relationships at the top, professional duos generally seem to be difficult to sustain. One reason is that the individuals that comprise the dyad are usually extremely powerful individuals and have a strong degree of independent self-control (Lee and Tiedens, 2001) that may lead to rivalry and attempts to control each other. Another factor increasing chances of failure may lie in the fact that in a number of situations members have been forced to work together, rather than having chosen the arrangement voluntarily. In mergers and acquisitions, the setting with the highest failure rate for executive duos, there is usually a duplication of ambition, as both co-CEOs or both co-chairs come from a position in which they called the shots in their respective companies. Yet another difficult setting for executive role-sharing is cases of joint ventures. Here, the members of the duo, in addition to having their agendas for the future of the joint endeavor, also have agendas associated with the companies they represent (Ariño and de la Torre, 1998). A political example is the *cohabitation* in France, where members with overtly opposing views must be able to work together.

Yablonsky (1955) put forward a hypothesis on the role that cohesiveness plays in a dyad. He posited that "The dyad can only maintain its position as the nucleus of its own atom when there is a strong cohesiveness in its structure" (p. 359). He provides an example of police department detectives who work together and consider themselves to be partners. As Yablonsky explains, "Because of the dangerous nature of their work it practically becomes an all-or-none form of dyad. This is either they work closely with and accept the other fully; or if there is any lack of confidence they tend to work 'together' but yet shift for themselves when the job becomes precarious" (p. 360).

Sharing the top job in a dyad allows complementary skills to be gained, while preserving the individuality of the executives (Simmel, 1950, pp. 134–135). As Lee and Tiedens (2001) argued, high-powered individuals have a more independent self. The dyad allows the preservation of this individuality and independence. When two people join forces at the top, together they allow the fundamental dualities in executive work to be addressed: internal versus external duties, controlling versus entrepreneurial orientations, and management versus governance tasks.

Hambrick and Cannella (2004) demonstrated that it is expensive and not necessarily profitable for companies to have a CEO–COO structure. However, are there other downsides to tight professional couplings at the top? When embarking on a strong relationship at the corporate top or deciding on the appointment of professional duos, it is also worth considering the cons: the costs, the dilemmas, and the tension it may create for the organization and its stakeholders. Moreover, it is worth thinking in terms of optional designs and whether a return to the solo model makes sense. Some voices may be skeptical that such sharing at the top is realistic, especially given that executives spend most of their careers aspiring to get the top job.

Finally, if a blueprint for making the professional duo arrangement function is to be established, the following issues need to be addressed. First, it is important to think about how one can convince a CEO, for example, to share a job and a title. Individuals who have been involved in these processes recognize that it is difficult and that it may take a long time. Second, professional duos may be easier to create when starting an enterprise from the ground up. As research has demonstrated (for example, Ruef, Aldrich, and Carter, 2003), it is founding teams rather than solitary individuals that embark on the creation of a new company. Although the sharing of founding efforts has been well documented, the survival and seamless operation of a duo – or a larger constellation at the later stages of the enterprise – has been studied far less. Moreover, the development of a duo is often far from smooth, as some anecdotal evidence from our conversations with executives has shown.

When hierarchical and professional duos are established in an organization, does it need to be restructured to accommodate the shared arrangements? Are special communication efforts necessary on the part of the professional duo in order to clarify and affirm its way of operation? These questions need to be addressed when considering professional duos as an alternative to the traditionally unitary model of vertical structures.

Committed dyadic partnerships have different degrees of coupling – from a sporadic collaboration in a dyad, through joint performance of tasks in a professional duo (e.g. co-CEOs, co-founders), to joint career decision-making and moves in a united career, which we explore in detail in Chapter 6. Not all dyads become formalized into professional duos, and not every professional duo links its members' trajectories into a united career.

Professional duos are dyads with joint responsibility and role performance, knitted together by an authority line (for hierarchical duos) or by high levels of trust and shared cognition (for partnership duos). As an alternative to solo executives, professional duos are most widespread and resilient when compared to other small-numbers arrangements, as they help in dealing with basic dilemmas inherent in the work at the corporate apex. Professional duos constitute an important small-numbers corporate governance structure that addresses the contingencies we described earlier, and they provide an alternative for overcoming the limitations of solo management.

We are convinced that job-sharing in the executive suite is not destined to failure if the top women and men are prepared for what lies ahead. Through a better understanding of the implications of sharing the top position, it can be a successful endeavor, both for the individuals involved and for the company they lead. Furthermore, we propose that awareness of when and how to exit such power-sharing arrangements is required in order to avoid such personal and professional costs as damaged reputations due to the high visibility of the dyad's uncoupling.

In this chapter we have examined professional duos. In the next chapter we take one step forward, to the small-number options of trios and larger constellations.

5 | *Trios and bigger executive constellations*

> I found that there were definite advantages in having a team of three at the head of the business rather than simply myself and the chief executive. It made it easier to discuss and settle issues with the chief executive, which could have been potentially divisive. If a matter has to be resolved, two people can find themselves at odds and the only solution is for one to give way to the other. This is a normal feature of coming to decisions, but it puts a strain on the relationship between the two people involved. The win/lose situation can often be avoided if a third person, in whose impartial judgement the other two have confidence, is party to the discussions.
>
> Cadbury, 2002, p. 126

TITIAN's *Allegory of Prudence* startles the visitor to the National Gallery in London with an image of three men's heads above a triple-headed beast (wolf, lion, and dog) that hints at the three ages of man – youth, maturity, and old age. The inscription in Latin above them reads *Ex praeterito praesens prvdenter agit ni futuractione detvrpet* (From the past the man of the present acts prudently so as not to imperil the future).[1] These powerful images and the message have been used as an illustration in a recent article (Pradera, 2004, p. 17) on the three-headed structure of Spain's Partido Popular (PP), a political party on the centre-right of the political spectrum, currently in opposition. The trio is the party's founding father (Manuel Fraga), its

---

[1] http://www.nationalgallery.org.uk (accessed on November 13, 2004).

honorary president (a position introduced specifically for José María Aznar, former prime minister of Spain and previous president of the party), and the current party president, Mariano Rajoy. The article alluded to the potential political games in which these three could engage. At the apex of a political party, where strong identification with a single figure is necessary, such a three-headed structure could be problematic (Pradera, 2004, p. 17). Although trios have been relatively problematic and unstable small-numbers structures, they have also been largely instrumental in achieving political agendas, as the historical and business examples in this chapter reveal. In this chapter we examine small-numbers structures of three or more individuals as an alternative to solo executives and professional duos in the design of corporate power.

In Chapter 4 we discussed the relevance of professional duos in addressing dichotomous organizational needs. We suggested that trust is essential in integrating the complementary contributions and capabilities of the members of the duo and in making the arrangement balanced and effective. However, in addition to dichotomous organizations, there are also polychotomous ones (Senger, 1971). Such organizations pose a range of demands upon a leader, which can be better addressed by appointing multiple leaders of equal rank (Senger, 1971). These multiple leaders can form a total constellation of specialists, "one that allows or aids the system to establish a full orbit in its dimensions of necessary movement" (Bales, 1955, p. 79). Structures of three or more individuals are characterized by "distinctive processes of the dynamics of power" (Blau, 1969, p. 199) that cannot be observed in a dyad.

Small-numbers teams at the corporate apex received increased attention in the 1960s and early 1970s, and such empirical studies as the examination of the executive role constellation at a mental hospital were conducted (Hodgson, Levinson, and Zaleznik, 1965). Conceptual articles also appeared on plural chief executives (Daniel, 1965) and co-managers (Senger, 1971). These studies highlighted the belief that a team at the top magnified "the capacities of the top office to deal with the full range of its responsibilities" (Daniel, 1965, p. 74). There has been a recent renewal of interest in plural chiefs (e.g. Gronn, 2002; O'Toole, Galbraith, and Lawler, 2002; Sally, 2002). However, in the main, the focus has been on professional duos, leaving the discussion of trios and quartets on the sidelines. Guided by Simmel's (1950) argument that the mere number of people in the group has implications for the behavior of its members, we place particular emphasis in this chapter on small-numbers structures of threesomes and foursomes. In this sense, we examine executive role constellations and executive offices. The executive office or the office of the chief executive – both terms that have been used in the literature – denotes "a structure with permeable boundaries that speeds the flow of strategic and operational information among the executive decision makers" (Rivero and Spencer, 1998, p. 65).

An executive role constellation is a "matrix of interpersonal relations, with its specialization, differentiation, and complementarity of roles" (Hodgson, Levinson, and Zaleznik, 1965, p. 12). It "can be made up of a varying number of people performing certain roles that are interrelated in a number of different ways" (Hodgson, Levinson, and Zaleznik, 1965, p. 485). In this matrix or system, the division of labor takes place at both the emotional and the administrative tasks levels (Hodgson, Levinson, and Zaleznik, 1965). In addition, the notion of role constellation is meant to "imply an emerging and evolving system rather than a static, formally defined group or a simple aggregate" (Hodgson, Levinson, and Zaleznik, 1965, p. xii).

This chapter is organized into four major sections. We begin by tracing the historical origins of political structures of three or more individuals, including the First and Second Triumvirates of ancient Rome, and, moving to more modern times, we discuss, among other things, political structures found in the 1920s at the forefront of political power in the USSR, and since 1996 in the presidency of Bosnia-Herzegovina. Then we provide a conceptual background on triads, drawing primarily on the work of Simmel (1950), Hodgson, Levinson, and Zaleznik (1965), and Krackhardt (1999), to determine what differentiates the corporate power structure of a trio from that of a duo. Next we examine different types of threesomes at the organizational apex, referring to Caplow's (1956) typology of coalitions in a triad and Simmel's (1950) strategies: mediator/arbiter, *tertius gaudens* (the third who rejoices), and *divide et impera* (divide and rule). Finally, we illustrate Simmel's strategies with examples drawn from the business world. In doing so, we expand the range of strategies proposed by Simmel with two particular instances: those of a legitimator (a strategy observed in the professionalization of technological start-ups) and an integrator (a strategy characteristic in a generational transition in family firms). In this discussion we focus mainly on the small-numbers structures of three executives, although we eventually broaden the discussion to include teams of four individuals.

Historical triumvirates

The term triumvirate comes from the Latin *tresviri* or *triumviri*. In ancient Rome such three-man arrangements were popular in the management of activities in the judicial, religious, and administrative spheres, as the large number of terms in the following definition of triumvirate from the *Encyclopædia Britannica* suggests:

Tresviri capitales, or tresviri nocturni, first instituted about 289 BC, assisted higher magistrates in their judicial functions, especially those relating to crime and the civil status of citizens. Tresviri epulones, originally a board of three priests, was created in 196 BC to take charge of the banquet of Jupiter, the key event in the festivals of the Ludi Romani and Ludi Plebeii. Tresviri monetales were in charge of the mint for Rome and Italy during both the republic and the empire . . . Boards of three persons, usually elected, called triumviri agris dandis assignandis (sometimes also judicandis) and triumviri coloniae deducendae were frequently placed, respectively, in charge of assignments of land and in charge of the founding of colonies during the last three centuries of the republic. (3rd–1st century BC)[2]

This quotation reveals the ubiquity of trios in the governance of various administrative and religious functions in ancient Rome. However, it does not provide details on the evolution of these structures of threesomes. Two renowned historical examples that cast light on the dynamics and instabilities of the threesome structures are the First and Second Roman Triumvirates. The title *tresviri rei publicae constituendae* (triumvirate for organizing the state) was granted in 43 BC for five years to the group known as the Second Triumvirate, consisting of Mark Antony, Marcus Aemilius Lepidus, and Octavian (later Emperor Augustus). Under that arrangement they received absolute authority, described in the annals as dictatorial. The First Triumvirate, that of Pompey the Great, Julius Caesar, and Marcus Licinius Crassus, began in 60 BC and operated with no sanctioned powers; rather it was

---

[2] "Triumvirate," *Encyclopædia Britannica*, http://www.britannica.com/eb/article?tocId = 9073449 (accessed November 14, 2004).

simply founded on the basis of an informal understanding of the three powerful leaders. The secret trio was characterized as complementary: "Crassus had the money, Pompey the military prestige, and Caesar, though patrician in origin, had the *populares* on his side and the dignity of pontifex maximus" (Le Glay, Voisin, and Le Bohec, 1996, p. 137; italics in original). The triumvirate was not exempt from problems and disagreements, however, and ended in 53 BC with the death of Crassus. The remaining duo ceased officially with Pompey's death in Egypt, leaving Caesar as the sole ruler of Rome.

Unlike the First Triumvirate, which was based on a secret agreement, the Second Triumvirate was not only public but also sanctioned by a legal document (Le Glay, Voisin, and Le Bohec, 1996). Its members – Mark Antony, Octavian, and Lepidus – not only divided the Roman world and took charge of different geographical areas, but also shared missions among themselves. Over time, Lepidus was not only isolated but also removed from even nominal membership of the triumvirate. It is worth noting that both the secret and public triumvirates were forged for the pursuit of political interests and power ambitions and were dissolved for the same reasons several years after their establishment, leading to solo rulerships.

Another example of a triumvirate, situated at the historical time of a swing from republicanism to autocracy, is that of the Consulate of Napoleon Bonaparte, with Bonaparte as First Consul together with Sieyès and Pierre-Roger Ducos as Second and Third Consuls with advisory powers. Sieyès played an essential role in the orchestration of the arrangement. He and Bonaparte had planned a *coup d'état* that was carried out on Brumaire 18–19, Year VIII (November 9–10, 1799) when the directors were forced to resign and the new government, the Consulate, was established.[3] Sieyès and the Brumarians' initial plan in supporting the *coup d'état* had been to install a strengthened executive composed of a powerless Grand Elector and two co-equal Consuls under parliamentary control (Markham, 1970). However, it was rejected and replaced by an arrangement in which the First Consul held all executive power. This arrangement formally ended in 1804 when Bonaparte crowned himself Emperor and replaced the two consuls, creating the positions of *prince impérial* for his brothers Joseph

---

[3] "Napoleon I," *Encyclopædia Britannica*, http://www.britannica.com/eb/article?tocId = 16214 (accessed November 10, 2004).

and Louis. Thus the Consulate trio had become instrumental to a solo leader in instituting his rule.

Another illustration of an instrumental and unstable trio is the one Stalin established in order to obtain a firm grip on political power in the USSR. In the years when Lenin was no longer able to sustain his position because of health problems and Trotsky was considered heir apparent, Stalin formed a triumvirate with Grigory Zinovyev and Lev Kamenev. The trio not only detained Lenin under house arrest but also dominated the Politburo. The trio succeeded in isolating Trotsky as a rival and seized power upon Lenin's death. Like other political triumvirates, this one ended up with Stalin assuming the leadership of the party and the country single-handedly.[4]

But not all threesome structures are unstable. US President Roosevelt, his "trouble-shooter" Taft, who was Secretary of War and, for a period, Secretary of State, and Root, Secretary of State provide an example of a smoothly running political trio. The three men worked together so closely and so harmoniously that they came to be known as the Three Musketeers.[5]

Although famous trios can be found at the head of state or political organizations, institutionalized foursome structures have been rare. A peculiar foursome structure – known as the Gang of Four – was at China's political forefront from 1966 to 1976, until the death of Mao Zedong. The group comprised Mao's third wife, Jiang Qing, as well as Wang Hongwen, Zhang Chunqiao, and Yao Wen-yuan. Chairman Mao's team was responsible for implementing the harsh policies that became known as the Cultural Revolution. Those four, initially low-ranking officials in good standing with Mao had united forces in manipulation and rose to high positions in the government and the Communist Party at the beginning of the Cultural Revolution. By restraining the media and propaganda outlets, the group gained control over the following crucial areas: intellectual education, basic theories in science and technology, teacher–student relations, school discipline, and party policies regarding intellectuals.[6] After Mao's death in 1976,

---

[4] "Union of Soviet Socialist Republics," *Encyclopædia Britannica*, http://www.britannica.com/eb/article?tocId = 42051 (accessed November 13, 2004).

[5] "Taft, William Howard," *Britannica Student Encyclopædia*, http://www.britannica.com/ebi/article?tocId = 208675 (accessed November 14, 2004).

[6] "Gang of Four," *Encyclopædia Britannica*, http://www.britannica.com/eb/article?tocId = 9035993 (accessed November 11, 2004).

the Gang was held jointly responsible for its crimes at the forefront of the Cultural Revolution.

Sometimes threesome and foursome structures are assembled not for the pursuit of individual interests but for group interests and agendas, when collaboration in a joint undertaking is essential. This was the purpose behind the adoption in 1996 of a tripartite presidency in Bosnia-Herzegovina, where a Bosnian, a Serb, and a Croat represent the people that constitute the nation and function as a collective head of state, rotating the chair of the presidency every eight months.

All these examples of political and government threesome or foursome structures point to the diversity of reasons for which such structures come into being: the covert or overt pursuit of power and privilege, the performance of complex activities that require diverse capabilities, or the representation of different collective interests in a joint enterprise, to name three possibilities. Another observation that could be made from reading the pages of the historical annals is that, unlike duos, threesome and foursome structures usually develop their own identity. Hence they are referred to by invoking this collective identity, e.g. a triumvirate, a consulate, or a gang of four. Furthermore, they are relatively short-lived structures. Triggered by interpersonal disagreements, changing interests or context, or shifting coalitions, they have been prone to dissolution or to transformation into a duo or a solo arrangement.

The historical examples outlined in this section are diverse manifestations of a well-studied sociological structure – the triad. A triad, defined in the austere language of social network analysis, is "a subset of three actors and the (possible) tie(s) among them" (Wasserman and Faust, 1994, p. 19). In the following examination of triads, we seek to achieve two particular distinctions: to consider how a triad differs from a dyad, and to investigate how triadic types differ from one another.

Differences between structures of professional duos and trios

Simmel (1950) considered the size of the group to be an essential determinant of variations that can be observed in the structure of social relations, suggesting that an increase in number is associated with a change in the character of relationships within the group. Before we discuss the differences between triads and dyads, two characteristics of Simmel's approach are worth noting. First, Simmel's use of the triad was "apparently intended to emphasize the crucial distinction between a pair and any group of more than two" (Blau, 1969, p. 199). According to Simmel (1950), "the further expansion to four or more persons by no means correspondingly modifies the group any further" (Simmel, in Krackhardt, 1999, p. 186). Thus, the crucial change in behavior occurs when the structure expands from a duo to a trio. Second, Simmel's primary interest was in *Verbindungen zu dreien* (associations of three parties), which made reference to much more loosely organized and multi-leveled phenomena than the structured and integrated groups of three persons that are connoted by the term "triad" (Levine, Carter, and Gorman, 1976). Although we acknowledge the breadth of Simmel's notion, our interest in small-numbers structures at the top leads us to focus on the narrower definition of a triad as a three-person group.

Triads differ from dyads in several respects: permanence and stability; individual and supra-individual identities; affection; bargaining power and conflict resolution; and role-sharing and separation. Triads are considered to be more enduring structures than dyads (Simmel, 1950). Dyads reveal an impending sense of death, whereas triads manifest a sense of durability (Mills, 1958). One of the reasons for the apparent stability of the triad is the development of a special supra-individual identity, which provides a focal point for the three members, attaching them to the object that represents the relationship as a whole or as a collectivity (Mills, 1958). This supra-individual identity also restricts the individualities and public behaviors of the participating members (Krackhardt, 1999).

In addition to permanence and collectivity, affection is another differentiator between trios and duos. In the dyad, there is exclusivity in the relationship and an affection that may culminate in intimacy; whereas in the triad it tends to be either restricted to a subpart or checked (Mills, 1958). Another take on that is provided by Goffman (1990 [1959]), who defined a team as "any set of individuals who cooperate in staging a single routine" (p. 85). The bond that Goffman suggested binds the team together is one of reciprocal dependence and familiarity, a kind of intimacy without warmth. Triads have been found restrictive not only in terms of the members' individuality and affection but also with regard to their bargaining power. However, they can also be enabling, particularly in conflict resolution, because a third member can often bring balance and reconciliation, which is not the case with dyads, where polar positions can be sustained. Furthermore, because triads comprise too many individuals for role-sharing, role separation is more characteristic than it is for dyads, therefore reducing the need to rely on trust.

These traits of the triad reinforce each other and reveal the extent to which a component of the triad may be easily replaced by a new member. Thus, triads favor the emergence of politics at the top and the building of coalitions to overcome the power of a *tertium*. As a consequence, what on some occasions can be a stable and enduring structure can become an unstable and transient arrangement over time.

Simmel's (1950) work stimulated a prolific line of inquiry on triads (Levine, Carter, and Gorman, 1976). Mills (1953), for example, conducted a pioneering study at the Harvard Laboratory of Social Relations on interaction patterns in forty-eight three-person groups, and confirmed Simmel's basic point of the propensity of a threesome to break into a pair and a singleton (Levine, Carter, and Gorman, 1976). A study by Strodtbeck (1954) revealed that this type of break-up did not occur in the familiar group of father, mother, and an adolescent, which Levine, Carter, and Gorman (1976) believe creates a misleading impression that coalition formation within families is not significant. As many case histories have shown, there is room for building and using coalitions in family businesses.

In an attempt to develop Simmel's ideas further, Mills (1958) raised a series of questions that call for a more refined understanding of the differences between dyads and triads. He proposed that it was necessary to pay attention to both the adding of numbers to, and the subtracting of them from, duos and trios – to acquire a better understanding of both the transitions from dyads to triads and the transition from triads to dyads.

Another area of Simmel's original contribution that requires further refinement concerns the stability of trios, about which evidence has been relatively inconclusive. On the basis of their study of the executive trio at the top of a mental hospital, for example, Hodgson, Levinson, and Zaleznik (1965) concluded that "Pairings of top executives may prove to be the most stable of all role constellations" (p. 487) and triadic constellations "are perhaps the most intrinsically unstable of all. Triads always have that 'third party' who is somewhat 'in between' and two others" (p. 487). We discuss the lack of agreement on the

stability of dyads and triads in the concluding chapter when we analyze the insights provided by the adoption of a contingency view of
small-numbers corporate power structures and governance. In the next
section we describe different types of triads and argue that, depending
on the power distribution among other characteristics of the triadic
relationship, some triads can be more stable than others.

Types of trios

An essential feature of structures of threesomes is the interactions that
occur among their members. One approach to the study of these interactions is provided by game theory, originated in the work of John
von Neumann and Oskar Morgenstern (1944). Game theory has provided important insights on interactions, in particular on multi-person
games of strategy in which the concern is with essential coalitions and
power indices (Kelly, 2003), and has influenced sociological thinking
(Swedberg, 2001). Unlike game theorists, with their rational consid-
erations, social psychologists have focused on the "expectations stem-
ming from the perceptions and motives of the participants" (Vinacke
and Arkoff, 1957). When examining triads sociologically, the focus
becomes the significance of having three elements in a structure
(Simmel, 1950) and the outcomes of the members' interactions when
they differ in rank and power (Caplow, 1956). Reviving the work of
Simmel, Caplow (1956) examined six types of triads (see Figure 5) to
determine if one member is more or less powerful than another and
if the two remaining individuals, by joining their forces in a coalition,
can rule out a third element.

Given the distribution of power among the members of a triad, certain coalitions among the individual members are more likely than
others (Caplow, 1956). For example, on rare occasions, if at all, both
historically and in business life, we have three individuals who are
absolutely equal in terms of competencies, resources, power, ranks,
and related characteristics. Hence the Type 1 triads of Caplow's typology are rare and represent an idealized type of triad. Furthermore,
based on Bales' method of interaction process analysis, Caplow (1956)
argued that in a triad "If the two most active members show a mutually
supportive pattern, then their relationship is characterized as solidary.
Otherwise it is described as conflicting, dominant, or contending"
(p. 492). As a general trend, Mills (1953) had affirmed Simmel's

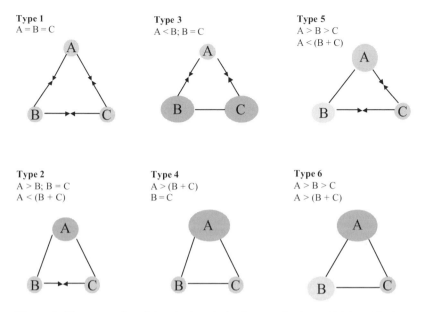

Figure 5. Six types of coalition in the triad. (*Source*: Caplow, 1956, p. 491.)

proposition that "the primary tendency in the threesome is segrega-
tion into a pair and an other: the more active members form a solidary
bond and the least active member is isolated" (Caplow, 1956, p. 492).

In the next section we use the insight gained from the historical
examples and the sociological work on the theory of triads to grasp
the peculiarities of executive trios and larger executive constellations.

Dynamics of executive role constellations

Small-numbers power structures of three or more individuals could
occupy a place on a continuum from constellation to aggregate. The
former denotes a highly specialized and differentiated complementary system of executive roles characterized by a symbolic character
and a group identity, whereas the latter refers to an unspecialized,
undifferentiated system of interchangeable roles that lacks identity
(Hodgson, Levinson, and Zaleznik, 1965). As described, the aggre-
gates are "in antithesis to executive role constellations" (Hodgson,
Levinson, and Zaleznik, 1965, p. 489). These are executive groups
that have failed to achieve (or have been hampered by social pressures

Symmetrical

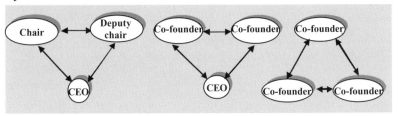

Non-symmetrical

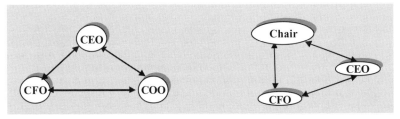

Figure 6. Examples of symmetrical and non-symmetrical executive constellations.

from achieving) the adequate role specializations, differentiations, and complementarities for their individual contigencies.

Executive role constellations could be further subdivided into symmetrical and non-symmetrical types (Cadbury, 2002). An example of a symmetrical executive trio is the so-called "triangle of equals" (Cadbury, 2002), consisting of chair, chief executive, and deputy chair. Also it can comprise co-founders of a start-up company who share decision-making power equally or of co-founders and a hired CEO who is given equal standing and the responsibility to professionalize the business. Non-symmetrical trios might be formed by a chair, CEO, and CFO; or by a CEO, COO, and CFO – any trio in which the members differ in rank and power (Cadbury, 2002). Figure 6 illustrates some examples of symmetrical and non-symmetrical executive role constellations.

Forming an executive role constellation

There are several questions that could be addressed when discussing the dynamics of executive role constellations.

(1) How do trios arise: from an already formed and functioning pair, or *de novo*, in which three parties come together without previous history?

(2) How do they operate?

(3) What integration mechanisms keep them together?

(4) How – in the words of Mills (1958) – do the affective, behavioral, and cognitive aspects of the original dyad change (together or separately) with the arrival of the third member?

(5) And in cases of dissolution, and moving back to a pair or a solo small-numbers structure, what is the effect on the affective, behavioral, and cognitive aspects of the relationships of those who remain?

We now try to address these issues by providing business examples. Executive role constellations can form in various cases of transition, including the start-up of a business when a team of co-founders contributes complementary capabilities, resources, and expertise; in moving from the first to the second generation in a family firm, when the children of the co-founders jointly take the reins of the company; in the integration of the activities of companies following a merger or an acquisition to secure representation of the parties involved; in the governance of multi-party alliances, in which each party seeks representation in the executive and governance functions of the new venture; or when a professional duo seeks a way to resolve its disagreements and hires a *consigliere*.

Here we briefly mention a few examples of how and why executive role constellations come into being. When it began operations, Covisint, the business-to-business electronic supplier exchange that was co-founded by the big three car manufacturers DaimlerChrysler, Ford Motor Company, and General Motors, was run by three co-CEOs, representing each founding firm. Initially there was a fourth member, a consultant, whose role as a *consigliere* was to secure the functioning of the power structure. Over time, in order to improve accountability, the design of the corporate office eventually moved to two and finally to a single CEO at the helm of the company.

Another instance of the formation of vertical structures of threesomes and foursomes is at the start-up stage of new ventures in which several individuals join forces to help build the enterprise. What characterizes such small-numbers structures at the forefront of new businesses is their complementarity of expertise and access to contacts, as well as the affectivity that usually binds them prior to their embarking on a professional relationship. As Ruef, Aldrich, and Carter (2003) have observed in the case of US start-ups, these are founded primarily with family and friends. For example, Harley-Davidson Motor Company was incorporated in 1907 by four co-founders William Harley and the brothers Arthur, Walter, and William Davidson. Sun Microsystems was born in the early 1980s from the efforts of a foursome – the ambition and vision of Vinod Khosla, the practical manufacturing and personal skills of Scott McNealy, and the technological genius of Andy Bechtolsheim and Bill Joy. They were later joined by a fifth element, the skillful marketing and sales person, John Gage, with the formal title of Chief Scientist (Southwick, 1999).

In 1994, DreamWorks was founded by Jeffrey Katzenberg (*de facto* Chief Executive), Steven Spielberg (*de facto* Chief Creative Officer), and David Geffen (considered the entrepreneurial force behind the enterprise). *Forbes* interviewed the three co-founders individually and received their accounts of how they came to found DreamWorks. In the words of Steven Spielberg:

I give very little thought to the corporate evolution, because that's not my job here. That's not what I'm supposed to do . . . I get a headache when these guys start talking about refinancing and things like that. It just goes right over my head. And that's why I insisted, when Jeffrey [Katzenberg] approached me to form DreamWorks . . . that David [Geffen] had to come along as a full partner. And I said "Jeffrey, you know, you and I need an adult in the mix". (Kafka and Newcomb, 2003b)

In that interview, Spielberg acknowledged that he worked principally as a creative partner. Katzenberg recognized that Geffen was the entrepreneur, "certainly among the three or four greatest entrepreneurs in the entertainment business, ever" (Kafka and Newcomb, 2003a). What Geffen pointed to, in turn, was not only their complementarity of skills but also the opportunity for each of them to pursue his own wants, needs and desires:

It gives Steven the opportunity to do all things he always wanted to do without ever having to go ask anybody for permission. It gives Jeffrey the opportunity to build an animation company and a movie distribution and marketing company from scratch a second time. And it's given me the opportunity to stay in business with [DreamWorks Records executives Mo Ostin, Lenny Waronker, and Michael Ostin], who are people I have been in business

[with] virtually my entire life. And to be able to support all of these people and be in the background, which is what I prefer, and not on the line. So it services us all. (Kafka and Newcomb, 2003c)

This quotation reveals that the glue that binds a constellation is not only the complementarity of competencies and networks of contacts but also the availability of space for each individual member to develop a preferred area of activity.

Functioning of executive role constellations

How do trios and foursomes operate? At the opening of Joseph Conrad's *Heart of Darkness*,[7] Marlow begins telling his dark colonization tale to his friends. They are on the *Nellie*, a cruising yawl, all bound by the special "bond of the sea," which – as the narrator reveals – "Besides holding our hearts together through long periods of separation, it had the effect of making us tolerant to each other's yarns – and even convictions" (Conrad, 2000, pp. 15–16). The scene is evocative of many of the elements of collaborative pairing: trust, intimacy, openness, egalitarian relationship, acceptance of differences in perspectives, and a kind of empathic attention (Farrell, 2001). Similar bonds and tolerance are needed not only on board a yawl but also in the executive suite, when top executives form executive constellations to address the complexity of the top job.

Another evocative metaphor on how executive constellations function is that of the "second skin." In an article about the Oscar-winning Spanish film director Pedro Almodóvar, his team was portrayed as his second skin, connecting him with the world (Millás, 2004). The metaphor of skin alludes to a characteristic of the team members as nerve endings with sufficient sensitivity to detect the stimuli that can damage or favor the film director. At first glance it may seem that this team insulates the director from the world but, at second glance, Millás argues, it becomes clear that the opposite is true; it helps him relate to the world. At third glance one becomes aware of the fact that it does both: insulates and connects him according to which is better at each moment. To make the parallel with our small-numbers structures at the corporate helm, the team is annexed to the leader or top executive and

---

[7] First published in J. Conrad, *Youth: A Narrative with Two Other Stories.* Edinburgh: W. Blackwood and Sons, 1902.

may perform the same or similar functions as a co-leader or a co-CEO, for example – without the formal sharing of the position, however. The team can handle part of the work complexity, facilitating the range of the relationships in which the leader is involved.

For a trio or a constellation of four individuals to function well at the top, fine-tuning and mutual understanding are essential. An example from fiction is provided by Alexandre Dumas' (1844) story *The Three Musketeers*, first serialized in the newspaper *Le Siècle*. It narrated the experience of Athos, Porthos, Aramis, and their new friend, D'Artagnan, who joins the adventures of the closely knit trio and converts it into a well-balanced quartet. The musketeers' famous motto – "All for one, and one for all!" – is revealing of the type of union that can exist in small-numbers constellations.

Further examples of this necessary synchronization and improvisation can be drawn from the world of music. Murnighan and Conlon (1991) have detailed the dynamics of particularly intense groups of four – the professional string quartets composed of two violinists, a viola player, and a cellist – whose collective task is "to reach a high level of coordinated sound" (p. 166). A curious differentiation in string quartets is the one that exists between the European- and American-style quartets. In the European style, the quartet is expected to sound in unison, whereas in the American style it sounds like four voices that have been combined harmoniously (Murnighan and Conlon, 1991). This differentiation may have parallels in the business world, as suggested by Cadbury's (2002) distinction between (1) triumvirates of a chair, CEO, and senior director or a chair, CEO, and CFO, in which the individualities and their expertise matter, and (2) the office of the chair, where the three members are expected to act as one.

Murnighan and Conlon's (1991) inquiry into the dynamics of string quartets emphasizes the importance of reciprocal interdependence, which is complete and immediate. There are some parallels between the ability to be a good member of an executive constellation and that of being a good quartet player: "the ability to listen and respond to each other was the most important characteristic that differentiated quartet players from soloists" (Murnighan and Conlon, 1991, p. 165). We consider it useful to discuss in some detail the roles of the members of the quartet and some of the implications drawn by Murnighan and Conlon (1991) on the basis of their study. There are different positions within the quartet and each has different musical responsibilities: first violinist, second violinist, viola player, and cellist. The first violinist is the musical leader of the quartet, and the one most easily heard by the audience, even in European-style quartets. It is essential for the first violin to have the "audition," the musical vision. The second violinist ("second fiddle") is expected to provide a complementary sound and echo the first fiddle. Also, along with the viola player, the second fiddle forms the middle of the quartet. The viola player has a linking position because they team up not only with the second violinist but also with the cellist, with whom the viola player forms the bottom of the quartet. The cellist constitutes the base of the group and lays the foundation in order to enable the rest of the strings to shine. A requirement is that the cellist be completely dependable. Finally, another essential require-ment is for "each player to have a soloist's skills but not a soloist's temperament" (Murnighan and Conlon, 1991, p. 167). These musical roles can have parallels in foursomes at the top, in which some of the figures are more visible to the stakeholders by the nature of their posi-tions (e.g. chair, CEO) while others are essential supporters who are less exposed to public attention (e.g. a COO).

Simmel (1950) found that a change from a structure of three to a structure of four created insignificant changes in behavior. However, we believe some differences could be identified. In the cases of four co-founders, for example, decision-making could become more difficult than it would in a trio because there is no odd element to reconcile the parties in cases of opposing opinions. Instead the foursome could split into two pairs, leading to a sustained difficulty in reconciling views. On the basis of the examples we have examined, we speculate that decision-making will be easier and speedier in structures of three than in structures of four.

In the next section, we move to the exploration of strategies in trios and illustrate them with business examples.

Strategies in executive role constellations

Cadbury (2002) considered two main types of triumvirate – one he described as being composed of equals (chair, chief executive, and deputy chair) and the other as being hierarchically constructed (chair, chief executive, and financial director, with the latter reporting to the CEO). He also noted that some companies have used the office of the chair as a structural arrangement; however, he did not discuss its problems. In this section we discuss strategies in formal teams at the top, like the office of the chair; and informal constellations, which, although not denoted as an office in the company's organization chart, function as such in reality.

In the discussion of the strategies of three members in executive constellations, we build on Simmel's (1950) original depiction of the different roles a third member can play in the triad. Simmel examined the mediator and arbiter roles (the mediator facilitates, while the arbiter takes a position in favor of one or the other of the two remaining parties); the *tertius gaudens* who benefited from the juxtaposing of the other two; and the *divide et impera* in which a duo is weakened by infusing rivalry into their relationship. Below we illustrate Simmel's strategies with their approximations from the business world. We have expanded the range of strategies proposed by Simmel with two particular instances – those of the legitimator (a strategy observed in bringing professional management to technological start-ups) and the integrator (a strategy characteristic of generational transitions in family firms). We have derived the roles of the legitimator and the integrator from the examples we encountered. As they did not fit neatly into the strategies defined by Simmel, yet were representative of such important types of organizational context as high-tech start-ups and family businesses, we decided to include and illustrate them accordingly.

The following five examples are used to illustrate the different strategies. The strategy of the mediator is illustrated with the case of Citigroup at the time of Robert Rubin as a *consigliere* for Weill and Reed who had together formed the Office of the Chairman. The strategy of the *tertius gaudens* is illustrated by Sumner Redstone, the CEO of Viacom, who, after the departure of Mel Karmazin as a COO, appointed two co-COOs and co-presidents, from whom he could choose his heir apparent. The third example is that of an attempted *divide et impera* strategy at the time of Josep Vilarasau – former CEO of Spain's largest savings bank, La Caixa – who, in his attempts to retain the executive powers when moving to the position of chair, divided the CEO position between two professionals.

In addition to these illustrations of Simmel's strategies, we are advancing two more strategies in contemporary trios. The first is that of the legitimator, which can be illustrated by Eric Schmidt's appointment as a CEO of Google with the purpose of bringing professional management expertise to the two technically savvy co-founders, Brin and Page. The second is the strategy of the integrator, which can be found in family businesses and is exemplified here with James Tisch, CEO of Loews, who is considered to be an integrator of the "Office of the President," which he holds together with Andrew and Jonathan Tisch (James' brother and cousin, respectively). Below we shed light on each of these strategies and the examples that illustrate them. Table 1 summarizes the main points of the discussion that follows.

Mediator strategy

The mediator strategy is one of Simmel's classic scenarios, in which a third person mediates the tensions or facilitates the interactions of an existing pair. As an illustration of the mediating role, we consider the employment of Robert Rubin (former US Secretary of the Treasury and former successful co-COO and co-CEO at Goldman Sachs, together with Stephen Friedman) by Citigroup's co-CEOs and co-chairs at the time, Sandy Weill and John Reed. As the Citigroup's communiqué on October 26, 1999 revealed, "Mr. Rubin will serve as Chairman of the Executive Committee of the Board and will work with Mr. Reed and Mr. Weill, Chairmen and Co-Chief Executive Officers, in a newly constituted three-person office of the Chairman."

Rubin became a "trusted advisor," "a true *consigliere*" (Loomis, 2003, p. 124) and was considered to be well suited to satisfy Weill and Reed's need to improve their working relationship and decision-making. The following account by Rubin reveals how the trio used to operate:

Since now I was the third member of the office of the chairman, though not a co-CEO, I suggested that we have a meeting once a week, called the "Office of the Chairman Meeting," with the three of us as well as Chuck Prince, Citigroup's general counsel, acting as secretary. I would function as facilitator to try to help John and Sandy work through decisions. John was fine with the process, but it was Sandy who really used these meetings, arriving with a prepared agenda. He would say, "I've got these five things I want to talk about today." And we would go through them one by one. These meetings helped John and Sandy somewhat, but making decisions and setting direction continued to be very difficult. (Rubin, in Rubin and Weisberg, 2003, pp. 308–309)

Despite these attempts to improve the functioning of the co-CEO arrangement at Citigroup, voices were raised by the executive team

Table 1. *Roles and games in the triad: an illustration*

Role in a triad	Political game	Illustration
Mediator	A third mediating party in a professional duo of equally ranked executives provides impartial judgment and allows contentious issues to be discussed and settled. It can also provide the pair with complementary capabilities (Cadbury, 2002). If a mediator takes a position, however, it can destabilize over time, and even lead to termination of a professional duo.	Citigroup (1999–2000): Robert Rubin was appointed a member of the Office of the Chair to facilitate decision-making and collaboration between the co-CEOs and co-chairs, Sanford (Sandy) Weill and John Reed.
Tertius gaudens	A CEO who appoints two equally ranked executives as lieutenants, letting them know that they are heirs apparent and initiating competition between them. This competition can be beneficial for the firm, as the two will try to prove themselves capable for the top job. It can also be beneficial for the CEO, who can pick a new CEO that would allow the old CEO to remain an active chair. Yet, it may well be detrimental to the partnership of the two co-lieutenants.	Viacom (2004–): After the departure of Mel Karmazin, Sumner Redstone as chair and CEO appointed Tom Freston and Leslie Moonves co-presidents, co-COOs and his heirs apparent, creating competition between them.

Divide et impera	A chair seeking to maintain active involvement and additional executive power may try to weaken the CEO position by splitting it between two executives. The game can change, however, if these joint CEOs manage to gain sufficient autonomy in their respective domains, thus narrowing the initially expected power by the chair to representative functions.	La Caixa (1999–2003): Josep Vilarasau sought to maintain executive power as a former CEO of the entity in his new position as chair by splitting the CEO position into two positions and assigning two different areas of responsibility to Isidre Fainé, president and CEO of La Caixa, and to Antoni Brufau, president and CEO of the La Caixa Group (Perez, 2004).
Legitimator	A CEO with professional management capacity can be hired to complement the competence of technically minded co-founders. The third party may have power over the co-founders who control the stock because of his or her standing as a legitimator to external stakeholders and the support from the board.	Google (2001–): CEO Eric Schmidt gave credibility to the venture with his professional management expertise that complemented the technically minded co-founders Sergey Brin and Larry Page in transforming Google into "a self-sustaining affair." Schmidt has a veto vote and back-up from the board, but the co-founders together control large amounts of stock.
Integrator	A CEO from the family in a family-controlled business can maintain harmony at the top by integrating the roles and inputs of other second-generation family representatives in a consultative manner and by downplaying status and power in decision-making.	Loews (1999–): Jimmy Tisch (CEO) provided integration at the head of the second-generation family firm (founded by brothers Larry and Bob Tisch) by working in an Office of the President structure with Andrew Tisch (Jimmy's brother), who oversaw Lorillard and Bulova, and with Jonathan Tisch (their cousin) in charge of the hotel business.

that pointed in the direction of choosing a single "North Star" (Rubin and Weisberg, 2003, p. 310), an issue that was brought to the attention of the board by the two co-CEOs. The board decision was to keep Weill, which put an end not only to the trio but also to the Weill–Reed pair. Rubin kept his responsibilities as a chair of the management committee. As the press came to describe the situation:

In a tense, fractious Sunday meeting of Citi's board in February 2000, director Rubin was at one point asked whether he'd consider taking the CEO's job himself – he said no, adamantly – and then was asked whom he would support as a single CEO, Weill or Reed. On the grounds that the company's management was by that time almost entirely made up of executives whom Weill had brought with him from Travelers, and that the management team was very good, Rubin picked Weill – in effect, throwing him the victory. The total experience, says Rubin understatedly, "left me with the feeling that the odds of co-CEOs working together effectively in a corporate setting are actually very low". (Loomis, 2003, p. 120)

If one reads Rubin's account of the events in his recent book (Rubin and Weisberg, 2003), his involvement in choosing the CEO is clearly downplayed. If he had taken a side and chosen, he would have had to have moved away from a mediating role to become an "arbiter," which is a variety of the first strategy. The arbiter, as described by Simmel, takes a side and influences a decision, which is beyond the scope of intervention of the mediator.

Tertius gaudens strategy

An interesting situation in a trio manifested itself recently at Viacom, with the departure of Sumner Redstone's long-time lieutenant, Mel Karmazin. Sumner Redstone appointed not one, but two, executives – Tom Freston and Leslie Moonves – to replace him. Furthermore, the two newly appointed co-COOs and co-presidents were aware they were being chosen as the potential heirs apparent from whom Redstone's successor would be chosen. The press described the situation as an "uneasy game." Initial speculations of the likelihood of one or another candidate winning over the other, point to the fact that "Freston has an edge as the dance begins. He has a longer relationship with Redstone and global experience. And he seems almost universally liked, a rarity in the entertainment industry, where backbiting is common" (Gunther, 2004). In initiating such a competition between the two co-COOs with whom he forms the executive trio, it could be speculated Redstone is aiming to turn their competition to his own advantage – choosing the candidate that fits best with him and his plans to be an active chair once he departs from his executive duties:

> In the meantime Freston will have every incentive to fix Paramount's movie operations, and Moonves will turn up the heat to drive radio growth. Once he's picked a new CEO – and perhaps lost another talented operating head – Redstone plans to remain a "very active" chairman. In other words, Freston and Moonves had best remember who's still in charge. (Gunther, 2004)

Divide et impera strategy

In the classic accounts of Simmel on strategies in a triad, the *divide et impera* strategy is played by a third element that creates frictions between the other two in order to attain a dominant position or another gain. An example that approximates this strategy is provided by what occurred at the top of Spain's largest savings bank – La Caixa (Perez, 2004). In 1999, then-CEO Vilarasau was required to move up to the position of chair. According to interpretations in the media, he wished to maintain his executive powers in this new position but to limit the attention to detail. For this purpose he considered dividing the CEO's job into two and appointing Isidre Fainé and Antoni Brufau as equals (Perez, 2004). However, in accordance with Catalan legislation, they were unable to hold the co-CEO title. To resolve this issue, Antoni Brufau was appointed CEO of La Caixa Group. Isidre Fainé, in turn, was appointed CEO of La Caixa, the bank entity. The initial intent to maintain executive power in the hands of a strong chair by dividing the CEO job between two executives, however, seemed not to unfold as expected. The CEOs of La Caixa and CaixaHolding managed to gain autonomy in their respective domains, thus limiting the Chair's responsibilities to representative functions (Perez, 2004). This peculiar two-headed structure was inherited by Ricardo Fornesa who replaced Vilarasau, and finally ended – by mutual agreement – when in October 2004 Brufau was appointed head of Repsol, in which La Caixa was an important shareholder. No one was appointed to replace him, which left Fainé as a single-headed CEO.

Legitimator strategy

Google, the search engine business, is run by a triumvirate consisting of the CEO Eric Schmidt and the two emblematic co-founders and Stanford buddies, Larry Page and Sergey Brin. The appointment of Eric

Schmidt as a CEO and chair of this successful business was the result of continuous pressure by the board, in response to pressures from investors, to bring professional management talent into the company in order to help it grow in a sustainable, profitable way:

> Google was becoming a household word, serving up an estimated 60 million searches a day. But it still had no real way to make money. Revenues dribbled in, mostly from licensing the search service to other sites. For more than a year, the board pressed Brin and Page to get professional help, and in early 2001 they recruited Eric Schmidt. The fit looked perfect: He had deep technical roots (a PhD in computer science and a run as CTO of Sun) and leadership experience too – he had just spent four years as CEO of networking pioneer Novell.
>
> Most important was that even though Schmidt, now 48, was almost old enough to be Brin's or Page's father, he wasn't interested in pushing them aside, or in replacing the culture they had created . . .
>
> Schmidt focused instead on transforming Google into a self-sustaining affair. Shortly after he arrived, he and the top execs got much more aggressive about generating revenue. (Vogelstein, 2003, pp. 108, 110)

The following account sheds some light on the operation of the trio:

> Page, Brin, and Schmidt say they run the company as a triumvirate. Adds Schmidt: "Larry and Sergey have become my best friends. We have lunch every Saturday at [sub chain] Quiznos. Larry rollerblades in these itty-bitty shorts. He still looks like a college kid. And Sergey comes in from a diving lesson. These are special times."
>
> Schmidt understands that investors like to know that someone is in charge – and explains that, in the triumvirate, his is the last word. "We seldom disagree," he says. "If we do, we put it to a vote and whoever gets two votes wins. If it's a particularly egregious disagreement and it's important enough, I'll override them and they'll be mad at me for a while." What about the fact that Brin and Page control large amounts of stock? "They have the final trump, but they'd never use it – then they wouldn't get to see all the people they've gotten used to eating lunch with," he says, implying that he and the people he's hired would leave. (Vogelstein, 2003, p. 112)

By far the best explanation of how the triumvirate at the top of Google works is provided by the section "Executive Roles" in a letter entitled "'An Owner's Manual" for Google's Shareholders' from the two co-founders, Larry and Sergey, to their shareholders. Because it is revealing of their roles, relationships, and interactions, we have quoted it extensively:

We run Google as a triumvirate. Sergey and I have worked closely together for the last eight years, five at Google. Eric, our CEO, joined Google three years ago. The three of us run the company collaboratively with Sergey and me as Presidents. The structure is unconventional, but we have worked successfully in this way.

To facilitate timely decisions, Eric, Sergey and I meet daily to update each other on the business and to focus our collaborative thinking on the most important and immediate issues. Decisions are often made by one of us, with the others being briefed later. This works because we have tremendous trust and respect for each other and we generally think alike. Because of our intense long term working relationship, we can often predict differences of opinion among the three of us. We know that when we disagree, the correct decision is far from obvious. For important decisions, we discuss the issue with the larger team. Eric, Sergey and I run the company without any significant internal conflict, but with healthy debate. As different topics come up, we often delegate decision-making responsibility to one of us.

We hired Eric as a more experienced complement to Sergey and me to help us run the business. Eric was CTO of Sun Microsystems. He was also CEO of Novell and has a Ph.D. in computer science, a very unusual and important combination for Google given our scientific and technical culture. This partnership among the three of us has worked very well and we expect it to continue. The shared judgements and extra energy available from all three of us has significantly benefited Google.

Eric has the legal responsibilities of the CEO and focuses on management of our vice presidents and the sales organization. Sergey focuses on engineering and business deals. I focus on engineering and product management. All three of us devote considerable time to the overall management of the company and other fluctuating needs. We are extremely fortunate to have talented management that has grown the company to where it is today – they operate the company and deserve the credit.[8]

In an article in the *Wall Street Journal*, Eric Schmidt has provided the third party's view of their triumvirate's operation, which points in the same direction as suggested by the two co-founders:

We run as a triumvirate . . . The way it really works is that if it's really important, (one of us) drives the three of us to agree. It has been a great personal partnership. When I was recruited, the goal was to build a culture that could scale from this extraordinary thing that Larry and Sergey had built. And so it required a different management function, a leadership approach

---

[8] http://google-blog.dirson.com/an-owners-manual.html (accessed December 6, 2004).

. . . We, in fact, drive to consensus. Now, if two people agree, then the third person is yelled at for a while and vice-versa. And by the way, it rotates around. Think about partnerships – a three-person partnership is just more complicated than a two-person partnership. But the fact of the matter is that there are many things that I told Larry and Sergey I just want them to own . . . Most of the issues, we operate together. So we do the product reviews together; we do business reviews together; we do the deal reviews together. They typically lead the employee meetings, with me assisting. I lead the management meetings. (Mangalindan, 2004, p. B1)

The accounts of the three members of the triumvirate at Google – the two co-founders and the CEO – point to several important characteristics of their relationship *à trois*. First, the addition of the third element of the trio is justified; Eric Schmidt contributes an impeccable track record as a professional manager as well as a science background and experience with high-tech companies – something that could provide external legitimacy (with investors) and internal legitimacy (with employees, given the peculiar culture at Google). Second, the accounts emphasize role separation (each of the members of the trio has a position and a domain of responsibilities). At the same time they share information on a regular basis, in both formal and informal forms of exchange and jointly perform reviews and decision-making tasks. The comments of both the co-founders and the CEO emphasize the importance not only of the well-structured professional relationship but also of the integration of the work of the three through a strong bond: the tie of mutual trust and respect.

Integrator strategy

In 1999, the brothers Larry and Bob Tisch, founders of Loews, a holding company with principal subsidiaries in finance, tobacco, hotels, and watches, created the Office of the President to secure the harmonious functioning of the company under the second generation represented by their sons. James Tisch, Larry's heir, assumed the role of president and CEO. His brother, Andrew Tisch, took on the role of chair of the Executive Committee, overseeing businesses such as Bulova and Lorillard, while their cousin, Jonathan (Jon) Tisch, took responsibility for the company's hotel business and became chair and CEO of Loews Hotels. Although James (Jimmy) Tisch is the one who formally calls the shots, he acknowledged in a recent *Fortune* interview that he always does that in consultation with the other two members of the executive office:

Jimmy, 51, is his father's most direct heir at Loews. He is the CEO. Along with his brother Andrew, 54, and cousin Jonathan, 50, he is also part of the office of the president, a management arrangement established by his father and uncle in 1999. The Tisches assiduously downplay issues of power and status – it's part of the way they maintain family harmony – and sure enough, Jimmy insists he relies on his brother and cousin in running Loews. ("I can say things to my brother and cousin that I can't say to anyone else," he says.) But he is clearly the man in charge. (Brooker, 2004)

In a companywide meeting "to show the passing of the torch from the founders to the next generation of the Tisch family" (Hurley, 2000), a song was performed that provides some insight into the character of the Loews trio:

> Loews Corporation
> Sings of tradition
> And as a family
> Greets the millennium.
> Like the three tenors
> You have your mighty three
> Andrew, Jon and Jimmy
> Singing in harmony.

The founding Tisches' partnership worked well because the brothers were opposites who understood and respected each other's strengths: Larry's financial acumen and Bob's sales capabilities. An important example for the second-generation trio was this founding pair:

Larry and Bob had worked out their different roles at Loews without letting sibling rivalries or jealousies interfere. Neither brother tried to trump the other or gain power over the other. Though most people assumed Larry ran the show, both held the title of CEO. Their sons knew they were supposed to act the same way. When Jimmy was still in his 30s, it was clear that he was going to run Loews one day. It is the sort of thing that can tear a family apart. But the younger Tisches accepted their roles. Today Andrew oversees Lorillard and Bulova, and Jonathan is in charge of the hotels. And none of the three ever makes a major business decision without consulting the other two. (Brooker, 2004)

Therefore, we can acknowledge the importance of the corporate culture and the personal example of well-functioning professional duos and trios for the continuity of small-numbers power structures in an organization. In the case of Loews, the founding pair has managed to transmit the values of role-sharing and integration to the generation that will succeed them. In a similar way, for several decades the pairs of co-CEOs at the helm at Goldman Sachs served as an example of power-sharing to the new breed of department co-heads and co-COOs, hence paving the way for perpetuating the small-numbers structures.

The termination of executive role constellations

Professional trios and larger constellations discontinue their power-sharing arrangements for a variety of reasons. The dissolution could be the outcome of political games and infighting, in which a leading coalition forms – either within the trio or quartet or with the support of outside individuals – to oust one of the members. An example is the ousting of Corzine as a co-CEO of Goldman Sachs by the coalition of Thornton, Thain, and Paulson; Paulson was a co-CEO with Corzine at the time (Spiro, Silverman, and Reed, 1999). It can be part of a larger process of structural realignment and generational change, as in the case of the departures of Matti Alahuhta and Sari Baldauf, who since 1992 had been members of the "gang of four" around Nokia's CEO Jorma Ollila (George, 2004). After more than a decade of continuity at the top, during which the tightly knit team has converted Nokia into a leading technology group, Ollila argues that "in a period of change for the industry, Nokia must adapt its structure and management team" (George, 2004, p. 8). The changes in the market pose new require-ments for management, as Nokia's chief executive reveals: "It's a very different era in terms of management requirements: in terms of skills, know-how, how you build your customer relationship" (George, 2004, p. 8).

Concluding remarks

In this chapter we introduced another small-numbers option to solo executives and professional duos in the design of the corporate top – the structures of threesomes or larger executive constellations. We pro-vided historical and recent examples of trios or larger groups governing countries and businesses in order to demonstrate both their ubiquity and their complex nature and political agenda. With the help of sociol-ogy, mainly the work of Simmel (1950), we highlighted the behavioral consequences at the top, which occur when the structure of the apex is a triad rather than a dyad. Further distinction was made among types of triads, depending on the distribution of power and hence the nature of possible coalitions. In examining the dynamics of structures of three-somes, we focused on the strategies that the third member in a trio can employ. Using recent business cases, we illustrated Simmel's (1950) classic categories of mediator, *tertius gaudens*, and *divide et impera*, and suggested two additional strategies – that of the legitimator and the integrator – both of which are aimed at addressing phenomena such as the professionalization of management in high-technology start-ups or the balancing efforts after generational change in family businesses.

We have concluded from our exploration of small numbers of three-somes and foursomes at the top of the companies "that there is still enough dissatisfaction with traditional structures to encourage inno-vative approaches to the task of the company direction" (Cadbury, 2002, p. 127). These approaches may pave the way to binding, long-lasting partnerships of the individuals who have adopted them, leading to the unity of their careers, a phenomenon we discuss at length in Chapter 6.

6 | *United careers of small numbers at the top*

[I]f you are a passionate leader, intuitive and charismatic, look for a trustworthy and confident manager to counterbalance you. If you are a lover of numbers, security and rigor, try to share your career with a loony visionary.

Cubeiro, 1998

For six years, we shared a job at Fleet Bank: vice president, global markets foreign exchange. One desk, one chair, one computer, one telephone, and one voice-mail account. We had – still have – one résumé. To our clients and colleagues, we were effectively one person with the strengths and ideas of two . . . when we look for a new job, we will look together. If one of us wants to leave our next position, the other will leave as well . . . For the foreseeable future, we are a package.

Cunningham and Murray, 2005, p. 125

THE AUGUST 2004 issue of *Vanity Fair* carried an article entitled "So Very Valentino," which claimed to provide a "never-before look at the devoted, passionate 'family' behind one of the world's richest fashion empires" (Tyrnauer, 2004, p. 94). It was the story of the fashion designer Valentino Garavani and "his business partner, onetime boyfriend, alter ego, and closest companion" (Tyrnauer, 2004, p. 96), Giancarlo Giammetti. Countess Consuelo Crespi, the Rome-based fashion editor of American *Vogue*, summarized their strengths succinctly as "the brains of Giancarlo mixed with the talent and determination of Valentino" (Tyrnauer, 2004, p. 96). Like the professional duos we examined in Chapter 4, Valentino and Giancarlo constitute yet another odd couple with complementary characters, talents, focus, and temperament (according to their own descriptions in the *Vanity Fair* article, one is "supercalm" and the other is more "agitated"). They are "the perfect Mr. Inside/Mr. Outside team" (Tyrnauer, 2004, p. 102), the article suggests. The designer and his committed business partner talk about the special intuition they have developed: "Giancarlo and I understand each other completely without speaking," says Valentino (Tyrnauer, 2004, p. 102).

Giancarlo is the enabler and protector of Valentino's talent, which allows Valentino to make the designs of his liking. This pairing reminds us of our first case – the one that started us on our journey, studying small-numbers structures and careers, and has kept us inspired and motivated while writing this book. In preparing that case, we observed how Spanish film director Pedro Almodóvar has been protected and enabled by his brother and producer, Agustín Almodóvar, to make the movies of his liking. Relationships like those of Garavani and Giammetti and the Almodóvar brothers are far more dyed-in-the-wool and enduring than are those we observed for professional duos, trios, and quartets, in which the sharing of positions was usually time-bound. The commitment, the mutual, intuitive understanding, and the affection are so deep in the two cases in point that the individuals have gone beyond a temporary professional collaboration and have connected their careers. In such instances of united careers, there is a symbiosis in the professional and emotional domains, which is conducive to meaningful work trajectories and personal lives for each of the individuals involved and to success for their joint enterprise. In this chapter we examine the characteristics and dynamics of such long-term binding relationships and governance structures and explore the career implications for the individuals involved.

Up to this point in the book we have examined the professional collaborations of small numbers at the top of corporations, focusing on the professional exchange of these duos, trios, or foursomes over time. In this chapter we go a step further – from the professional duos we introduced in Chapter 4 and the trios and quartets we discussed in Chapter 5 to an increasingly committed partnership of united careers of professionals at the top.

United careers, as demonstrated later in this chapter, represent a true collaboration. Identifying united careers is not a straightforward process, as the strength of the relationship and the joint career decisions and moves cannot be easily deduced from job titles. Perhaps this is one of the reasons why such plural careers, although more widespread than generally believed, have been left unattended for so long by career theorists.

To begin, we provide some examples of united careers in the domains in which they are most frequently found: in the creative sectors, science, and business start-ups. Then we define the united career in comparison and contrast with other career phenomena and strategies, such as job-sharing, dual careers, and mentor–protégé relationships. We proceed by examining four cases of united careers that have different origins and represent diverse types of professional duos and a variety of businesses. We focus on the career coupling and the mechanisms used by the individuals to connect and coordinate their joint trajectories. Finally, we explore the implications of such career coupling for corporate power structures and governance, for the individuals involved, and for the organizations in which their united careers may be manifested.

Propensity to unite careers

Career scholars broadly define careers as "the evolving sequence of a person's work experiences over time" (Arthur, Hall, and Lawrence, 1989, pp. 8–9). Through their career behaviors, individuals are able to create companies and shape organizational structures and actions (Weick, 1996; Alvarez, 2000; Inkson and Arthur, 2001). Careers, however, are not necessarily individual phenomena. A growing number of people in committed relationships choose not to have independent jobs but to join efforts in the creation of a new venture, hence wiping out the boundary between personal and work life (Marshack, 1998, pp. ix–xi). These joint entrepreneurial efforts could take the form of a solo entrepreneur with a supportive spouse – copreneurs who, in addition to love, share the ownership and management of their family firm (Marshack, 1998, p. 19). Furthermore, research on American entrepreneurs reveals that they tend to undertake new ventures in teams rather than individually, choosing their collaborators primarily from among their kith and kin (Ruef, Aldrich and Carter, 2003).

Career studies on intra-role transitions have focused on the increasing complexity of managerial jobs in response to a greater number of boundaryless organizational structures (Sullivan, 1999, p. 470). Managers are expected to have a wider range of competencies and abilities and to synthesize insights from different mind-sets (Gosling and Mintzberg, 2003). The increasing complexity of today's organizations is influencing not only the work of managers but also the career patterns they follow, pushing them toward an array of innovative, boundaryless arrangements (Arthur, 1994; DeFillippi and Arthur, 1994).

One manifestation of this increasing plurality, not yet embraced by career theory, is the case of two or more individuals choosing to bind their professional trajectories together over time. We denote this career binding as united careers, distinguishing it from the professional duos, trios, and foursomes that we examined in Chapters 4 and 5. We argue that the united careers exhibit a tighter coupling of the relationship because, in addition to task collaboration, the individuals consider each other's trajectory when making career decisions and undertake joint career moves. The complementary Stan Laurel and Oliver Hardy style of duo in comic cinema has been frequently replicated in the business world in a range of contexts from banking, manufacturing, and entertainment to retail and electronics. Yet the coupling of careers prevails in three areas: creative sectors, science, and start-ups – especially in those cases where creation and invention is imperative to the business. In order to provide clues about the spread of the united career phenomenon, we briefly mention some of the most noteworthy examples in these three areas.

Creative sectors. Durable collaborations are frequently found in creative enterprises such as entertainment, advertising, and fashion, where creative people team up with other like-minded professionals in duos or larger collaborative circles in order to sustain stylistic innovations and push them forward (Greenfeld, 1989; Farrell, 2001). Or they may be found between creative and business professionals, bridging the domains of art and commerce (Becker, 1982; Alvarez and Svejenova, 2002a, 2002b). Committed creative duos or circles of three, four, or more artists have flourished in a number of settings:

- *painting*: the Impressionists (White and White, 1965; Farrell, 2001)
- *architecture*: the Scottish brothers Robert and James Adam, creators of the Adam style, who designed and built some of the most famous

buildings in England and Scotland during the last half of the eigh-
teenth century[1]

- *film*: the Coen brothers (De Felipe, 1999)
- *literature*: the writers Joseph Conrad and Madox Ford, who strongly
  influenced each other's writing (Farrell, 2001)
- *music*: the British string quartets with long-term collaboration
  (Murnighan and Conlon, 1991) or the long-lasting jazz trios, such
  as that of the pianist Keith Jarett with bassist Gary Peacock and
  drummer Jack DeJohnette (Fordham, 2002)
- *advertising*: creatives who recurrently team up in the development of
  campaigns and move together between agencies (Vagnoni, 1997).

In addition to partnerships of creatives, stable collaborations are also
formed between creative and business professionals. Such has been the
case of Quebec's show business talent Guy Latraverse and his management partner Rénald Paré at Sogestalt Télévision (Leblanc and
Lapierre, 2001). Among film directors there is a tendency to couple their careers with producers who are close to them and provide
them with autonomy and resources (Alvarez, Mazza, Strandgaard, and
Svejenova, 2005). In fashion, one of the long-lasting career duos is
that of Yves Saint Laurent and Pierre Bergé (Tyrnauer, 2004). Also,
the luxury brands of the group LVMH (Louis Vuitton Moët Hennessy)
have been co-managed by a designer in charge of the aesthetic conception and an entrepreneur responsible for commercialization (Sibillin,
2001). Music recording is also propitious for enduring art–business
career couplings, such as that of Gloria and Emilio Estefan, the most
powerful couple of Latin musicians in the United States, who have
sustained an affective and professional relationship over three decades
(Townsend, 2000).

Science. Science is another setting for the durable coupling of talent (Zuckerman, 1967) and the manifestation of the phenomenon of
united careers. Examples of Nobel Prize winners with "seamless scientific and domestic collaboration" include Pierre and Marie Curie, and
Irène Joliot-Curie and Frédéric Joliot. The advances of Sigmund Freud's
psychoanalytic theory could be traced back to his friendship and long-
term intellectual exchanges with Wilhelm Fleiss (Farrell, 2001). Scholarly accomplishments of such dyads are found to be greater and more

---

[1] "Adam, Robert," *Encyclopaedia Britannica* http://www.britannica.com/eb/article
?tocId = 121. (accessed November 15, 2004).

lasting than they might have been had they worked individually (Pycior, Slack, and Abir-Am, 1996).

Business start-ups. Entrepreneurs tend to undertake new ventures in duos or small teams rather than individually (Ruef, Aldrich, and Carter, 2003). United careers are frequently observed among entrepreneurs, especially in familial entrepreneurship and copreneurship situations (Marshack, 1998; de Bruin and Lewis, 2004). Harvey and Robert Weinstein co-founded and co-ran Miramax Films, one of the most inventive and successful film companies in the United States. William Harley and the brothers Arthur, Walter, and William Davidson established and built the Harley-Davidson Motor Company together. The high-tech industry also provides a series of relevant examples, like the co-founders of the Hewlett-Packard Company, Stanford buddies William R. Hewlett and David Packard (Kaplan, 2000, p. 34) and the introverted Bill Gates and the socially adept Steve Ballmer, who met at Harvard in the early 1970s and later started Microsoft (Heenan and Bennis, 1999). The number of examples that can be found at the start-up stage of an enterprise and sustained throughout years of business growth and expansion is extensive.

Contrary to traditional depictions of careers as individual and independent undertakings, our examples hint at long-term collaborations in which the careers of two or more professionals unfold together: united careers.

Defining united careers

Individuals who have bound their trajectories in united career patterns possess stronger and more durable ties than do professional duos and larger constellations because joint career decisions and moves are added to their task collaboration. Business and political landscapes show many examples of executives who – beyond working together for a particular assignment or for a specific phase of a project – interlock their careers for a long period. They become a unit both at work and in professional development. Their joint path is an entity in itself, one that differs from either individual's separate career, raising motivations and outcomes that cannot be pursued independently. Yet in spite of the inherent academic appeal of these relationships, the existing literature is either scant or peripheral to our interests in providing an understanding of the requisites of joint career advancement. Characteristics such as openness and disclosure; detailed knowledge of each other, and the subsequent predictability of reactions; uniqueness of the interaction; as well as the capacity of the involved individuals to handle conflict are indicative of professional duos with strong relational foundations (Gabarro, 1987).

It is precisely the union and unison of career moves that differentiates united careers from professional duos. In the words of two executives who have joined their careers: "when we look for a new job, we will look together. If one of us wants to leave our next position, the other will leave as well" (Cunningham and Murray, 2005, p. 125). United careers differ from dual careers, in which spouses or partners pursue separate career paths (Rapoport and Rapoport, 1965a, 1965b, 1969; Hall and Hall, 1978, 1979; Blossfeld and Drobnic, 2001). They are distinguishable from mentor–protégé couples, for which the career interventions are primarily unidirectional, usually from the mentor to the protégé (Farrell, 2001). Even in cases of informal mentorship characterized by closeness and intimacy (Kram, 1985; Ragins, Cotton, and Miller, 2000), there is no shared decision-making on career issues or joint career moves, which is essential in our definition of united careers. Finally, united careers do not mean that an individual is expected to sacrifice her or his trajectory to support unconditionally the career of the other. Rather, they constitute symbiotic mutualism in career decisions, moves, and outcomes (Alvarez and Svejenova, 2002a), whereby the individuals who have united their careers experience more satisfying careers than the ones they could have developed individually. On account of relational cohesion (Lawler and Yoon, 1996), that special attachment to the relationship which develops over time with successive satisfactory exchanges, the members place particular value on staying professionally connected and thus enjoying a more meaningful and satisfactory career. As two executives with united careers explain: "The fact is, we've found a working relationship that not only is rewarding and freeing for us but, we are convinced, offers our employers and customers more quality and commitment" (Cunningham and Murray, 2005, p. 125).

We propose the following definition of united careers, which serves to differentiate them from the professional or personal career arrangements we discussed previously (e.g. dual careers and mentor–protégé dyads):

United careers are durable, coordinated task collaborations in the working lives of two or more professionals in which the career of one individual evolves with that of (an)other individual(s) through a series of vertical, lateral, or cross-organizational moves that have been jointly decided and undertaken.

It is a distinctive feature of united careers that for the duration of the coupling the career motives, moves, decisions, and achievements of one individual cannot occur or be understood separately from those of other individual(s). Furthermore, we argue that by bringing together and coordinating by the means of a committed relationship the respective career competencies of two members – the know-why, know-how, and know-who competencies (DeFillippi and Arthur, 1994) – united careers could better address the requirements that professionals face as a consequence of organizational complexity.

Illustrating united careers

In Chapter 4, we discussed the potential trajectories along which a dyad could evolve and suggested that it could become a professional duo, which could continue operating, be terminated, or – alternatively – be extended in scope to become united careers. These trajectories may be initiated from a dyad that has an affective or working genesis and whose members either share a role or maintain separate roles. In order to shed light on some of the defining characteristics of united careers, we examine four cases as illustrations. Before proceeding, however, we introduce two dimensions of distinction in the development of united careers. The first dimension is genesis: the career unity could arise from a working relationship or from an affective relationship – from the presence of a family tie or a bond of friendship, for example. The siblings Almódovar (El Deseo) and Valls (Banco Popular) provide us with two examples of affective genesis. We have chosen Whitehead and Weinberg (Goldman Sachs) and Ibuka and Morita (Sony Corporation) as examples of working genesis. The second dimension is that of role differentiation. Two of the pairs with united careers have shared a position (the Valls brothers and Whitehead and Weinberg). The other two partnerships have maintained distinctive roles and positions (the Almodóvar brothers and Ibuka and Morita).

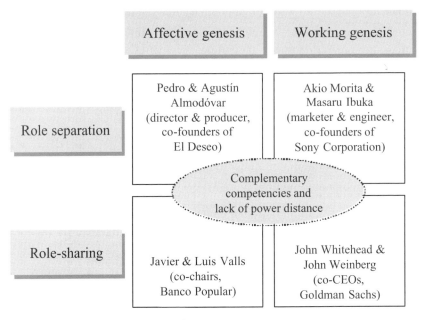

Figure 7. Illustrating the united career.

Thus, our first career pairing represents a strong case of coupling: the careers of the Spanish film director Pedro Almodóvar and his brother-producer Agustín. Their professional relationship has an affective genesis and role separation, with distinctive responsibilities (director and producer, respectively). The second career duet – that of the brothers Javier and Luis Valls, who, until October 2004 shared the chair of the Spanish bank Banco Popular – illustrates another affective genesis, with position-sharing, that lasted for fifteen years. The third example of united careers exemplifies a working genesis with position-sharing. Unlike the former two cases in which the tandem's genesis was a sibling link, this example had its origins in office proximity at Goldman Sachs, and the two Harvard graduates – John Weinberg and John Whitehead – had later become co-chief executives of the company. The fourth case is that of Sony Corporation's co-founders – marketer Akio Morita and engineer Masaru Ibuka, who met as members of a task force during World War II.

We analyzed the cases of united careers (see Figure 7 for a summary) focusing on the following issues: genesis and complementarities, professional collaboration, and the transition into an enduring united career. Additional themes of relevance to understanding the trajectories of each pair with united careers were also considered.

Pedro and Agustín Almodóvar at El Deseo

As we have mentioned repeatedly, the symbiotic careers of the siblings Pedro and Agustín Almodóvar started us on further explorations of two phenomena: small numbers at the top and united careers. In its different forms (formally since 1985 when they co-founded El Deseo), their relationship in cinema-related fields has lasted over three decades. The Almodóvar brothers represent a dyad of affective genesis and a professional duo with role separation – that of film director and film producer. In comparison, had we explored the Coen brothers as a film-making professional duo with united careers, they would have represented role-sharing (not role separation), because both Joel and Ethan are involved in script-writing, directing, and producing.

The Almodóvar brothers' professional partnership developed on the basis of their strong sibling relationship, firmly embedded in the family values prevailing during the 1950s in their birthplace, Spain. In the words of Agustín, "It is an affective relationship, based on mysterious, irrational things, related to fraternity." Their shared childhood and the early adulthood away from home, in Madrid, during which Pedro introduced his younger brother, Agustín, to his social circles and professional interests, strengthened their sibling relationship to one of extremely strong affection and trust. Pedro Almodóvar emphasizes the long and intimate relationship with his brother, and the understanding that exists between the two of them:

Agustín has always been my first spectator. When an idea occurs to me, the first thing I do before I develop it is to tell him about it. He is always there . . . the person who understands me best and who has always comprehended in a very profound way everything I have done. (Pedro Almodóvar, quoted in Strauss, 2001, p. 65)

In the press book of one of his films, writing in the third person about the relationship between Agustín and himself, Pedro Almodóvar acknowledges the longevity and exclusivity of their bond: 'They love, respect, understand and support each other.'' The brothers' accounts reveal an extremely strong, mutually affective relationship, which involves commitment beyond what is customary for integrated working relationships or kin dyads.

Along with the strong affection and trust, their complementarity and role separation leads to a well-balanced collaboration, far beyond what might be expected from the role descriptions (or in this case, the film credits). In the accounts of Pedro Almodóvar, again written in the third person in a film's press-book:

Agustín is not only the right hand of Pedro . . . The two of them are complementary, even physically they fit as two pieces of a puzzle called El Deseo, S. A., or the Almodóvars . . . The two of them [are] perfectly balanced, as if they belonged to the same body, to a single criterion, exercised with the same sensibility. His [Agustín's] collaboration goes beyond what the film credits reveal. Almodóvar Agustín is the encyclopedia which continuously nurtures Pedro so he can tie down his stories and characters.

This single criterion, the same sensibility and exchange of ideas, reflects what Farrell called "instrumental intimacy" in creative work – the merging of cognitive processes in a pair and the open exchange of half-finished work in progress (Farrell, 2001, pp. 150–151). Farrell defined it as follows: "Instrumental intimacy occurs when each begins to use the mind of the other as if it were an extension of his own . . . The boundaries between the self and other diminish until the members are able to think out loud together as if they are one person" (p. 157).

If we focus on the two brothers as a professional duo, their relationship is characterized by role separation. Broadly speaking, Pedro is in charge of the vision of the movies, the script-writing and the film-directing; his brother is in charge of film production and the management of their production company. Although the projects are clearly driven by Pedro's artistic vision and expressive needs, the professional relationship between the two brothers is not hierarchical, as both of them have made clear on several occasions. Pedro needs Agustín's support to gain greater control over his artwork and to avoid the inevitable tension between art and business that manifests itself in sterile opposition, mismatched intentions, or formal disagreements with producers (De Felipe, 1999). Asked about how Agustín reacts to his scripts, Pedro Almodóvar explains, "Agustín has so much respect for me that, for fear that he might distract me, he will never give me his opinion as a producer during the gestation phase of the script" (Strauss, 2001, p. 65).

As Agustín acknowledges, the result of this tight collaboration "beyond what the film credits reveal" allows Pedro's creativity to flourish:

In our work with Pedro in El Deseo, nothing is wasted. All the creative energy is directed to the movie. We are not a traditional production company but rather a team around an artist . . . With Pedro we have a solid personal project and our work consists of making this cinematic dream a reality, providing him the necessary equilibrium. (Agustín Almodóvar, quoted in Strauss, 2001, p. 67)

Since the mid-1980s, the two brothers have followed a united career trajectory as the director and producer of all Pedro Almodóvar's films. Pedro has had the opportunity to work with other producers, but has preferred to rely on the partnership with his brother-producer. Just as Agustín's professional trajectory as a film producer is closely linked to the career of his brother-director, Pedro's career cannot be understood without referring to his brother Agustín's collaboration and support.

Agustín traces his relationship with Pedro as a film director back to 1972 when he started following him in the making and showing of his short movies. In the early 1980s he was an actor and assistant in Pedro's feature films. At that time he had graduated in chemistry and was working as a chemistry, physics, and mathematics teacher at a high school, a career he finally abandoned in 1985. The brothers then established their own production company, El Deseo, and formally joined their trajectories as film director and producer.

Pedro Almodóvar wanted to start his production company with, as El Deseo's press director Paz Sufrategui told us, "somebody who was going to understand him intimately, from the essence, from the first idea of a film" (Alvarez and Svejenova, 2002a, p. 195). Agustín's decision to support Pedro was grounded in strong affective ties and a firm belief in his brother's talent: "I took a vital decision – to abandon my career . . . for love of Pedro . . . [and] to see the happiness and coherence of the career of a gifted person." An indispensable condition for his complete dedication, he added, was his relationship with Pedro, based on loyalty, affection, and fraternity – and ultimately – on his "love of Pedro." These quotations emphasize both the affect- and cognition-based trust in their career unity.

As Agustín has acknowledged, apart from the personal satisfaction of seeing the advancement of his gifted and loved sibling, becoming involved in film production and in the running of a production company offered a much more exciting and rewarding occupation than that of a chemistry teacher. As Pedro recognizes, working with Agustín has provided him with the structure and organization that has given him all the freedom needed for his movies and an eclectic support for the nourishment of his ideas. Hence, the joint trajectory of an artist and his or her trustee, which may be further embedded in their independent production company, is a different path from that followed by an artist alone. The artist, who is often unable or reluctant to assume business responsibilities for the production of his or her art, receives support in these activities from a trusted partner. The partner enjoys an interesting occupation and obtains personal satisfaction from helping a beloved and gifted person.

Luis and Javier Valls Taberner at Banco Popular

The careers of the brothers Luis and Javier Valls Taberner were united for over three decades at the apex of, historically speaking, the most profitable independent Spanish bank, Banco Popular. Their long *durée* integrated career trajectories were first joined as chair and deputy chair (1972–1989) and then as co-chairs (1989–2004). The coupled careers ended in October 2004 with the resignation of Luis Valls, whose decision to leave the shared position was grounded in the desire to secure a smooth succession at the top of the banking entity. But in the intervening years, Luis and Javier Valls succeeded in becoming a model of successful professional and career pairing at the top of a Spanish bank, in an industry characterized by strong consolidation through mergers, acquisitions, and the proliferation of short-lived, failing professional duos at the apex of the consolidated banks. The Valls brothers were a professional duo grounded in affection and trust. They have said that they would not have minded sharing the apex with one or two more co-chairs if they could have been like brothers to them – referring to the importance of the affection and mutual understanding that the sibling relationship provides (Castro, 1991). In fact, their late brother Pedro Valls Taberner had also been with Banco Popular for decades, developing the human resources aspects of the bank and acting as a member of the bank's board of directors. In this sense, Pedro, Luis, and Javier Valls could be considered as a trio with united careers. In the words of Luis Valls (1989):

For 25 years two levels have operated in the bank: the professional or executive level, and the political level. At the political level, among others, there
have been three of us, three brothers, one in the front office, another in the
back office, and the third out on the street. It is – it has been – an effective
division of roles, of use of time and capabilities. The back office, the kitchen,
has always attracted me. But basically at bottom, we have all worked with
the mentality of a chairman. At no time – in this long journey of 25 years –
have we had problems getting on with one another, problems of hierarchy
or mutual understanding. If there is a difference of opinions, one of us gives
way.

This quotation aptly summarizes some of the pillars of successful
united careers. First, united careers work well when the individuals
are on the same journey, ready to weather storms together and iron
out disagreements. Second, complementary capabilities and division
of labor enhance the sustainability of the career unity, and a common
mind-set ("the mentality of a chairman") helps to provide a common
vision for the organization. Last but not least is the nature of the relationship, marked by mutual understanding, a willingness to give way,
and the absence of power differentials. On the importance of the lack
of a hierarchy, Luis Valls (1989) wrote the following highly revealing
account:

It is well known that when two people – two heads – embark together upon
a long trip, there always comes a time when they fight, or return having
fought . . . But two conditions have to be present for them: the trip has to be
long enough and there must not be any hierarchy between the two because
of similarities of age, social condition or professional rank. If there is a clear
hierarchy between them, it is obvious that there are not two heads. Sharing
things – ideas, hobbies, tastes, exhaustion – helps to prevent fighting. There
is no doubt that having the same blood, sensibility, criteria, and vision of
the game greatly reduces the scope for disagreement. The likelihood of conflict is slight when there is no need to discuss the decision because there is
"instinctive" consensus about the goals or how to achieve them. The guarantee that nothing will break the co-existence lies not only in the absence of
disagreement between the two people but also in the lack of distance between
them.

One of us had the privilege of interviewing Luis and Javier Valls on
December 19, 2001, in their office in the bank's building at Calle José
Ortega y Gasset, 29 in Madrid. It provided an opportunity to obtain
a personal impression of their chemistry and their synchronization,

as well as their style differences. During the interview they would laugh together at the many coincidences in their preferences and tastes. Returning from a trip abroad, they would find that they had bought the same sweater. They revealed that they intuitively coincide and, when disagreements arose, one of them easily yielded to the other.

Luis and Javier Valls are described in a range of press articles as being different, both in character and way of life, yet a complementary and well-balanced pair, an example of yin and yang (Castro, 1991). Luis Valls has been portrayed as introverted, intellectual, thoughtful, a keen reader and writer. In the interview he would come up with insightful remarks or stories about other siblings with close collaboration (e.g. John and Robert Kennedy). The Spanish press labeled him the "Florentine Prince of Spanish banking," precisely because of his political acumen, his capacity for strategizing, and his irony. Javier has been defined as extroverted, vivid, and communicative, a person who talks and jokes about practical issues and is capable of doing so in many different languages.

The Valls brothers also emphasize the strong trust that exists between them. In the interview they remarked, not without irony, that the only place they went together was to the Bank of Spain. The rest of the professional duos, sharing the top position as a result of mergers and acquisitions in the Spanish banking system, tended to go everywhere together to keep an eye on what the other said and did. A clear manifestation of this trust and affection dates back to 1972, when Luis Valls had to convince the board of directors to appoint his brother Javier as the bank's deputy chair. In doing so, he talked about the "value of affection," about how trust is not taken for granted but avowed on a daily basis, and that "Javier and I have a life-long relationship and many years together here, in the bank" (Goñi, 1992). This reference to the value of trust and affection confirms what we identified in Chapter 4, in our discussion of professional duos, as useful integration mechanisms associated with governance roles at the top.

The two siblings followed separate career paths before joining Banco Popular (e.g. Luis Valls used to work as a university professor). They joined with the help of their cousin Félix Millet Marystani, the chair of the bank at the time. It was he who in 1959 offered the position of deputy chair to Luis Valls and in 1972 the position of chair. In 1972 Javier Valls was appointed deputy chair, thus initiating the first formal interlocking of his career with that of Luis Valls. About three months before the formal announcement, the financial sections of the popular press in Spain were already informing the public at large that "Banco Popular will have two presidents before 1992" (Cifuentes, 1989). It actually happened sooner than expected, and on April 25, 1989 Javier Valls was appointed co-chair at a regular meeting of Banco Popular's board of directors.

The Valls brothers explained in the interview that role-sharing at the top had not been their invention; rather, they were copying a structure that had already been established by banks of the stature of Spain's Banco Bilbao Vizcaya at the time it merged with Banesto, or Deutsche Bank. They revealed they had had the idea of role-sharing before 1989 but, as there had been no precedent at that time, they had preferred to wait until other banks consolidated this form of governance as a means of reconciling power struggles after merger and acquisition activities. This comment hints at the need for the legitimization of role-sharing as a governance form before adopters decide to employ it in the design of their vertical power structures. When Spanish legislation made it possible and there were other cases available as precedents, the brothers announced that they would be sharing the position of chair. Despite the availability of precedents, the role-sharing formula was not considered clear enough in terms of accountability by the Trade Register in Spain, and the Valls brothers had to take turns in the position, specifying at every moment which one of them was the *primus inter pares*. Commenting on the way the brothers work together, Castro (1991) revealed:

For days at a stretch the Valls brothers don't even see each other. Each goes about his business without getting in the other's way. There is no need for that; the getting along well is written in the blood. There is an intuitive agreement between them, but each organizes his life and his work with flexibility.

This quotation points to the importance of this intuitive understanding, which serves as an integrator of the relationship. Furthermore, it supports Glaser's (1963) and Gronn's (1999) observations that for professional duos to jell, each partner needs sufficient space and autonomy to exercise personal responsibilities. The Valls brothers acknowledge that "when you both think the same way and take the same decisions even without consulting one another, then there are no frictions." However, other Spanish banks that have adopted the professional duo solution to facilitate post-merger integration have not had such a positive experience. At Banco Santander Central Hispano (BSCH), José María Amusátegui left before his shared mandate with Emilio Botín had come to its planned conclusion, and after what was considered by the press to be a clash of egos. Similarly, Emilio Ybarra withdrew from role-sharing at the helm of Banco Bilbao Vizcaya Argentaria (BBVA) with Francisco González earlier than had been originally agreed. The main difference between the Valls brothers and those failed professional duos in Spanish banking is the high level of trust that comes with the sibling bond and the many years of joint operation in Banco Popular without infighting. In mergers and acquisitions, complementarity and lack of distance are unlikely because both heads have a background in running integral operations.

In October 2004, the 78-year-old Luis Valls resigned as co-chair. His place was taken by the 42-year-old Ángel Ron, until then the CEO of Banco Popular, who is now co-chair with the 74-year-old Javier Valls. Luis Valls' comments in the Spanish press revealed that his withdrawal as a co-chair and a board member were related to the efforts being made to achieve coherence in the succession at the top of Banco Popular. The role-sharing structure was maintained because the Valls brothers had previously acknowledged that it provided an opportunity for smooth transitions at the political layer of the company. The two brothers attribute the success of their united careers to their complementarity; the lack of power distance or ambition to have the other's position (when they served as chair and deputy chair, for example); and their deep trust and readiness to yield to one another when differences of opinion arose.

John Weinberg and John Whitehead at Goldman Sachs

John Weinberg and John Whitehead initiated their relationship in the early 1950s, after having joined the investment bank Goldman Sachs within three years of one another. Their collaboration developed initially because of the physical proximity of their offices and the lengthy discussions, during lunch breaks, of their visions for the future of Goldman Sachs:

From his first day at the firm John Weinberg was seated at a desk facing Whitehead, only inches apart in the old squash court. For lunch the pair walked over to Scottie's Sandwich Shop, which served the thickest corned beef sandwiches . . . Over and over Weinberg and Whitehead would reorganize the firm in their heads, making plans for how it would be different if they ever got their shot. (Endlich, 2002, pp. 109–110)

By the time the so-called "two Johns" became joint chief executives in 1976, they had worked together for about a quarter of a century. Their formal (self-) appointment as co-CEOs of Goldman Sachs was a fruit of their joint decision-making, a feature of what we defined as united careers:

While Levy [Goldman Sachs' CEO at that time] lay unconscious, Whitehead and Weinberg met alone without consulting their partners and summarily decided to anoint themselves the firm's leaders. The pair presented the plan to the management committee, which rubber-stamped the decision and paved the way for another smooth transition of power. (Endlich, 2002, p. 110)

The duo was welcomed with skepticism by the top consulting companies:

Upon hearing the news of their ascendancy, Marvin Bower, then head of the highly respected consulting firm McKinsey & Co., called immediately to offer the pair his congratulations and issue a warning. While both were men of great talent and either could lead the firm capably, the structure they had put in place, he informed them, simply would not work. (Endlich, 2002, p. 111)

Contrary to all the skepticism manifested by the business community about the success of their role-sharing arrangement, the professional duo proved everybody wrong through the arrangement's longevity and effectiveness in expanding the company. The duo played the co-chief executive roles by taking joint responsibility for the entire firm. Still, each had the opportunity to exercise his core capabilities and work in his preferred domains of action. Whitehead was in charge of the long-term direction and budgets and Weinberg focused on clients and new business development. Weinberg was the soul of the company and the continuation of its legacy, being the son of Sidney Weinberg, the man at the top of the company at the time of the founding families, the Goldmans and the Sachs. Whitehead had more business experience, with a higher profile outside the firm. He was the strategist of the firm, its visionary. So not only did Weinberg and Whitehead have some day-to-day complementarity in their expertise and style, they also shared the responsibilities and accountability for the performance of the firm.

Weinberg and Whitehead were more than a professional duo at the top, as "their long careers had moved in lockstep" (Endlich, 2002, p. 110). In their career unity, they managed to create – out of a small family business – a professional organization that competed in many of the world's major business centers. In 1984 Whitehead retired from business to become part of President Reagan's administration in the USA, thereby uncoupling his career from Weinberg's to pursue an individual career trajectory. However, it is worth noting that this professional duo with united careers dissolved not because of frictions and disagreements but because of the opportunity of one of its members to pursue a personally appealing and rewarding career path. Hence it reveals a different exit strategy for united careers – one driven by the availability of a highly satisfying professional occupation for one of the individuals in a domain where he or she cannot be joined by the other member of the professional duo.

Finally, it is important to acknowledge that John Whitehead and John Weinberg initiated, through personal example and the introduction of company practices, the discovery, development, and promotion of professional duos as part of the culture at Goldman Sachs. Although Weinberg remained the sole chief executive of the firm with the exit of Whitehead, another pair had been identified as having the potential to share roles at the top (initially as co-COOs and then as co-CEOs) and had been promoted together – Stephen Friedman and Robert Rubin. For Weinberg, "The big question was to decide whether [Friedman and Rubin] would be able to do what John Whitehead and I did" (Endlich, 2002, p. 184). He gave them a five-year transition period, gradually handing over more responsibility. Friedman and Rubin acted informally as co-CEOs after Whitehead's departure. In 1985, they were appointed to co-head the fixed income division, and in 1987 they became co-vice chairs and co-COOs. In Chapter 4 we referred to the accounts of Robert Rubin on how satisfactory their work as a professional duo was (Rubin and Weisberg, 2003).

Masaru Ibuka and Akio Morita at Sony Corporation

The first chapter of John Nathan's (1999) book *Sony: The Private Life* concentrates on the founding fathers of Sony Corporation. The chapter begins, revealingly:

At the center of the postwar social organism called Sony Corporation stands one of business history's most productive and intriguing relationships. For over forty years, Masaru Ibuka and Akio Morita grew Sony together, from adjoining offices, reveling in each other's company. Their personal secretaries, women who devoted themselves to their well-being for dozens of years . . . like to remember them facing each other on the rug, playing with a prototype that Ibuka had snatched from the hands of one of his engineers and carried upstairs gleefully to show Morita. (p. 1)

The two men who co-founded Sony Corporation had complementary talents. Ibuka was the dreamer and visionary, an inventive genius, passionate about technology, who had graduated in mechanical engineering from Waseda University. Morita was pragmatic, a master of negotiations and marketing with a degree in physics from Osaka Imperial University. He was an elegant man, with the aristocratic delicacy of an eldest son raised, according to tradition, as a prince. His large, old family was involved in sake brewing and other business ventures. As Sony Corporation's official website describes it:

Throughout their long partnership, Ibuka devoted his energies to technological research and product development, while Morita was instrumental in leading Sony in the areas of marketing, globalization, finance and human resources. Morita also spearheaded Sony's entry into the software business, and he contributed to the overall management of the company.[2]

Ibuka was considered to be a pure and simple soul; Morita was known for his appetite for success and recognition (Nathan, 1999, p. 3). Similar to Agustín Almodóvar's role in the career of his brother and film director Pedro, and that of Giancarlo Giammetti in the trajectory of the renowned fashion designer Valentino, Morita's role was to protect Ibuka, to support his boldest dreams and visions, and to help him in realizing them.

In Chapter 4, in the discussion of what makes for a successful professional duo, we suggested that it is important that its members speak with a single voice. This is noted as characteristic of the partnership of Ibuka and Morita:

If Ibuka and Morita had serious disagreements over the years, they resolved them privately. Regarding company policy they spoke with one voice; no one in or outside Sony ever heard either of them criticize the other. Nor has anyone who has ever seen them failed to remark on the exclusive bond that seemed to unite them in a mysterious way. (Nathan, 1999, p. 2)

---

[2] http://www.sony.com/SCA/press/morita_bio.shtml.

Makoto, Ibuka's son, further described this strong and binding relationship:

They were closer than lovers, even Mrs. Morita felt that. They were bound together by a tie so tight it was more like love than friendship. The connection was so deep that not even their wives could break into it when they were together. Even now, when they're both sick, when Mr. Morita comes to visit my father or my father pays Mr. Morita a visit, they sit together in silence, holding hands, the tears running down their cheeks, and they're communicating without words. That's the kind of friendship they always shared. (Nathan, 1999, p. 2)

Another revealing account from people in the inner circle of the co-founders of Sony Corporation comes from Kazuaki, Morita's younger brother, who defines their relationship as marked by intimacy:

It was truly strange. Men usually get along really well for three or maybe five years and then there's some kind of an argument. But they managed for such a long time, right up against each other, matching perfectly in their work lives and their personal lives. They were incredibly lucky to have found each other. I never saw anything like that combination! (Nathan, 1999, pp. 2–3)

The beginning of this impressive professional and personal partnership dated back to 1944, when Ibuka, twenty-four years old at the time, and Morita, thirteen years his senior, found themselves together during World War II in a task force that had been given the task of developing a heat-seeking missile "in time to turn the tide of the failing war" (Nathan, 1999, p. 4). For almost a year, they spent a great deal of time together, brainstorming technology. By themselves, they were discussing the post-war future of Japan, in a way similar to Weinberg and Whitehead's discussions about the future of Goldman Sachs. The work on the task force was followed by Morita's visits to Ibuka's company, where the two men were thought to have developed deeper mutual regard (Nathan, 1999). Then Ibuka and Morita lost touch, meeting again only after a story on Ibuka's inventions was published in the post-war *Asahi Shimbun*, Japan's second largest newspaper. Morita read the article, contacted Ibuka, and initially became involved with Ibuka's company on a part-time basis, while fulfilling a teaching commitment. The formal incorporation of the company took place on May 7, 1946. Ibuka was appointed managing director and Morita took the role of general manager.

One of the many articles following Akio Morita's death emphasized the fact that his entire career had been united to that of his partner and co-founder of Sony Corporation, Masaru Ibuka. This successful career unity was due to their complementarities, but also to the extremely strong and binding personal relationship that allowed them to endure crises and difficulties. They developed a special intuition for one other, connecting their minds through what we previously defined as instrumental intimacy (Farrell, 2001). In 1976, Ibuka stepped down as chair of Sony Corporation, retaining a strong advisory connection with the company until his death in 1997. Morita died in 1999. Their partnership has left a trace in the annals of the great business achievements of the twentieth century.

Drawing implications from the cases

United careers are sustainable over time when attention is paid to a range of issues. First, it is important that the individuals who embark on united careers develop a deep understanding of each other's talent, character, and style, and choose their united professional occupations accordingly. As identified in Chapters 4 and 5, for the professional side of the relationship to develop successfully, it is essential to shape the roles of the two or more members accordingly. Role and task differentiation is necessary in order to provide the individuals with their own domain of action; role integration is needed in order to coordinate these domains and complete a common project. The development of intimate understanding and shared cognition between the partners facilitates the coordination of their activities and the resolution of conflicts. The most successful united careers reflect the importance of giving freedom to the partner who feels strongly about an idea. Finally, the pairs also refer to spending both work and social time together, which increases their knowledge of one another and the strength of their bonding.

Implications of united careers

Examining united careers allows us to introduce small numbers (e.g. duos, trios, and foursomes) as a unit of analysis in career studies, a stream of research that has tended to focus on the individual or the organization. Small-number structures are not only theoretically meaningful phenomena, but also increasingly relevant, with implications for governance, individual careers, and organizational practices.

Implications for corporate power structures and governance

Our explorations into examples of united careers revealed that the corporate power arrangements of small numbers are more likely to be productive and to endure if embedded into united career patterns. In those cases, the individuals involved would care deeply about the relationship and try to reconcile their differences in amicable ways in order to perpetuate it.

Furthermore, what we encountered is an important distinction in the genesis of small-numbers power structures and governance and united careers, which may have influenced their longevity and success. We distinguished between affective and working genesis, the former referring to friendship and family relationships and the latter acknowledging the work context as a source of the relationship. On the basis of the examples cited, we hypothesize that small numbers with affective genesis may have a higher propensity to be successful and survive because they encompass a strong commitment to the relationship that precedes the professional collaboration. This is, no doubt, a simplistic interpretation, as the many cases of troubled family businesses would demonstrate. We believe it is important to study the phenomenon of united careers further in order to gain a better understanding of the mechanisms that contribute to better collaboration, in cases of both affective and working genesis. In this sense, small numbers at the top have been found potentially suitable for resolving power conflicts, as a recent report on family businesses has acknowledged Mass Mutual Financial Group and Raymond Institute, 2003). In every fourth family business surveyed, the participant acknowledged that they are considering role-sharing as part of their succession planning. An understanding of the ways in which role-sharing can be incorporated into a well-integrated design is a topic that deserves far greater academic attention.

The longevity of small numbers and united careers arising from working relationships could be improved, and their operations could be more successful if they were appropriately designed for role separation, role-sharing, and the integration mechanisms. Professional duos and larger constellations are better balanced if they are able to turn their working collaborations into affective ones and combine the benefits of both affective and cognitive trust (McAllister, 1995), which are together the glue that holds the partnership together.

Finally, exits from small-number structures and united careers must be understood in order to diminish organizational and individual costs. These issues are discussed in the following sections on the individual and organizational implications of united careers.

Implications for individuals

Increasingly complex occupations place extensive demands on the necessary competencies and mind-sets of professionals, and on the roles that need to be played. It is difficult for an individual to possess all the relevant knowledge and expertise and to be able to switch through a series of organizational roles (Ashforth, Kreiner, and Fugate, 2000). Furthermore, the nature of the top job, whether in a big corporation or a smaller family business, requires trust, an intimate understanding, and support. Mature individuals who possess the qualities to meet these criteria may want to consider developing a career with a trusted *alter ego* who provides complementary capabilities and committed support. An important first step is to understand the critical requirements and interdependencies arising from the nature of the occupation and the available personal career competencies and limitations; and to realize the need for complementary knowledge, abilities, style, and access to critical networks. It is also crucial to identify an individual who is able, at both the professional and personal level, to develop a working partnership based on trust; that is, to find the right partner, "because you're utterly dependent on each other" (Cunningham and Murray, 2005, p. 130). In addition to having the know-why, know-how, and know-who career competencies (DeFillippi and Arthur, 1994), the development of a united career would require a "liaison career competence," which is associated with the skills and attitudes necessary for the sustenance of close and enduring partnerships.

As revealed by the cases we presented in this chapter, affective bonds with strong cognition-based trust foundations are usually a good basis for developing a task and career coupling. Time is also an important dimension in partnerships. In order for united careers to form, a continuity of collaboration and joint experiences, as well as escalating emotional and material exchanges (Hodgson, Levinson, and Zaleznik, 1965) are needed. Executives who are contemplating united career arrangements must be able to share power with another person and be willing and able to accept another person's point of view, not only with regard to work, but also with respect to career direction. It is important to assess periodically the benefits and trade-offs of a united career. Although it may provide rewarding and freeing working relationships with higher quality and commitment to employers and customers (Cunningham and Murray, 2005), it may also lead to difficulties in making career moves (e.g. less flexibility or slower speed), as each new career opportunity must provide room for two professionals rather than one. Moreover, personal circumstances and needs may produce changes that cause a drift away from career unity and back to individual trajectories (e.g. John Whitehead moved from a united career with John Weinberg to an individual path). Given today's increasingly fragmented organizational and career experiences, united careers could provide individuals with continuity and coherence in their professional lives. In view of the committed and smooth collaboration that characterizes them, they could also lead to enhanced contributions to fulfilling organizational objectives.

Organizational implications

Organizations – particularly those with hybrid identities, requiring the coordination of a range of competencies (Glynn, 2000) – should consider practices of hiring, developing, and promoting professionals in duos and teams. Cianni and Wnuck (1997) have argued that strong teams could move collectively to higher organizational levels, using team-based experiences in developing individual members' career paths. In the rest of this chapter we provide some ideas and illustrate them with examples of business practice.

Hiring small numbers. More applied research should be performed on the practices of companies that have realized the potential of dyads and have actively promoted them. In the influential Californian studio Nissan Design International, cars are designed by "odd couples" consisting of an intuitive creative and an analytic creative who have been hired in pairs by the unit's founder and former president, Jerry Hirshberg, in the belief that this odd coupling leads to frictions that enhance creativity (Leonard-Barton, 1995b; Cubeiro, 1998). Monsanto's "two-in-a-box" program pairs a scientist with a marketing or finance person as co-leaders of a global product division in this multi-national chemical company (Sally, 2002). A similar "two-in-a-box" approach is practiced at Intel, with two people sharing the CIO seat (Foremski, 2003). Hiring pairs requires special selection mechanisms, ones that are sensitive to the potential synergies that an organization could realize from teaming up their talents.

Job and career-sharing practices, however, are not necessarily known or accepted in a wealth of organizations. Executives seeking to embark on a united career may have to explain to and negotiate with different stakeholders to gain legitimacy and support for their shared work arrangement. As two executives with joint careers explained: "The real challenges came almost exclusively from a lack of management support and our immediate colleagues' suspicions about our arrangement . . . We continually had to explain ourselves; we were always on trial – which was a drag on our time, not to mention our morale" (Cunningham and Murray, 2005, p. 128).

Developing Career policies that are attentive to united careers or well-balanced professional duos could contribute to organizational efficiency and creativity. Such career policies may also contribute to the further diffusion and legitimation of small numbers at the top and united careers, due to what Monica Higgins calls "career imprinting" in her recent book *Career Imprints: Creating Leaders Across an Industry* (Higgins, 2005). As she explains in an interview: "Career imprinting refers to the process by which individuals pick up or cultivate a certain set of capabilities, connections, confidence, and cognition due to their work experiences at a particular employer" (Higgins, quoted in Stark, 2005). It could be argued, then, that organizations open to position- and career-sharing practices, may leave an imprint on their employees and influence them to transfer and continue using such arrangements to organizations they join or create throughout their careers.

Promoting small numbers. Goldman Sachs systematically screened and selected individuals with the potential to jell as professional duos, providing them with joint career appointments and monitoring and assessing their chemistry, synergies, relational quality, and cohesion (Endlich, 2002, p. 179). A professional duo with complementary competencies and styles could be a source of competitive advantage for the organization. Not realizing the importance of pairing and promoting its members individually may destroy effectively functioning work units. As Belbin (1981) argued, a common mistake is that "Pairings of proven effectiveness are often broken up to fill managerial gaps or even as well-intentioned acts of management development, with little realization of how much the interdependence of two people contributes to the running of a successful unit" (Belbin, 1981, p. 129). As a consequence of such interventions, professional duos are more easily sustained and stable at the top than on the way up, as they are usually difficult to notice: "Since role relationships are not readily discernible, they are likely to be ignored whenever career progression is being considered" (Belbin, 1981, p. 130).

"Exiting" in small numbers. Professional duos may decide to exit together, moving on to a different organization or project, as is often the case for creatives in advertising (Vagnoni, 1997). They could also exit together, with each member of the duo then following an individual path. In November 2003, the top duo at Gucci, Domenico De Sole and Tom Ford, announced that they were quitting their top posts together after failing to reach an agreement over the renewal of their contracts. No announcement was made, however, as to the duo continuing its tight collaboration elsewhere. In fact, potential individual plans and moves were discussed in the press.

It is difficult to provide advice to the human resources department of a corporation on what constitutes united career management, perhaps because the linking of careers depends on the individuals' decisions to connect their trajectories rather than on organizational attempts to maintain professional duos over time. Yet organizations must be aware of the existence of such united careers when promoting individually, especially if specific competitive advantage may reside in a dyad whose members have connected their professional trajectories.

In the case of united trajectories, one member's problems could negatively affect the career of the other member. The idea of united careers as united destinies is illustrated by the memorable words of the former Spanish prime minister Felipe González, spoken at the time that charges of corruption jeopardized the career of his vice-president, Alfonso Guerra. "They will get the two of us for the price of one," he said at the time, signaling the end of the coupling of their political destinies, united at that time by twenty years of partnership.

In this chapter we explored some career underpinnings of small numbers at the top and defined a distinctive career pattern – the united career – with implications for governance and career theory and practice. In order to address the particularities and dynamics of united careers, career theory should open up to a new level of analysis that has received little attention: the dyad, or in the cases of committed teams or collaborative circles, the relevant small-numbers structure of individuals such as a trio or quartet. Following Simmel's (1950) seminal sociological work on small numbers, it could be expected that united careers of duos would have different characteristics and dynamics from those of trios or quartets. Further research is needed to examine and document these differences.

The examples we have gathered from the business press, books, specialist magazines of arts and science, and the study of four different cases as illustrations of career-related phenomena in duos, have revealed heterogeneous pairs, ranging from professional duos centered on work collaboration to stronger and more durable associations encompassing work collaboration and joint career decision-making – what we called united careers.

Our most difficult challenge was to differentiate the small-numbers structures we discussed in Chapters 4 and 5, particularly the long-term relationships, from the cases of united careers. In our view, the strong differentiating element between the two is the joint decision-making regarding professional trajectories and the interlocked career moves and outcomes that characterize coupled careers. Over the course of the evolution of this career coupling or relationship, there are many crossroads at which one or both members must decide if they are willing and able to continue on a common path, or if their interests and ambitions have drifted apart. In the united career, there is an element of committed union, as a criterion for decision-making and acting upon the professional future of the duo. It is the special attachment to the relationship, the relational cohesion, that evokes contributing behavior and congruent work (Lawler and Yoon, 1996). In this sense, affective exchange theory (Lawler, 2001) could provide a useful framework for understanding careers as plural rather than individual phenomena.

It seems that, if affection exists prior to professional collaboration, neither member of the pair or larger constellation builds a fully individualized professional project: remaining united is the prime objective. Moreover, we would suggest that an affective genesis makes it easier for the small-numbers structure to deal with difficult situations and crises, and gives the relationship a special stickiness and sustainability. In other words, preserving the relationship may have priority over individual career aspirations. This will not be the case of duos glued together only by extensive task collaboration, as individual career motives and aspirations would tend to dominate over the duo's longevity. A characteristic of a dyad's dynamics that is pertinent to achieving success in united careers is the extensive investment in each other's well-being and efficacy.

Family and friendship ties provide a natural environment for developing a close relationship that can grow into professional and career collaboration. Office proximity may serve the same function, as it did in the case of Weinberg and Whitehead's pairing. College conviviality seems to provide the time and space and be conducive to affection and mutual awareness, and thereby to the formation of professional duos. Hewlett and Packard met at Stanford, for instance; Gates and Balmer at Harvard; and Jobs and Wozniack at Berkeley. Less known outside of their country but involved in equally exciting partnerships, the trio behind the quirky UK smoothie company Innocent met while they were students at Cambridge. Kaleil and Tom, the protagonists of the documentary *Startup.com*, met in high school. "Magnet places," such as schools, universities, art studios, or hospitals that attract like-minded professionals and provide access to relevant networks are good catalysts for duos and united careers (Farrell, 2001). Universities could purposefully promote the exploration of career pairings by providing opportunities for work on joint assignments.

Committed unions thrive on both strong cognition- and affect-based trust. Without trust, the members of a duo are highly unlikely to develop profound awareness of each other's motives, abilities, and professional and personal needs, or to accept self-imposed limitations on their career options. Affection is a necessary but insufficient condition for the development of united careers. Members of the successful united careers represented in our examples not only had strong mutual affection, but were able to collaborate efficiently in top management or governance tasks (Ibarra, 1992). They scored highly on all the dimensions along which working relationships develop: openness and disclosure, extensive knowledge of one another, predictability of reactions, uniqueness of their interaction, and the capacity to handle conflict and disagreement (Gabarro, 1987). Cognition-based trust is built faster on the basis of existing personal affection in time-honored friendships or family ties. In other words, although both affect- and cognitive-based trust are needed for a united career to thrive, the former seems to be a faster and safer foundation for developing the latter.

Complementarities of the duo's competencies and styles are important to its stability and longevity. For any given degree of affection and trust, a duo is more evenly balanced and more likely to last and expand to united careers if its members assume complementary tasks or contribute to the same tasks with complementary styles and competencies. We were able to see for ourselves the uniqueness of each member of the Valls and Almodóvar couples, while at the same time observing their complementarity. Hence, a useful metaphor regarding professional duos that make it to the stage of forming lasting united careers is that of yin and yang, the symbols of complementary forces in harmony and equilibrium.

Although the multiple and varied requirements for the success of united careers restrict their frequency, when they function well, as in the cases of the Almodóvar and Valls brothers or that of Morita and Ibuka or Weinberg and Whitehead, the organizational synergies and professional and personal rewards of such associations are extremely high for each member of the duo.

Finally, another important issue in united careers is their exclusivity. Some professionals embark on a decade-long exclusive relationship with a trusted *alter ego*; other professionals are more pragmatic or more in need of a range of relationships and maintain several committed partnerships in a united career path over time. Whatever the pattern, the important point is that careers – traditionally viewed as individual trajectories – come in many different shapes and sizes of small-numbers phenomena. This relational view of careers is perhaps better able to depict the true nature of our professional lives.

In this chapter we have sought to demonstrate and acknowledge the phenomenon of united careers. More research is needed on the dynamics of united careers that begin, in the absence of family ties or early friendship, with a working relationship. Furthermore, as suggested by Sullivan (1999), more attention should be paid to dysfunctional career outcomes and to the viability and meaning of united careers for women and minorities. Finally, the social and organizational context in which the united career occurs needs to be taken into account (Blau, 1969; Gabarro, 1987). As Blau acknowledged, "Crusoe and Friday were a dyad that existed in isolation, but most associations are part of a broad matrix of social relations" (Blau, 1969, p. 199).

This chapter is an invitation to build on the idea of small numbers, to rethink traditional academic ideas and individual and organizational

practices relating to careers as individual and independent undertakings, and to open them up to opportunities provided by united career
trajectories. United careers are examples of the richness and variety
of professional arrangements in an increasingly boundaryless context.
They could help solve some of the tensions facing professionals in
today's complex organizations, and could serve as a platform for a
fulfilling professional and personal life.

Conclusion: From small numbers to corporate governance regimes

"Do you know," I said, "that it is necessary that there also be as many forms of human characters as there are forms of regimes? Or do you suppose that the regimes arise 'from an oak or rocks' and not from the dispositions of the men in the cities, which, tipping the scale as it were, draw the rest along with them?"

"No," he said. "I don't at all think they arise from anything other than this."

Plato, *The Republic*, Book VIII, 543 e.

MUCH HAS BEEN written on solo structures and executive roles. However, as argued in the Introduction, a book on duos, trios, and larger executive constellations that share governance positions is timely. In Part I of the book we situated the phenomenon of small numbers at the top in the field of organization studies and outlined its most relevant debates. We also introduced our two main theoretical lenses – contingency theory and role theory – through which we investigate the phenomenon. In Part II of the book we concentrated on the phenomenon itself, undertaking a presentation and discussion of examples of the basic types of small-numbers structures: professional duos, trios, and larger constellations. We also delved into the domain of career theories, seeking to grasp the particulars of executives' united careers, the most integrated case of small numbers.

In this concluding chapter we first undertake a comparative analysis of the alignment of the small-numbers arrangements with the main contingencies that corporate power structures need to address. This is, as announced in the Introduction, the specific aim of the book.

Second, drawing on the comparison, we generalize to arguments for the structuring of corporate power in general. For this is the general aim of the book. We propose to apply the notion of regime, which originated in political sciences, to the design of vertical structures. We propose three basic corporate governance regimes: Rules, Politics, and Trust. Finally, we offer suggestions for further research in the area.

Small-numbers structures and contingencies

In Chapter 1 we identified the six most eventful contingencies that must be factored into the design of executive structures. Two of these contingencies are located in the external environment: strategic uncertainty and normative environment. Two others reside in the internal environment: strategic decision-making tasks and political dynamics. The final two contingencies derive from the executive environment: status and career systems, and interpersonal relationships at the top. These contingencies manifest contradictory requirements, rendering problematic the executives' task of designing their own structures. Because small numbers at the top provide a good balance between the differentiation of executive roles (aimed at control) regulated by law or governance codes, on the one hand, and their integration (aimed at decision making) through productive interpersonal relationships, on the other, they are a good option to be considered by the designers of corporate political structures. Most other existing options are biased toward the control function of corporate governance.

In the following paragraphs and in Table 2 we assess the alignment or fit of vertical structures – solo, duos, and trios – with specific political contingencies. The degree of fit ranges from "poor fit," in which a vertical power structure is considered unable to address well a critical contingency; to "very good fit," in which the executive structure of the firm is believed to warrant an optimal alignment with the contingency. We also distinguish an intermediary level, or "good fit," which indicates that one design option, although not the best, is better capable of addressing a contingency than is a design that has been classified as "poor."

The following discussion is useful, not so much for our particular assessment of the fit as for the recognition of the need for open-mindedness in the exploration of the several blueprints of vertical structures available, including small numbers at the top.

Table 2. *Alignment of small-numbers structures with corporate power contingencies*

	Solo	Duos	Trios
Contingencies			
External			
Strategic uncertainty	Poor	Good	Very good
Normative environment	Very good	Poor	Poor
Internal			
Strategic decision-making tasks	Poor	Very good	Good
Political dynamics	Poor	Good	Very good
Executive			
Status and career systems	Very good	Poor	Good
Interpersonal relationships	Poor	Very good	Good

It is also worth noting that in our comparative discussion of small numbers, we consider them to function as ideal types: as executive structures possessing adequate degrees not only of differentiation and specialization of competencies and tasks of the individuals involved, but also of integration through such mechanisms as joint cognition, trust, and affection, which secure timely information-sharing, healthy debate, and quality of decision making. Thus, for the purposes of the comparison, we are considering only well-functioning small-numbers structures, and leave the discussion of their potential dysfunctional features to follow our comparative analysis. As for the case of horizontal structures and their basic types (functional, multi-divisional, matrix, and network), vertical structures present, in practice, a wide variety of hybrids, *ad hoc* combinations, and transitional arrangements, which makes their alignment with the corporate power contingencies situational.

Based on the descriptions of alignment in Table 2, we offer some comments on the propensity of each structure to address the essential contingencies in corporate governance.

Solo executives

As previously discussed, a solo structure refers not to an executive governing a complex organization single-handedly but to one who does not share a top role with others or is not accompanied by a trusted executive constellation. We hypothesize that the solo option is very good for satisfying the requirements of the external contingency, normative environment. This design option allows unequivocal accountability in the case of legal, social, and ethical scrutiny of decisions, and provides an opportunity for control by other executives who do not have close interpersonal ties with the solo executive. We also believe that solo executive leadership is the option best equipped to address the executive contingency of status and career systems, which reflects generalized individualism in cadres. Achieving a solo position at the top is still a potent career motor for many executives.

Solo structures, however, are less capable of responding to strategic uncertainty than are either duo or trio structures. The pressure to make quick decisions based on large amounts of ambiguous data may overwhelm the cognitive capabilities of solo executives. Solos' capacity for mutually adjusted collaboration is obviously marginal, since it is a solipsistic structure. Coping with political dynamics may be more difficult for solo executives than for pairs or trios of executives, given that political moves often require alliances or even executive constellations to be played safely and successfully and ideally preemptively. Similarly, dealing with the peculiarity and high intensity of relationships at the top may be difficult for solos, who operate without companionship in the workplace.

Hence, under conditions of strategic complexity, uncertainty, and turbulence, the solo option, dominant in practice, does not yield good strategic decisions and adequate management of the corporate political structure.

Professional duos

We believe that the professional duo offers a very good alignment with the internal contingency, strategic decision-making tasks. As Hodgson, Levinson, and Zaleznik (1965) have acknowledged, the pairing is an effective structure for decision making in complex environments. If the mix of competencies, backgrounds, styles, and contacts of the two executives is appropriate and successfully integrated, the professional duo provides better decision-making capability at the top than can a solo executive who relies on individual capacities or a loosely knit team.

The pair structure is especially suitable for addressing the organizational dualities discussed in Chapter 2. In facing the internal–external dilemma of organizations, for example, one member of the pair can focus attention and energy on the internal tasks and responsibilities and the other can perform external tasks while simultaneously integrating these tasks through the nature and strength of their relationship. The duo's relationship, if based on trust and affection, provides each individual with both task support and the emotional support essential to work at the top.

Because of the emotional support inherent in the executive duo, we argue, it is an option well-fitted to the executive contingency of interpersonal relationships. Interpersonal relationships *à trois* are far more complex and intense than are pair relationships because, rather than one relationship, the threesome requires three essential ties to be balanced.

Duos, like solo designs, have limited ability to match all six contingencies. They are, for example, a poor fit with the demands of the normative environment because of their blurred accountability, and because close interpersonal relationship goes against the "social distance" postulate of codes of good governance practice. Two at the top provide an odd structure for an executive status system based on an individualistic *Weltanschaung* and for the corporate hierarchy. Two at the top can, for example, lead to confusion and mixed loyalties among employees. It is difficult to assign reputations to the individuals in a duo, to judge their individual capabilities, and to assess the outcome of their pairing relative to that of a solo professional's contribution. These limitations of executive pairs provide us with an understanding of the lukewarm reception they often elicit, despite the benefits they can offer.

It is necessary to reflect further on the path dependency of professional duos and the effects of the nature of their genesis on their survival and their ability to address the critical contingencies at the top. In the case of individuals who initiate a professional, role-sharing duo as a result of the merger of their companies, for instance, we often notice inbred volatility of the pair structure, which may be attributed to the overlapping competencies and ambitions of the members or to their conflicting agendas. This volatility can also result from the absence of past collaboration and awareness of each other's characteristics, styles, and trustworthiness. Hence, a professional duo with its genesis in the merger of two companies is unlikely to offer a good fit with the executive contingency of interpersonal relationships. Furthermore, the internal contingency of political dynamics is more acute in such cases, as the merging camps may have recently been competitors. In cases of such highly contested executive partnerships, in which competition rather than collaboration is brought into the shared position, it could be better to have a solo executive rather than a divided duo heading the united companies. Another option could be to "stabilize" the duo with the introduction of a third element – in the role of mediator rather than arbiter – that could help balance the duo and improve its working relationship.

Professional duos that have been built on the ground of an existing affective relationship (e.g. siblings, close friends), we argue, are more likely to establish a strong working bond of mutual respect and collaboration. They are also more prone to developing a strong attachment to the relationship, which acts as a barrier to the exit of a member of the duo. Hence these cases are also more likely to unite their careers over time. On the other hand, duos who have been forced into position-sharing on the grounds of a weak, non-existing, and even, at times, poor working relationship, are more likely to have difficulties creating a long *durée* bond.

The executive pairs thrive in organizational environments in which their dyadic relationship is not isolated. It is usually embedded in a triad or a larger relational structure, which can influence their dynamics and lead to either their stability or their termination. Hence in considering a professional duo as an alternative to a solo executive, it is worth accounting for the relational fabric in which the duo is embedded. Less fertile soil for the survival of the duo is the highly politicized environment in which separate superiors with conflicting interests have appointed them or in which each of the position-sharing executives maintains a separate camp of loyal followers.

Trios and larger executive constellations

A trio of executives is a very good design option for alignment with the external contingency of strategic uncertainty; in particular, it fits well with goal definition and the goals–means association. That is, if two heads are better than one, three heads could be better than two when addressing uncertainty and complexity. This is not only a matter of a broader range of competencies or a more accurate perception of the environment. The trio's ability to resolve conflicting views on the means–ends connections tends to be superior to that of the duo precisely because of its uneven number, the presence of a third member allowing two differing or even polar views to be brought closer together.

In addressing the internal contingency of political dynamics, the trio is an ambivalent structure. On the one hand, it can provide a good fit if the trio is a balanced coalition. On the other hand, it can be a poor fit, as it is more vulnerable than other small numbers to the effects of shifting coalitions. Furthermore, the trio's stability is the one most contingent on the personalities occupying the power structures and their interpersonal relationships.

Like a duo, a trio at the top is a poor fit with the normative environment. If two at the top cloud accountability, a trio worsens it, as trios have even greater difficulty than do duos with liability and with controlling executive practices and performance. As to strategic decision making, a trio is less efficient in the tasks of strategic alignment than is a duo because the essential element in performing these tasks is mutual adjustment. It is easier for duos to achieve that adjustment than for trios, in which interactions and internal coalitions may obstruct the needed coordination.

Having a trio at the top is neither a poor option nor a best option; rather it provides a good enough fit for individuality and interpersonal relationships at the top. In a trio, the intensity of relationships could be magnified through the interactions of three people and the formation of internal coalitions. Furthermore, a supra-individual identity can develop in trios, further complicating the intensity of its relationships. A triad preserves the individuality of a member better than a dyad does, and because individuality is essential for jobholders at the top, a trio can be good at addressing the status and career-system contingency.

A comparison of the capacity of the different small-numbers arrangements to provide an alignment with the six basic contingencies germane to the design of governance structures yields general configurations, none of which fully or simultaneously satisfies the relevant environments. This lack of complete fit is due, as discussed in Chapter 1, to the numerous relevant contingencies making contradictory demands on the design of vertical structures. As Gresov (1989) pointed out, the units facing conflicting contingencies are precisely those more prone to poorly fitting designs and poor performance. It is not surprising, then, that there are many reports on the dissatisfaction of top executives regarding the design and functioning of executive committees (Nadler, Spencer, and associates, 1998), CEO positions (Khurana, 2002), boards of directors (Carter and Lorsch, 2004), and even general shareholder meetings (Alvarez, Gifra, and Ricart, 2005). As Eccles and Nohria (1992) warned, structures are transitory (as environments change they become obsolete), unsatisfactory (no environment can be fully adapted to), and insufficient (organizational adaptation cannot be done only with structures, it also requires the other organizational elements, such as systems and skills, to be aligned). These characteristics, as well as the imperfection, ambiguity, and uncertainty that Coffey, Athos, and Raynolds (1968) attributed to top organizational jobs, are especially true of the structuring of corporate power.

Executives design the apex of their organizations, selecting among different alternatives in ways that, at a minimum, satisfy the indispensable demands of the external and internal environments and their four basic contingencies. However, executives also decide among possible designs on the basis of their professional or personal preferences for status and career systems and interpersonal relationships at the top, thereby adapting to the executive environment.

The principle of equifinality – the ability to reach the same end by following different paths or, in this case, by using different vertical arrangements – makes choice in structural design possible and establishes contingency theory as being practitioner-friendly (Gresov and Drazin, 1997). Small numbers at the top increase the options available for the satisfaction of the executive environment.

Unfortunately, however, the dominant discourse of corporate governance reforms all over the world promotes one particular template for the structuring of corporate power – that of publicly traded companies in Anglo-Saxon business systems (Guillén, 2001), in which shareholders are equivalent to the sovereign people in democratic regimes, and which is more oriented to control than to decision-making (Pound, 1995). Although there is, therefore, potential for latitude in political design of the top, dominant ideologies of corporate governance have reduced the number and variety of models available, making it more difficult to profit from that latitude.

Corporate political regimes: rules, politics, and trust

The scarcity of frameworks for corporate political design can be also attributed in part to the difficulties of transferring into the business domain fundamental analogies that originated in politics (Kerr, 2004). These analogies could have ignited the theoretical or practical imagination for a variety of corporate political architectures. Exceptions on the theoretical side are Zald's (1969) idea of constitution applied to the charter of corporations and Davis and Thompson's (1994) innovative application of the metaphor of social movements to network organizations. A practical exception could be found in de Jong and van Witteloostuijn (2004).

Paradoxically, however, much of the reform in corporate governance practices is based upon and legitimated precisely by the application to business organizations of two complementary fundamental analogies forming the basis of the design of democratic political systems: the division of power (e.g. separation of legislative, executive, and judiciary power) and checks and balances as a principle for the design of political processes (e.g. control of the executive by the legislature, and resolution of conflicts between the two by an independent judiciary). Applications of these principles, based on an almost mechanical imagery, are reflected in the prescriptions of corporate governance reforms of a business, social, and even affective hiatus between executives and directors and between institutional and managerial actors: chairs of boards and CEOs are not supposed to be friends and independent directors led by the chair should be able to meet alone at least annually to avoid negative influences from the internal executive directors. These political analogies also suggest that owners or shareholders are equivalent to the sovereign people in democratic regimes.[1] The dominant model includes the tenet that this hegemony should be especially guarded because, agency theory *dixit*, internal executives are suspected of opportunism; therefore, shareholders and boards should establish stringent checks on them. Agency theory legitimates the transfer of the application of these two metaphors from politics to business. As mentioned in Chapter 1, agency theory is, under the guise of an economic theory, a truly political theory.

The very expression "corporate governance" is ideologically loaded. "Corporate politics" would be a more objective expression to denote the system and processes for decision making over the long term

---

[1] Contrary to this assumption, stakeholder theory, for instance, proclaims that shareholders investing in the stock market, given their short-term orientation, should be considered more as suppliers of financial resources than as owners *stricto sensu*.

of a corporation that bring together the managerial and institutional executives (O'Sullivan, 2000). It is "politics" because those systems and processes determine who has the greatest decision rights about the future of the corporation and the dominant claims on the value created. The more technical and neutral term "governance" is close to the word "government," which, in turn, refers to a specialization in policy implementation (not in sovereign policy decision-making). "Government," a word that has a similar connotation in many languages, disguises the true political and contested nature of the field.

None the less, one political analogy can be of great help in conceptualizing corporate power structures because it clarifies rather than disguises them: the notion of "regime." It is a political construct that has yet to be systematically employed in the discussion of the political structures of corporations with the exception of Courpasson (2000) and Clegg and Courpasson (2004). In political science, the concept of "regime" serves to classify the variety of political configurations. It generally includes the following components: (1) the basic legitimacy of a political system (e.g. democratic, monarchic, totalitarian); (2) the fundamental organization of the power structure (e.g. centralized versus decentralized, unified versus federal, presidential versus parliamentarian); and (3) the hegemonic social actor or class on which the regime relies (e.g. the bourgeoisie, the military) and the style with which that group exercises political leadership (e.g. liberal, conservative, authoritarian, enlightened). Most characterizations of political regimes (e.g. a federal republic, a parliamentarian monarchy) combine the first two of these three elements, which are always contained in the formal charter of the political systems. The dominant political actor and its leadership style, while profoundly affecting the functioning of a whole political regime, is most often without formal recognition,[2] as happens to most answers to the questions "Who rules?" and "*Qui prodest?*"

Clegg and Courpasson (2004) define regimes as "forms and practices of governance that are objectified and embodied in specific operational, administrative and managerial systems" (p. 543). In our opinion, the application of the notion of regime to corporate political structures has

---

[2] An exception could be "enlightened despotism."

several advantages. First, it refers, as corporate structures do, to general or systemic political configurations that satisfy some environments and contingencies better than others. Second, regime is an explicit political term (not merely technical or governance-like) that assumes a fundamental decision to satisfy some contingencies at the expense of others and to manage the consequences of that discrimination. A particular regime is not determined; it is not the only possible response to a specific configuration of environments. Third, the three basic components of a regime – legitimacy, power structure, and leadership – transfer nicely to the political structure of business corporations. The principal legitimacy, to which a corporate political structure could attend, could be, for example, the family owning a company, the co-founders of a venture, the venture capitalists, the state, or the shareholders. The power structure refers to the basic configuration of differentiation and integration of corporate governance roles and bodies, e.g. the existence (or not) of a functioning board or lead director, and of small numbers at the top. The dominant political actors could be, for example, the family, shareholders, venture capitalists, the board, or the internal executives. And their leadership style could be charismatic, participative, rule-based, despotic, or authoritarian. Leadership is more important in business organizations than in political organizations, if only because the rule of law is (still) less prevalent and pervasive in business and its leaders generally have greater latitude for action than do politicians or civil servants. Fourth, each of the "ideal" political regimes we propose – Rules, Politics, and Trust – aligns well, although not exclusively, with one of the three basic environments discussed in Chapter 1: external, internal, and executive environment respectively.

In the next pages we present each regime. The discussion is an "ideal" one – fittingly Platonic.[3] Besides pointing out the internal differences among Rules, Politics, and Trust, the intention of this exposition is to support our argument about the plurality of options for the political structuring of organizations and the usefulness of the concept of regime for that intention.

The *Rules* regime involves following the regulations and norms for the design of corporate power structures that are posed by the

---

[3] One could also say, fittingly Parsonian.

ever-increasing institutionalization of corporate governance.[4] This regime satisfies the standard pressures for good governance that the institutional environment places upon the companies. A fundamental tenet in that environment is that roles should not be co-performed and that constellations of executives who trust one another are to be regarded with suspicion, especially when bridging the managerial and ownership domains.[5] Furthermore, the political capital needed to govern the organization is provided by the legitimacy obtained by complying with extant good governance rules.

The regime of Rules is best represented by what we called the solo exercise of power. Small numbers at the top could also govern a Rules regime, but this would represent a departure from the most compact version of the ideal type of regime, and the leadership would need to compensate for this variance by, for instance, managing reputation intensely.

The regime of Rules goes beyond alignment with the normative environment that is being enforced by an ever-expanding and influential list of intermediaries in corporate legitimacy and governance norms:

---

[4] There are some signs that the institutionalization of corporate governance is reaching its limits: complaints abound over the costs involved in complying with the Sarbanes–Oxley Act; a backlash against the directors of Calpers, the pioneers and leading propagandists of corporate governance reform in the USA; and similar reactions that are beginning to occur in Europe.

[5] One example of the strength of the institutionalization of the individualistic assumptions of corporate governance appeared in the press in December 2004, as we were writing these conclusions. A series of reports depicted the power struggle at the pinnacle of EADS, the European defense group in which France and Germany have important stakes. This group has been led for years by well-functioning structures of co-chairs and co-CEOs. In December 2004, however, the French stakeholder tried to terminate the role-sharing arrangement and install a solo Frenchman at the apex. The December 10 issue of the *Financial Times* carried an editorial against the coup because of the strife it might generate and because such a change could endanger the successful balance of power that existed over the years of co-reign. However, the editorial also emphasized that "If EADS were a normal company there would be good reason to question its curious structures, with two co-chairman and two co-chief executives" (p. 12). The strength of the institutionalization of the individualistic assumptions of corporate governance is patent in this case: what is outside the prescriptions of the dominant rules is considered "curious," despite the evidence of their success.

Another example is the *Fortune* piece (Tomlinson, 2005) on the two-headed management structure at Unilever. The article contains strong criticisms of the dual structure, including petitions for its termination. However, it is not possible reasonably to relate any of the several performance problems of the company presented in the piece to Unilever's governance arrangement.

financial analysts, journalists, management gurus, stock exchange regulators, head-hunting firms, risk-assessment firms, issuers of reputation and good governance indices, and corporate governance watchdogs, for example. It represents a view of power in which the personality, emotions, passions, affections, and even the vision of the top office-holders – the executive environment – are not highly influential elements. Rules represent a regime of corporate power in which the main political actors do not have the willingness or competency to establish and exercise power in a personalized, distinct, tailored way. In adopting Rules, executives are capable of avoiding the legal, regulatory, and media scrutiny which is prompted by those who follow distinctive power structures. Consequently, it is a conception of vertical structures that is built on the assumption of the replaceability of executives at the top. It is power design by default. General rules do apply.

To frame this regime in terms of classical organizational theory, it could be said that the regime of Rules makes possible the phenomenon that Selznick called "displacement of goals," because under this regime organizational values (the specific equations of goals and ends making up a company's identity) are less important than is the process by which the rights of the shareholders are guaranteed. The focus on the legitimacy of the Rules regime often leads to the renunciation of leadership, which cannot be exercised without some Politics and Trust. Hence, within Rules, leadership becomes powerless and without guilt or responsibility (Courpasson, 2000). Rules make the exercise of corporate power as anonymous as a stock market with a highly dispersed ownership of shares. It is a further step in the rationalization, bureaucratization, and depersonalization of economic activities.

Politics is the regime that adapts primarily to the contingency of political dynamics in the internal environment, and to competition for status and careers in the executive environment. Cognitive and intellectual conflict over strategic decisions is prompted and generated by the ways in which roles at the top are designed, negotiated, distributed, and hierarchically ordered and coordinated and, as a result, by the way political resources are obtained and status and careers are achieved and protected (Garvin and Roberto, 2001; Roberto, 2005). Such conflict creates an intense ambience at the top, influencing, in turn, the nature of interpersonal relationships among executives.

The fundamental assumption of the regime of Politics is that heterogeneity of perspectives at the top is necessary in order to reflect the diversity of the corporate environment. It follows a homeostatic or isomorphic principle of design, characterized by the internal reproduction of the complexities of the external environment, with the expectation that sufficient adaptation will follow. This is the main hypothesis behind the resource dependency theory of organizations as applied to corporate political structures like board composition (Pfeffer and Salancik, 1978). This theory also asserts that power has an impulse to flow toward the units or the individuals that satisfy critical contingencies. However, Politics does not assume, Pangloss-like, that the best power structure emerges spontaneously. On the contrary, political leadership requires the deliberate activity of removing the obstacles to power's motion toward the locus of key interfaces with the environment. Obstacles to this natural social motion could include entrenched interests, a lack of knowledge about the causality between activities and results, the strength of other intermediate contingencies, or strong institutionalization of the old regime.

Inaugurated in Selznick's book *Leadership in Administration*, Politics is the option of those who believe in organizations as complex political arenas – so complex, in fact, that leading them should involve setting norms for the political games rather than deciding on all the issues of substance, which is an impossible and self-defeating endeavor. Because of the complexity of organizations and the unexpected consequences of actions, leaders prefer to keep open as many routes for power traffic as possible, and wherever possible to enact politics through actions that are less costly, less visible, less obtrusive, less risky, and less open to criticism (Alvarez, 2000). Therefore, the most fitting leadership style for the Politics regime is robust action, described in Chapter 2. Although some solo leaders such as Cosimo de Medici, Franklin Delano Roosevelt, and Motorola's Bob Galvin[6] have proven adept at it, theirs are extraordinary examples. Robust action is more easily exercised in small numbers. In the Politics regime, duos, trios, and other small constellations of executives who are diverse in their competencies and styles are the ideal configuration of roles at the top.

The structure of roles is the key to the Politics regime because, as mentioned, tampering with role structures is the most direct way to

---

[6] See Gentile and Jick (1987).

motivate top managers to play the games that will prompt conflict and debate, resulting in the best strategic adaptation. Whereas in the Rules regime, legitimacy overrides the other two fundamental ingredients of any regime – power structure and leadership – in Politics, even though the power structure is dominant, the other two components are still important. Legitimacy is a *sine qua non* condition, because without it the norms by which executives play games cannot be enforced (Weber, 1978; Jackal, 1988; Ocasio, 1994). Leadership is also essential to Politics because, in its absence, competition could become too personal and destructive and could impede mutually adjusted coordination.

The regime of *Trust* is built upon strong, committed relationships of people at the top. Relationships can be especially intense at the apex because of the high uncertainty and ambiguity of the decision-making tasks (see Chapter 2), as well as the emotional needs prompted or heightened by working in a reduced, extremely demanding ambience with a small number of other executives. Hence Trust is a regime oriented primarily to the satisfaction of the executive contingency of interpersonal relationships. It promotes role-sharing and emphasizes role integration on the basis of committed, cognitive and affective bonds, rendering the top job less lonely and more satisfactory.

Trust is most frequently found in family businesses, in new ventures, or in the early stages of the development of organizations, where smaller size allows for interpersonal coordination rather than coordination managed through formal hierarchies. Another usual site for the application of Trust is in those temporary or permanent organizations that exhibit important internal differentiation, such as art and management in creative projects, or science and management in R&D labs and that, as a consequence, require high integration. Prescribed rules and political dynamics could be obstacles to achieving the mutual adjustment and coordination which such cases require. The Trust regime has two main alternatives in terms of leading political actors. In one alternative, it is a strong solo executive, either a charismatic founder of the firm, or a corporate savior, who transmits trustworthiness to the external, internal, and executive environments. The other alternative is that of a professional duo or a larger constellation as a leading actor, in which trust characterizes the interpersonal relationship and occurs within the small-numbers structure. The Trust regime emphasizes the importance of close and committed relationships as integrating mechanisms of the roles at the top – integration which at that height in the organizational pyramid cannot happen only on the basis of rules and political games. Hence Trust places an emphasis not only on the political actors in an organization but also on their integrated and coordinated action.

The legitimacy element in the Trust regime is the relationship, not only between the co-founders, family members, or executives who share roles, but also between them and the range of stakeholders who have vested interests in the business or whose actions could affect the organization. This legitimacy has been considered in some cases as limiting organizational efficiency, because the sustenance of the relationship dominates, as in the case of united careers, and less emphasis is placed on the maximization of performance in the organization. This limitation has been of great concern to the current proponents of governance reforms, who have argued that by emotionally and professionally distancing the executives at the top, their focus could be maintained on creating value for shareholders.

In the Trust regime (especially in its second alternative, as a relational characteristic, and not an institutional system's one), small-numbers executive arrangements as well as united careers are accepted options for corporate power design. Last but not least in our analysis of leadership, shared leadership is acknowledged.

In the current institutional environment, it is impossible to design a power structure that does not contain a significant number of Rules and at least some ingredients of Politics and Trust. Rules or its dominant ingredient, legitimacy, cannot be ignored by any regime (Bendix, 1956; Courpasson, 2000) because our second contingency – the institutional environment – is strong and becoming stronger by the day, especially in firms operating in the stock market. Some Trust is also essential for any regime because hierarchies and norms cannot account for all the coordinating dynamics. In any regime, collaboration requires at least a modicum of trust. And without Politics, corporations would lack diversity. That is, each regime has a dominant component and always contains some elements of the other two. The Rules regime is characterized by the dominance of legitimacy over structure and leadership. Trust exhibits the dominance of the leadership domain over legitimacy and structure. The regime of Politics shows its maximum intensity in the power structure element, but also keeps more intensity in the other two elements – legitimacy and leadership – than do the other two regimes for their non-dominant components (Figure 8). Consequently,

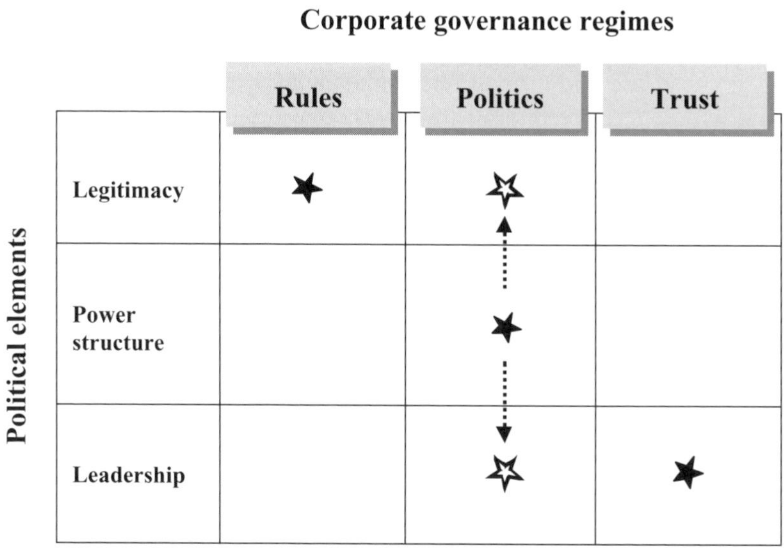

Corporate governance regimes

	Rules	Politics	Trust
Legitimacy	✦	☆ ↑	
Power structure		✦	
Leadership		☆	✦

Political elements (vertical axis label)

Figure 8. Relating corporate governance regimes and political elements.

Politics is the most complex and challenging to govern, but it is also the regime with the highest potential for making the most out of organized collective action.

Rules, Politics, and Trust are not isolated or disconnected from each other. They can also be located along dynamics of corporate evolution. The first user of the notion of political regime, Plato, in Book VIII of his *Republic*, posed a genealogy of implosion from the regime that he considered superior – aristocracy – to the other less noble regimes of timocracy, democracy, and tyranny. Plato's explanation for the *corruzione* of regimes was the deterioration of the strength and virtue of each regime's dominant actor and its leadership. In business settings, another dynamic may also play a role in prompting the succession of regimes: it is organizational growth. Organizational growth is an unstoppable process because organizations must keep receiving inputs from the environments and returning outputs to them (Katz and Kahn, 1978). Furthermore, as suggested by Greiner's (1972) article on the evolution and revolution as organizations grow, each growth phase brings new management and governance challenges. Moreover, and importantly for the case of corporate governance, when a corporation reaches a certain large size it draws the attention and activity of the regulatory environment. This visibility can occur because of its potential impact on society (e.g. employment of a large number of people) or because size and growth require financing from the stock market, and with external economic resources comes the special scrutiny that publicly traded companies receive.

We do not believe that there is a determined unidirectional evolution of corporate regimes, from less to more rational *à la Weber*, or from less to more corrupt *à la Plato*. Furthermore, we do not view regimes as closed blocks admitting only one version of each of them; as, for example, dyads and executive constellations can be at the head of any of the regimes. However, we do believe that understanding the dynamics of the emergence and collapse of corporate governance regimes is important in order to discover their political core, one that we labeled the executive environment in Chapter 1.

As long as adaptation to the external environment is accomplished, the greatest threat to the perpetuation of Rules lies in the abstraction and depersonalization of its leaders and their indifference to the displacement of the goals process. There is a fascinating paradox in the regime of Rules: solo executives are its predominant leadership, but this structural design is precisely the one in which individualism and distinctiveness is most suppressed. Rules constitute the most entropic of the regimes, and one in which, if the firm's performance fails, a paradoxical (for this regime) solution could be to bring in a strong, charismatic leader, a "corporate saviour" who is able to convey trust to the company's stakeholders.

The main potential disadvantage of the Trust regime is the subordination of the organization to the professional and personal limitations of that very leadership. It could be exemplified with the subordination of the organization to the hubris of an admired entrepreneur who does not want to or cannot surrender power, even if it means endangering the long-term prospects of the company or subordinating the organization to the united career of a duo, whose incumbents may see growth as a threat to the agreed-upon division of executive tasks and to their mutual bonds.

To the degree that Politics, based primarily upon the design and process of the power structure, is the regime that better maintains its two auxiliary orientations (legitimacy and leadership), its decay is less obvious and singular. The most relevant dangers for the Politics regime may reside in the division of the upper echelons into competing parties, and in the excesses of a robust action that traps the players in the political process and results in their losing sight of the organizational ends. Paradoxically, it could be that Politics might render agency theory true, in that it could produce players who are so savvy and skillful at playing short-term political games that strict controls should be established on them.

In summary, the notion of corporate political regime could be of great use in times when homogenization of corporate governance is being predicated and enforced. Corporate political regimes bring back plurality, choice, and latitude in the design of corporate governance. They also recognize the unparalleled importance of executives, both as designers of vertical structures and as the group for whom those structures are designed. Executives' first decision in corporate power design is how political they want to be: how much they are willing to engage in political dynamics, and how much they want this decision to impact the careers and the interpersonal relationships at the top. Power always is a personal matter, hence the quotation from Plato at the beginning of the chapter.

Research agenda

We have approached corporate structures from a mezzo perspective, with a focus on the role differentiation and integration of political structures at the top. Yet much work remains to be done at both micro and macro levels.

Micro work is necessary to shed more light on the local games that executives play when engaging in simultaneous intellectual and emotional conflict and when linking strategic tasks to the decision-making process. More anthropological works like those of Jackal (1988), Watson (1994, 1996), and Watson and Harris (1999) are needed in order to obtain a better close-up view of executives' work. Another worthwhile micro research endeavor is to study the specificities of the interpersonal relationships of top executives. This was a field that flourished in the 1960s and 1970s with the work of Athos, Gabarro, Lombard, Turner, Bennis, Schein, and other scholars, but it has not been updated, especially in regard to the executives laboring at the apex of organizations.

Although we have gained some insights into these interpersonal relationships through the readings and cases we encountered in working on this book, they are clearly insufficient. Further systematic work is in order. This is particularly important to us, given that our argument is precisely that executives' interpersonal relationships are the specific and only integrative device at the top.

We have emphasized that whether the individual or group at the top chooses the regime of Rules, Politics, or Trust depends on how the executives see themselves exercising power. This choice has to do with the political identity of the professionals at the top and is, in part, socially constructed by others, and decided upon, in part, by the same executives who design the corporate structures. We believe that knowledge about the process of generating such power identities has not advanced substantially since the work of McClelland (1961) and the group of clinical psychologists, led by Zaleznik and Kets de Vries, who concluded that the way in which executives exercise power is related to their self-images and inner theaters. However, the relationship between specific corporate power regimes and the process of creating power identities demands further attention and an in-depth study. We need to achieve as much understanding of this matter as we have of the impact of personal characteristics of CEOs on some strategic orientations (see, among others, Gupta, 1984, 1986; Gupta and Govindarajan, 1984; Miller and Dröge, 1986; Miller and Toulouse, 1986a, 1986b; Miller, 1991).

Macro work could improve our understanding of the management of the external conditions that may enable each of the basic regimes to endure and thrive – reputation-building and the management of different stakeholders, for instance, including, in the case of co-executives, the financial press. Another macro sequel to the arguments presented in this book should be an exploration of the association between regimes and types of organizations. Rules abound in publicly traded companies, Politics in professional and service firms (Greenwood and Empson, 2003), and Trust in entrepreneurial and family firms. Whereas those associations between regimes and types of companies may be those most frequently found today, a major point of this book is that there is considerable latitude for choosing the design of vertical structures, and that executives should consider what regime is best for their companies in addressing the key contingencies they face. That is, Trust or Politics, led by small numbers at the top, could also be an appropriate corporate power and leadership regime for a large corporation that obtains financial resources from the stock market – if they compensate for it with the legitimacy and leadership. In fact, we have provided numerous examples of small-number structures in these types of corporations.

We finished writing this book in the last days of 2004, the year of the first centenary of the publication of one of the founding books of sociology: Max Weber's *The Protestant Ethic and the Spirit of Capitalism*. In it, the German author described the mechanisms by which the systematic, calculating accumulation of capital was used by the Calvinists to shed doubts on their eternal fate. Once the original motives faded, it became the source of the secular rationalization of modern society "until the last ton of fossilized coal is burnt" (Weber, 2001, p. 123).

A *sine qua non* for the full deployment of the efficiency of capitalist organizations, of bureaucracies, is depersonalization – the suppression of purely personal feelings from the performance of roles. The depersonalization of economic and social life has long dominated the productive layers of organizations – their horizontal structures – which have been more prone to rationalization than vertical structures are, primarily because of the sequential and predictable nature of the tasks the former perform. The apex of organizations has, until recently, managed to escape bureaucratization. This situation has occurred because the focus of the institutional domains is more ideological than rational and because the judgments about goals and the goals–means relationship are unpredictable by nature. Furthermore, power in many companies is still entrepreneurial or is directly related to the founding phase (e.g. the significant participation of the founder and his or her family in the ownership and management of a business), a feature which Weber described in *Economy and Society* as forming the only exception to economic rationalization.

In the past few years, pressure has been mounting for corporate governance bodies to increase their vigilance, transparency, and accountability. Most of these changes were long overdue. However, social reforms are often characterized by an impetus and a bluntness of their own as they shake up the status quo, a force which cannot be made more subtle or selective or slowed down. Thus, social reforms often drag along other socially valuable phenomena that are not necessarily tied to the main object of the reform. The institutionalization of corporate governance threatens to eliminate the personal ties between executives, ties which bring them closer to each other and make the job environment at the apex more collaborative and humane. Such institutionalization also threatens to do away with all the politics germane to a group of people in charge of the definition of the ends and means of organizations. Paraphrasing Max Weber, we could say that corporate governance reforms at the beginning of the twenty-first century are becoming yet another step in the direction of incarcerating economic activities into the infamous iron cage.

Small numbers at the top constitute one of the last strongholds of resistance to an expanding regime of depersonalization and bureaucratization of governance in organizations, of economic life, and of society.

The ultimate rationale for employing small numbers at the top is the joy and strength derived from sharing with trusted others a position in the upper echelons of organizations which offers the greatest political leverage for unleashing the full potential of organized collective action. With this book, we hope to facilitate the release of this potential.

Appendix

Appendix table. Some examples of small numbers at the top

Organization	Names	Shared roles[a]	Period[b]	Activity	Financial data[c]	Web page
1. Accor Group	Gérard Pélisson Paul Dubrule	Co-founders, co-CEOs, & co-chairmen Founding co-chairmen	1983–1997 1983–present	European leader and one of the world's largest groups in hotels (including travel agencies, casinos, and restaurants) and services (innovative solutions to help organisations and public institutions create new ways to motivate and win the loyalty of their employees and citizens).	Sales: $ 8.59 billion Market value: $ 8.99 billion Profit: $ 0.38 billion *Source:* Forbes 2000	http://www.accor.com
2. Altadis Group	Pablo Isla Álvarez de Tejera Jean-Dominique Comolli	Co-chairmen	2000–present	The Altadis Group, created through the merger of Seita and Tabacalera, is one of the leading players in the European tobacco companies, as well as in the wholesale distribution sector. Altadis holds key positions in its three areas of activity. It ranks third in Western Europe in cigarettes, first in the world in cigars, and is one of the foremost distributors to convenience outlets in Southern Europe.	Sales: $ 9.45 billion Market value: $ 9.48 billion Profit: $ 0.46 billion *Source:* Forbes 2000	http://www.altadis.com

3. Ameritrade Holding Corporation	Mok Choe Raymond Dury	Co-chief information officers	June 2001–November 2001	Online brokerage industry. Through its Private Client and Institutional Client divisions, provides tiered levels of brokerage products and services tailored to meet the varying investing, trading, and execution needs of self-directed individual investors, financial institutions, and corporations.	Sales: $ 0.69 billion Market value: $ 7.05 billion Profit: $ 0.19 billion *Source*: Forbes 2000	http://www.amtd.com
4. Apple Computer Inc.	Steve Jobs Steve Wozniak	Co-founders	1976	Technology hardware, equipment, and software. Reinvented the personal computer in the 1980s with the Macintosh. Today, Apple continues to lead the industry in innovation with its award-winning desktop and notebook computers, OS X operating system, and iLife and professional applications. Apple is also spearheading the digital music revolution with its iPod portable music players and iTunes online music store.	Sales: $ 6.74 billion Market value: $ 8.50 billion Profit: $ 0.14 billion *Source*: Forbes 2000	http://www.apple.com

(*cont.*)

Organization	Names	Shared roles[a]	Period[b]	Activity	Financial data[c]	Web page
5. Arcelor	Joseph Kinsch Francis Mer	Co-chairmen	February 2002–May 2002	Arcelor, the merger of Aceralia, Arbed and, Usinor, is the world's biggest producer of flat carbon steel and long carbon steel, among the leaders in stainless steel production, and among the largest firms in Europe for distribution, transformation, and trading.	Sales: $ 25.77 billion Market value: $ 10.23 billion Profit: $ − 0.20 billion *Source:* Forbes 2000	http://www.arcelor.com
6. Banco Bilbao Vizcaya Argentaria Group	Francisco González Emilio Ybarra	Co-presidents	1999–2001	Banking. Global financial group with a solid position in the Spanish market and a leading franchise in Latin America. The principal business areas in which the BBVA Group operates are three: retail, wholesale, and Latin American.	Sales: $ 24.10 billion Market value: $ 44.67 billion Profit: $ 2.81 billion *Source:* Forbes 2000	http://www.bbva.com
7. Banco Popular Español Group	Javier Valls Luis Valls Javier Valls Ángel Ron	Co-chairmen Co-chairmen	1989–2004 2004–present	Global financial group. Banco Popular is the third largest banking group in Spain.	Sales: $ 3.32 billion Market value: $ 14.38 billion Profit: $ 0.67 billion *Source:* Forbes 2000	http://www. bancopopular.es/eng
8. Banco Zaragozano	Alberto Cortina Alberto Alcocer	Co-presidents	1997–2003	Banking. Belongs to the Barclays Group since 2003.	Total revenues: $ 0.235 billion Profit (before taxes): $ 0.070 billion *Source:* Banco Zaragozano (figures refer to 2002)[d]	http://www. bancozaragozano.es

9. Bed, Bath and Beyond	Leonard Feinstein Warren Eisenberg	Co-founders & co-chairmen	1971–present	Superstores selling predominantly better quality domestic merchandise and home furnishings.	Net sales (March 31): $ 3.6655 billion Net profit (March 31): $ 0.480 billion *Source:* Annual Report, 2003	http://www.bedbathandbeyond.com
10. Citigroup Inc.	John Reed Sandy Weill	Co-CEOs	1998–2000	Financial services. Citigroup is largely organized into five groups: Citigroup Global Consumer Group, the Global Corporate and Investment Banking Group, Citigroup Global Investment Management, Citigroup International, and Smith Barney.	Sales: $ 94.71 billion Market value: $ 255.30 billion Profit: $ 17.85 billion *Source:* Forbes 2000	http://www.citigroup.com
11. Corporación Financiera Alba	Juan March Delgado Carlos March Delgado	Co-chairmen	1998–present	Holding company. It forms part of Grupo March, one of Spain's leading business and financial groups, in which Banca March and Fundación Juan March are also included.	Revenues: € 1.118 billion Net profit: € 0.183 billion *Source:* Annual Report, 2003	http://www.cf-alba.com/index.cfm
12. Crédit Suisse Group	Oswald J. Grübel John J. Mack	Co-CEOs	2003–2004 (July)	Financial services in Europe and other selected markets. Investment products, private banking, and financial advisory services for private and corporate clients.	Operating income: $ 0.213 billion Net profit: $ 0.040 billion *Source:* Annual Report, 2003[e]	http://www.credit-suisse.com

(cont.)

(*cont.*)

Organization	Names	Shared roles[a]	Period[b]	Activity	Financial data[c]	Web page
13. Daimler-Chrysler	Jürgen E. Schrempp Robert J. Eaton	Co-chairmen	1998–2000	Automotive industry: its product portfolio ranges from small cars to sports cars and luxury sedans; and from versatile vans to heavy duty trucks or comfortable coaches.	Sales: $ 157.13 billion Market value: $ 47.43 billion Profit: $ 5.12 billion *Source:* Forbes 2000	http://www.daimlerchrysler.com
14. Diamond Entertainment Corporation	James Lu Jeffrey I. Schillen	Co-CEOs & co-chairmen	2002–present	Distribution and sale: videocassettes, DVDs, general merchandise, toys, and Cine-Chrome gift cards.	Revenues: $ 0.004 billion Gross profit: $ 0.001 billion *Source:* Yahoo Finance. Figures refer to 2002.	http://www.e-dmec.com
15. DreamWorks SKG	Steven Spielberg Jeffrey Katzenberg David Geffen	Co-founders	1994	Leading producer of live-action pictures, animated feature films, network and cable television programming, home video and DVD entertainment and consumer products. In July 2004, DreamWorks split off its animation unit, Dream Works Animation. Jeffrey Katzenberg is the CEO of the new independent company		http://www.dreamworks.com/ http://www.dreamworksanimation.com

16. e.Biscom	Silvio Scaglia Emanuele Angelidis	Co-CEOs	1999–2004	Italian network operator and telecommunications solutions.	Revenues: $ 6.81 billion EBITDA: $ 1.40 billion Net income: $ −2.59 billion *Source:* Annual Report, 2003[f]	http://www.ebiscom.it
17. EADS (European Aeronautic Defence and Space Company)	Arnaud Lagardère Manfred Bischoff	Co-chairmen	2003–present	A global leader in aerospace, defence and related services	Sales: $ 31.41 billion Market value: $ 18.7 billion Profit: $ −0.31 billion *Source:* Forbes 2000	http://www.eads.com
	Philippe Camus Rainer Hertrich	Co-CEOs	2000–2005			
	Nöel Forgeard Thomas Enders	Co-CEOs[g]	2005–			
18. Eurotunnel	Alastair Morton Andre Bénard	Co-chairmen	1987–1996	Eurotunnel manages the infrastructure of the Channel Tunnel and operates accompanied truck shuttle and passenger shuttle (car and coach) services between Folkestone, UK and Calais/Coquelles, France	Sales: $ 1.01 billion Market value: $ 3.29 billion Profit: $ −2.83 billion *Source:* Forbes 2000	http://www.eurotunnel.com
19. Exelon	John Rowe Corbin McNeill	Co-CEOs & co-chairmen	2000–2002	Public utility holding company that operates in energy delivery and generation	Sales: $ 15.81 billion Market value: $ 21.44 billion Profit: $ 0.79 billion *Source:* Forbes 2000	http://www.exeloncorp.com

(*cont.*)

(*cont.*)

Organization	Names	Shared roles[a]	Period[b]	Activity	Financial data[c]	Web page
20. Fiat Group	Gabriele Galateri Paolo Fresco	Co-CEOs	June 2002–December 2002	Motor industry. Design, manufacture, and marketing of cars, trucks, tractors, agricultural machinery, construction equipment, motor vehicle engines and components, and production systems.	Sales: $ 58.22 billion Market value: $ 6.92 billion Profit: $ −4.15 billion *Source:* Forbes 2000	http://www.fiatgroup.com/home.php?lang=en
21. Fortis	Hans Bartelds Maurice Lippens Jaap Glasz Maurice Lippens	Co-chairmen Co-chairmen	1990–2002 2002–2004	Integrated financial services provider active in the fields of banking and insurance.	Sales: $ 52.51 billion Market value: $ 30.19 billion Profit: $ 0.56 billion *Source:* Forbes 2000	http://www.fortis.com
22. Friedman Billings Ramsey Group	Emmanuel Friedman Eric Billings Russ Ramsey Emmanuel Friedman Eric Billings Richard Hendrix J. Rock Tonkel	Co-founders Co-CEOs & co-chairmen Co-CEOs & co-chairman Co-presidents	1989 1999–2001 2001–present 2004–present	Investment bank, institutional brokerage, asset management, and private client services.	Sales: $ 0.63 billion Market value: $ 4.23 billion Profit: $ 0.20 billion *Source:* Forbes 2000	http://www.fbr.com
23. Golden West Financial	Herbert M. Sandler Marion O. Sandler (wife)	Co-CEOs & co-chairmen	1963–present	The publicly held holding company for World Savings (savings and lending institution) and Atlas (an investment manager and distributor of no load mutual funds and tax-deferred annuities)	Sales: $ 3.84 billion Market value: $ 16.28 billion Profit: $ 1.11 billion *Source:* Forbes 2000	http://www.worldsavings.com/servlet/wsavings/golden-west/golden-west.html

# Company	Names	Titles	Years	Description	Financials	URL
24. Goldman Sachs	John Weinberg	Co-CEOs	1976–1984	Global investment banking, securities, and investment management	Sales: $ 22.84 billion Market value: $ 50.12 billion Profit: $ 2.54 billion *Source:* Forbes 2000	http://www.gs.com
	John Whitehead					
	Steve Friedman Robert Rubin	Co-chairmen	1990–1992			
	Henry M. Paulson Jon S. Corzine	Co-chairmen	1998–1999			
	John L. Thornton John A. Thain	Co-presidents & co-COOs	1998–2003			
25. Google	Larry Page	Co-founder	1998	Internet search engine services. Organizes the world's information and makes it universally accessible and useful.	Revenues: $ 0.966 billion Profit: $ 0.106 billion *Source:* Annual Report, 2003	http://www.google.com/intl/en/corporate/index.html
		CEO	1998–2001			
		Co-president	2001–present			
	Sergey Brin	Co-founder	1998			
		President	1998–2001			
		Co-president	2001–present			
	Eric C. Schmidt	Chairman	2001–present			
		CEO				
26. Guess	Maurice Marciano Paul Marciano	Co-chairmen & co-CEOs	1982–present	Design and market a leading lifestyle collection of casual apparel and accessories for women, men, children, and babies.	Net revenues: $ 0.637 billion Net earnings: $ 0.007 billion *Source:* Annual Report, 2003	http://www.guessinc.com
27. Hermès	Patrick Thomas Jean Louis Dumas	Co-chairmen	2004–present	Luxury and cosmetics.	Sales: $ 1.30 billion Market value: $ 7.57 billion Profit: $ 0.23 billion *Source:* Forbes 2000	http://www.hermes.com

(cont.)

Organization	Names	Shared roles[a]	Period[b]	Activity	Financial data[c]	Web page
28. Hewlett Packard	William R. Hewlett David Packard	Co-founders	1939	Technology hardware and equipment.	Sales: $ 73.06 billion Market value: $ 70.20 billion Profit: $ 2.54 billion *Source:* Forbes 2000	http://www.hp.com
29. Intel	Gordon Moore Bob Noyce[b]	Co-founders	1968	Semiconductor manufacturing and technology. Microprocessors, microchips, chipsets, motherboards, hardware components . . .	Sales: $ 30.14 billion Market value: $ 196.87 billion Profit: $ 5.64 billion *Source:* Forbes 2000	http://www.intel.com
30. Intesa BCI	Lino Benassi Christian Merle	Co-CEOs	2001–2002	Banking.	Net income $ 1.533 billion *Source:* Annual Report, 2003[i]	http://www.bancaintesa.it/piu/jsp/Home
31. JCDecaux	Jean Francois Decaux Jean Charles Decaux	Co-CEOs & co-chairmen of the Executive Board	1989–present	Advertising group. A world leader in outdoor advertising and the largest outdoor operator in Europe.	Revenues: $ 1.753 billion EBITDA: $ 0.4169 billion *Source:* Annual Report, 2003	http://www.jcdecaux.com
32. J&R Music and Computer World	Joe Friedman Rachelle Friedman (wife)	Co-CEOs & co-founders	1971–present	Electronics retailer. Also sells its products online and through a catalog.		http://www.jr.com
33. Keefe, Bruyette & Woods	Joseph J. Berry John Duffy	Co-CEOs	1999–2001	Full-service investment bank that specializes exclusively in the financial services sector.		http://www.kbw.com

Company	Names	Position	Period	Description	Financials	Website
34. Kraft Foods Inc.	Betsy Holden Roger Deromedi	Co-CEOs	2001–2004	Kraft Foods is a global leader in branded foods and beverages. Built on more than 100 years of quality and innovation, Kraft has grown from modest beginnings to become the largest food and beverage company headquartered in North America and second largest in the world, marketing many popular brands in more than 150 countries.	Net revenues (consolidated operation results): $ 31.010 billion Net earning: $ 3.476 billion *Source:* Financial Report, 2003	http://www.kraft.com
35. Laura Ashley Holdings	Ainum Mohd-Saaid Rebecca Annapillai Navaredham	Co-CEOs	2003–present	Women's and children's clothing and home furnishings.	Turnover: $ 5.058 billion Profit before tax: $ 0.055 billion *Source:* Annual Report, 2003[j]	http://www.lauraashley.com
36. Lehman Brothers Holdings Inc.	Joseph M. Gregory Bradley Jack	Co-COOs	May 2002–May 2004	Investment banking and financial services firm. It is a market leader in equity and fixed income, trading and research, investment banking, private equity, and private banking.	Sales: $ 17.10 billion Market value: $ 23.01 billion Profit: $ 1.47 billion *Source:* Forbes 2000	http://www.lehman.com

(cont.)

(*cont.*)

Organization	Names	Shared roles[a]	Period[b]	Activity	Financial data[c]	Web page
37. Marakon	Peter Kontes Jim McTaggart	Co-chairmen & co-founders	2000–2004	International management consulting firm that advises senior executives on the issues most impacting company performance and long-term value.	Revenues (2002): $ 0.014 billion *Source*: Marakon web page	http://www.marakon.com
38. Meritage Homes Corporation	Steve J. Hilton John R, Landon	Co-chairmen & co-CEOs	1997–present	Homebuilding industry. Meritage has delivered approximately 20,000 homes, ranging from entry level to semi-custom luxury. The company operates in rapidly growing states of the South and West of the USA, including five of the top ten housing markets in the country.	Revenues: $ 1.462 billion Net earnings: $ 0.094 billion *Source*: Annual Report, 2003	http://www.meritagehomes.com/home.html
39. Miramax Film Corp.	Harvey Weinstein Robert Weinstein (brothers)	Co-founders & Co-chairmen	1979–present	Produce and distribute films. Virtually created the independent film movement. (Miramax was purchased by Walt Disney in 1993, but the contract will be revised in 2005. Belongs to Walt Disney Studios Entertainment.)		http://www.miramax.com

40. New Line Cinema Corporation (a subsidiary of AOL Time Warner)	Michael Lyne Robert K. Shaye	Co-CEOs & co-chairmen	2001–present	Independent film company.	Revenues: $ 2.1934 billion Operating income before depreciation and amortization: $ 0.293 billion *Source:* Annual Report, 2003 (AOL Time Warner)	http://www.newline. com
41. News Corporation	Chase Carey Peter Chernin	Co-COOs	1996–2002	News Corporation is a diversified international media and entertainment company with operations in eight industry segments: filmed entertainment; television; cable network programming; direct broadcast satellite television; magazines and inserts; newspapers; book publishing; and other.	Sales: $ 20.16 billion Market value: $ 55.43 billion Profit: $ 1.22 billion *Source:* Forbes 2000	http://www.newscorp. com
42. Nike	Charles D. Denson Mark G. Parker	Co-presidents, NIKE brand	2001–present	Designs and markets a wide variety of athletic footwear, apparel, and equipment for competitive and recreational use.	Nike Inc. Sales: $ 11.25 billion Market value: $ 19.03 billion Profit: $ 0.81 billion *Source:* Forbes 2000	http://www.nike.com

(*cont.*)

(*cont.*)

Organization	Names	Shared roles[a]	Period[b]	Activity	Financial data[c]	Web page
43. Power Corporation of Canada	André Desmarais Paul Desmarais Jr.	Co-CEOs	1996–present	A diversified management and holding company, with holdings in leading financial services and the communications sector.	Sales: $ 12.10 billion Market value: $ 7.76 billion Profit: $ 0.41 billion *Source:* Forbes 2000	http://www. powercorp.com
44. Ralston Purina	W. Patrick McGinnis J. Patrick Mulcahy	Co-CEOs & Co-presidents	1997–1999	Production of pet products. On December 12, 2001, Ralston Purina Company was acquired by Nestlé S. A. Ralston Purina was then merged with a subsidiary of Nestlé.		http://www. ralstonpurina.com/ company
45. Regal Entertainment Group	Michael L. Campbell Kart C. Hall	Co-chairmen & Co-CEOs	1998–present	Regal Entertainment Group is the largest motion picture exhibitor in the world. The Company's theatre circuit, comprising Regal Cinemas, United Artists Theatres and Edwards Theatres.	Sales: $ 2.21 billion Market value: $ 2.97 billion Profit: $ 0.16 billion *Source:* Forbes 2000	http://www. regalcinemas.com/ corporate/about.html
46. Reliance Group	Anil D. Ambani Mukesh D. Ambani (brothers)	Co-CEOs	2002–present	Exploration and production of oil and gas, refining and marketing, petrochemicals (polyester, polymers, and intermediates), textiles, financial services and insurance, power, telecom and infocom initiatives.	Sales: $ 9.57 billion Market value: $ 18.40 billion Profit: $ 0.84 billion *Source:* Forbes 2000	http://www.ril.com

47. Research in Motion	James L. Basillie Mike Lazadiris	Co-CEOs	1993–present	Designer, manufacturer and marketer of innovative wireless solutions for the worldwide mobile communications market.	Sales: $ 0.32 billion Market value: $ 7.42 billion Profit: $ −0.16 billion *Source:* Forbes 2000	http://www.rim.net
48. Reuters America Inc.	Alexander Hungate Phil Lynch	Co-COOs & co-CEOs	January 2000–January 2001; January 2001– September 2001	Global information company providing indispensable information tailored for professionals in the financial services, media, and corporate markets.	Sales: $ 5.76 billion Market value: $ 9.73 billion Profit: $ −0.65 billion *Source:* Forbes 2000	http://about.reuters. com/home
49. Santander Group	Emilio Botín Jose María Amusátegui	Co-presidents	1999–2001	Banking group. Santander Group is Spain's largest banking group and the second biggest in the euro zone. Santander Group specializes in retail banking and has a strong presence in Europe and Latin America. The retail banking work generates 84% of the Group's net attributable income and is their main competitive edge. As well as retail banking they also have global businesses: asset management, corporate banking, investment banking, private banking, and treasury	Sales: $ 28.70 billion Market value: $ 44.67 billion Profit: $ 5.678 billion *Source:* Forbes 2000	http://www. gruposantander.com

(cont.)

(*cont.*)

Organization	Names	Shared roles[a]	Period[b]	Activity	Financial data[c]	Web page
50. SAP AG	Hennig Kagermann Hasso Platter	Co-CEOs & co-chairmen	1998–2003	Business solutions for all types of industries and for every major market.	Sales: $ 8.84 billion Market value: $ 54.10 billion Profit: $ 1.36 billion *Source:* Forbes 2000	http://www.sap.com
51. Sapient	Jerry A. Greenberg J. Stuart Moore	Co-CEOs, co-chairmen, & co-founders	1991–present	A business innovator that helps its clients achieve extraordinary results from their customer relationships, business operations, and technology.	Revenue (net sales of the Corporation): $ 0.254 billion Profit: $ 0.023 billion *Source:* Annual Report, 2004	http://www.sapient.com
52. Charles Schwab Corporation, Inc.	David Pottruck Charles Schwab	Co-CEOs	1997–2002	Financial services. The Charles Schwab Corporation is a financial holding company engaged, through its subsidiaries, in securities brokerage and related financial services. Charles Schwab & Co., Inc. (Schwab) is a securities broker-dealer with branch offices in forty-eight states, as well as a branch in the Commonwealth of Puerto Rico	Sales: $ 3.84 billion Market value: $ 17.09 billion Profit: $ 0.25 billion *Source:* Forbes 2000	http://www.schwab.com

53. Secured Services, Inc.	Shawn Kreloff Michael Dubreuil	Co-chairmen	2004–present	Identity and access management security software and services.	Expected revenues, 2004 $ 0.015 billion *Source:* Web page	http://www.secured-services.com/company/index.htm
54. SINA	Daniel Chiang Yongji Duan	Co-chairmen	2003–present	Leading online media company and value-added information service provider for China and for global Chinese communities.	Net Revenues: $ 0.116 billion	http://corp.sina.com.cn/eng/sina.index.eng.htm
	Hurst Lin	Co-COO	2003–present		Gross profit: $ 0.080 billion Net income: $ 0.031 billion *Source:* Annual Report, 2003	
55. J. M. Smucker Company	Timothy P. Smucker Richard K. Smucker	Co-CEOs	2001–present	The company is the market leader in fruit spreads, peanut butter, shortening and oils, ice cream toppings, and health and natural foods beverages in North America under such icon brands as Smucker's®, Jif,® and Crisco®. Has over 4,500 employees worldwide and distributes products in more than forty-five countries.	Net sales: $ 1.417 billion Net income: $ 0.111 billion *Source:* Annual Report, 2004 (April 2004 year ended)	http://www.smuckers.com/home.asp

(*cont.*)

Organization	Names	Shared roles[a]	Period[b]	Activity	Financial data[c]	Web page
56. Sony Corporation[k]	Akio Morita Masaru Ibuka	Co-founders	1946	Electronics Music Movies, television Video/online Games Robots Internet Services / Applications Business solutions	Sales: $ 63.23 billion Market value: $ 38.00 billion Profit: $ 0.98 billion *Source:* Forbes 2000	http://www.sony.net
57. Sony Pictures Classics (autonomous company of Sony Pictures Entertainment)	Michael Barker Tom Bernard Marcie Bloom	Co-presidents	1992–present	Produces, acquires and distributes independent films from America and around the world		http://www.sonyclassics.com
58. Spiegel Group	Michael R. Moran	Chairman of the Office of the President and Chief Legal Officer	1998–2001	On March 17, 2003 Spiegel, Inc. and its principal operating subsidiaries (with the exception of First Consumers National Bank) filed voluntary petitions for reorganization under chapter 11 of the US Bankruptcy Code in the United States Bankruptcy Court in the Southern District of New York.		http://www.thespiegelgroup.com/
	James Sievers	Office of the President and Chief Financial Officer				
	Harold Dahlstrand	Office of the President and Chief Human Resources Officer	1997–1999			

59. Sun Microsystems	Andy Bechtolsheim William Joy Vinod Khosla Scott McNealy	Co-founders	1982	Technology hardware and equipment. Solve complex network computing problems for governments, enterprises, and service providers; through virtualization and automation; through open standards and platform-independent Java technologies.	Sales: $ 11.20 billion Market value: $ 18.51 billion Profit: $ −1.45 billion *Source:* Forbes 2000	http://www.sun.com
60. Telecom Italia Group	Carlo Orazio Buora Enrico Bondi	Co-CEOs	2001–2002	Telecommunications services. As Italy's leading information and communication technology enterprise, Telecom Italia's status as one of Europe's most solid and profitable blue-chip companies.	Sales: $ 32.99 billion Market value: $ 46.57 billion Profit: $ −0.81 billion *Source:* Forbes 2000	http://www. telecomitalia.it
	Carlo Orazio Buora Ricardo Ruggiero	Co-CEOs	2002–present	The Telecom Italia Group comprises Telecom Italia, TIM, Finsiel, Olivetti Tecnost, Telecom Italia Lab, and Telecom Italia Media.		
61. Teledesic	William Owens Craig McCaug (co-founder with Bill Gates)	Co-CEOs	1998–2002	Communications: create a communications network that will enable cost-effective access to telecommunications services such as computer networking, broadband Internet, interactive multimedia, and high quality voice.		http://www.teledesic. com

(*cont.*)

(*cont.*)

Organization	Names	Shared roles[a]	Period[b]	Activity	Financial data[c]	Web page
62. TradeStation Group	William R. Cruz Ralph L. Cruz (brothers)	Co-founders, Co-CEOs, Co-chairmen	1996–present	Electronic trading platform that offers state-of-the-art direct-access order execution and enables clients to design, test, monitor and automate their own custom trading strategies.	Revenues: $ 0.060 billion Net income: $ 0.012 billion *Source:* Web page	http://www.tradestation.com
63. Unilever	Niall FitzGerald	Chairman Unilever PLC Vice-Chairman Unilever NV	1996–2004	Supplier of fast moving consumer goods across foods, home and personal product categories.	Sales: $ 50.70 billion Market value: $ 72.19 billion Profit: $ 2.24 billion *Source:* Forbes 2000	http://www.unilever.com
	Antony Burgman	Chairman Unilever NV Vice-Chairman Unilever PLC	1999–present			
	Paul Cesau	Chairman Unilever PLC Vice-Chairman Unilever NV	2004–present			
64. Verizon	Ivan Seidenberg Charles R. Lee	Co-CEOs	2000–2002	Providers of communication services. Directory publishers.	Sales: $ 67.75 billion Market value: $ 103.97 billion Profit: $ 2.57 billion *Source:* Forbes 2000	http://www2.verizon.com

65. Veronis Suhler Stevenson	John Suhler John J. Veronis Jeffrey T. Stevenson	Co-CEOs & co-founders	1981–present	Media merchant bank.	Revenues: $ 0.068 billion Income: $ 7.494 billion *Source:* Annual Report, 2003	http://www.vss.com
66. Viacom Inc.	Tom Preston Leslie Moonves	Co-COOs & co-presidents	June 2004–present	Media. Hold preeminent positions in broadcast and cable television, radio, outdoor advertising and online. Leader in the creation, promotion and distribution of news, entertainment, sports, and music.	Sales: $ 25.85 billion Market value: $ 68.66 billion Profit: $ 2.47 billion *Source:* Forbes 2000	http://www.viacom.com
67. Warner Bros. Entertainment Inc.	Terry Semel Robert Daly	Co-CEOs & co-chairmen	1994–1999	Every aspect of the entertainment industry, from feature films to television, home video/DVD, animation, comic books, interactive entertainment and games, product and brand licensing, international cinemas, and broadcasting.	Revenues: $ 8.774 billion Operating income before depreciation and amortization: $ 1.172 billion *Source:* Annual Report, 2003 (AOL Time Warner)	http://www2. warnerbros.com/main/ homepage/homepage. html

(cont.)

(cont.)

Organization	Names	Shared roles[a]	Period[b]	Activity	Financial data[c]	Web page
68. Yahoo! Inc.	Jerry Yang David Filo	Co-founders & Chiefs Yahoo	1995–present	Internet and media communications company that offers online navigational directories. It also provides online business services designed to enhance web presence of its clients.	Sales: $ 1.63 billion Market value: $ 30.50 billion Profit: $ 0.24 billion Source: Forbes 2000	http://docs.yahoo.com/info/pr/index.html

Notes: [a] Co-founders, co-chairs, co-CEOs, co-COOs, co-CIOs, etc.

[b] "Period" is the time over which the roles listed in the third column have been shared by the individuals listed in the second column. The term "present" refers to December 2004.

[c] The Forbes 2000 (http://www.forbes.com/2004/03/24/04f2000land.html, accessed January 7, 2005) is a comprehensive list of the world's biggest and most powerful companies, as measured by a composite ranking for sales, profits, assets, and market value. The list spans fifty-one countries and twenty-seven industries. Collectively, the Forbes 2000 account for a substantial amount of global business: Aggregate sales are $19 trillion; profits, $760 billion; assets, $68 trillion; market value, $24 trillion; and worldwide employees, 64 million. All figures are in US dollars and are the latest available. Market value is as of February 13, 2003.

Sources: Exshare, FT Interactive Data, Reuters Fundamentals, and Worldscope via FactSet Research Systems; Bloomberg Financial Markets.

[d] Original data in million €. To perform the conversion we have used the European Central Bank euro/dollar exchange reference rate on December 31, 2002 (€ 1 = $ 1.0487) (http://www.ecb.int/stats/exchange/eurofxref/html/index.en.html#info).

[e] Original data in million CHF. To perform the conversion we have used the Federal Reserve Swiss franc/dollar exchange reference rate on December 31, 2003 (CHF1 = $ 0.8078), (http://www.federalreserve.gov/releases/h10/Hist/).

[f] Original data in million €. To perform the conversion we have used the European Central Bank euro/dollar exchange reference rate on December 31, 2003 (€1 = $ 1.263), (http://www.ecb.int/stats/exchange/eurofxref/html/index.en.html#info).

[g] *Source:* Company website.

[h] According to Intel's silver-anniversary publication *Defining Intel: 25 ears/25 vents* (Intel Corporation, 1993), "Andy Grove joined Bob and Gordon soon after Intel's incorporation and eventually became the third head of the 'three-headed monster', as Bib called it, that led Intel" (p. 4).

[i] Original data in billion €. To perform the conversion we have used the European Central Bank euro/dollar exchange reference rate on December 31, 2003 (€1 = $ 1.263), (http://www.ecb.int/stats/exchange/eurofxref/html/index.en.html#info).

[j] Original data in million £. To perform the conversion we have used the Federal Reserve pound sterling/dollar exchange reference rate on December 31, 2003 (£1 = $ 1.7842), (http://www.federalreserve.gov/releases/h10/Hist/).

[k] Tokyo Tsushin Kogyo K. K. – Toyko Telecommunications Engineering Corporation – changed its corporate name to Sony in 1958.

References

Abrahams, P. 2002. "McNealy Expands Role as Sun's President Resigns," *Financial Times*, May 1.

Agor, W. H. 1986. "The Logic of Intuition: How Top Executives Make Important Decisions," *Organizational Dynamics* 14 (3): 5–19.

Aguilera, R. V. and Jackson, G. 2003. "The Cross-National Diversity of Corporate Governance: Dimensions and Determinants," *Academy of Management Review* 28 (3): 447–466.

Allen, C. T. 2003. "Empress Jingu: A Shamaness Ruler in Early Japan," *Japan Forum* 15(1): 81–98.

Allen, W. T. and Berkley, W. R. 2003. "In Defense of CEO Chair," *Harvard Business Review* 81 (9): 24–25.

Alvarez, J. L. (ed.) 1997. *The Diffusion and Consumption of Business Knowledge*. London: Macmillan.

Alvarez, J. L. 2000. "Theories of Managerial Action and Their Impact on the Conceptualization of Executive Careers," in M. Peiperl and M. Arthur (eds.), *Career Frontiers: New Conceptions of Working Lives*. Oxford: Oxford University Press, pp. 127–137.

Alvarez, J. L., Gifra, J., and Ricart, J. E. 2005. *Los accionistas y el gobierno de la empresa: análisis de la situación española*. Barcelona: Editorial Deusto.

Alvarez, J. L., Mazza, C., Strandgaard, J., and Svejenova, S. 2005. "Shielding Idiosyncrasy from Isomorphic Pressures: Towards Optimal Distinctiveness in European Film Organization," *Organization* 12 (6).

Alvarez, J. L., Miller, P., Levy, J., and Svejenova, S. 2004. "Journeys to the Self: Using Moving Directors in the Classroom," *Journal of Management Education* 28 (3): 335–355.

Alvarez, J. L. and Svejenova, S. 2000. "The Almodóvar Brothers' Film Factory: Unbinding Art Through Tight Relationships," Case DG-1331-E, Research Department, IESE Business School, Barcelona.

2002a. "Symbiotic Careers in Movie Making: Pedro and Agustín Almodóvar," in M. A. Peiperl, M. B. Arthur, and N. Anand (eds.), *Career Creativity: Explorations in the Remaking of Work*. Oxford: Oxford University Press, pp. 183–209.

2002b. "Pairs at the Top: From Tandems to Coupled Careers." Presented at the Inaugural Conference of the Harvard Business School European Research Center, Paris.

2003. *La gestión del poder. Breviario de poder, influencia y ética para ejecutivos.* Barcelona: Ediciones Granica.

Arco, S. 2004. "La nueva fragancia de los jóvenes Puig," El País Negocios, June 20.

Argyris, C. 1976. *Personality and Organization: The Conflict between System and the Individual.* London: Harper Collins.

1991. "Teaching Smart People How to Learn," Harvard Business Review 69 (3): 99–110.

Argyris, C. and Schön, D. 1974. *Theory in Practice.* San Francisco: Jossey Bass.

Ariño, A. and de la Torre, J. 1998. "Learning from Failure: Towards an Evolutionary Model of Collaborative Ventures," *Organization Science* 9 (3): 306–325.

Arthur, M. B. 1994. "The Boundaryless Career: A New Perspective for Organizational Inquiry," *Journal of Organizational Behavior* 65: 295–306.

Arthur, M. B., Hall, D. T., and Lawrence, B. S. 1989. "Generating New Directions in Career Theory: The Case for a Transdisciplinary Approach," in M. B. Arthur, D. T. Hall, and B. S. Lawrence (eds.), *Handbook of Career Theory.* New York: Cambridge University Press, pp. 7–25.

Ashforth, B. E., Kreiner, G. E., and Fugate, M. 2000. "All in a Day's Work: Boundaries and Micro Role Transitions," *Academy of Management Review* 25 (3): 472–491.

Ashforth, B. E. and Saks, A. M. 1995. "Work-role Transitions: A Longitudinal Examination of the Nicholson Model," *Journal of Occupational and Organizational Psychology* 68 (2): 157–175.

Athos, A. G. and Gabarro, J. J. (eds.) 1978. *Interpersonal Behavior: Communication and Understanding in Relationships.* Englewood Cliffs, NJ: Prentice-Hall.

Audia, P. G., Locke, E. A., and Smith, K. G. 2000. "The Paradox of Success: An Archival and a Laboratory Study of Strategic Persistence Following Radical Environmental Change," *Academy of Management Journal* 43 (5): 837–853.

Bacharach, S. B. and Lawler, E. J. 1980. *Power and Politics in Organizations.* San Francisco: Jossey-Bass.

Badowski, R. with Gittines, R. 2003. *Managing Up: How to Forge an Effective Relationship with Those Above You.* New York: Currency.

Baker, W. E. and Faulkner, R. R. 1991. "Role as Resource in the Hollywood Film Industry," *American Journal of Sociology* 97 (2): 279–309.

Balasz, K. 2002. "Take One Entrepreneur: The Recipe for Success of France's Great Chefs," *European Management Journal* 20 (3): 247–259.

Bales, R. F. 1955. "The Equilibrium Problem in Small Groups," in P. Hare, E. F. Borgatta, and R. F. Bales (eds.), *Small Groups*. New York: Alfred A. Knopf, pp. 449–490.

Ball, D. 2004. "Unilever Slashes Growth Forecasts," *Wall Street Journal Europe*, February 13–15.

Ballarín, E. and Boudeguer, R. M. 1993. "Banco Popular Español." Case DG-1064-E, IESE Business School, Barcelona.

Barber, B. 1983. *The Logic and Limits of Trust*. New Brunswick, NJ: Rutgers University Press.

Barley, S. R. 1990. "The Alignment of Technology and Structure Through Roles and Networks," *Administrative Science Quarterly* 35: 61–103.

Barnard, C. I. 1938. *The Functions of the Executive*. Cambridge, MA: Harvard University Press.

Barney, J. B. 1985. "Dimensions of Informal Social Network Structure: Toward a Contingency Theory of Informal Relations in Organizations," *Social Networks* 7: 1–46.

Bartlett, C. A. and Ghoshal, S. 1993. "Beyond the Reform: Toward a Managerial Theory of the Firm," *Strategic Management Journal* 14 (3): 23–47.

   1994. "Changing the Role of Top Management: Beyond Strategy to Purpose," *Harvard Business Review* 72 (6): 79–89.

   1998a. "Beyond the Russian Doll Management Model: New Personal Competencies for New Management Roles," in Hambrick, Nadler, and Tushman (eds.), pp. 70–97.

   1998b. *Managing Across Borders. The Transnational Solution*, 2nd edn. Boston: Harvard Business School Press.

Bebchuk, L. A. 2004. "The Case for Increasing Shareholder Power." Discussion Paper 500, John M. Olin Center for Law, Economics, and Business, Harvard Law School, Cambridge, MA.

Becker, H. 1982. *Art Worlds*. Berkeley: University of California Press.

Becker, H. and Useem, R. H. 1942. "Sociological Analysis of the Dyad," *American Sociological Review* 7 (1): 13–26.

Beersma, B., Hollenbeck, J. R., Humphrey, S. E., Moon, H. K., Conlon, D. E., and Ilgen, D. R. 2003. "Cooperation, Competition, and Team Performance: Towards a Contingency Approach," *Australian Journal of Psychology* Supplement 55: 115–119.

Belbin, R. M. 1981. *Management Teams*. Oxford: Butterworth-Heinemann.

   1998. *The Coming Shape of Organization*. Oxford: Butterworth-Heinemann.

   2000. *Team Roles at Work*. Oxford: Butterworth-Heinemann.

Belbin, R. M., Aston, B. R., and Mottram, R. D. 1976. "Building Effective Management Teams," *Journal of General Management* 3 (3): 23–24.

Bendix, R. 1956. *Work and Authority in Industry*. New York: Wiley.

Biddle, B. J. 1986. "Recent Developments in Role Theory," *Annual Review of Sociology* 12: 67–92.

Birkinshaw, J., Nobel, R., and Ridderstale, J. 2002. "Knowledge as a Contingency Variable: Do the Characteristics of Knowledge Predict Organization Structure?", *Organization Science* 13 (3): 274–289.

Blair, M. M. 1995. *Ownership and Control: Rethinking Corporate Governance for the Twenty-First Century*. Washington, DC: The Brookings Institution.

Blau, P. M. 1964. *Exchange and Power in Social Life*. New Brunswick, NJ: Transaction Books.

   1969. "The Structure of Social Associations," in W. L. Wallace (ed.), *Sociological Theory*. London: Heinemann, pp. 186–200.

   1974. "Presidential Address: Parameters of Social Structure," *American Sociological Review* 39 (5): 615–635.

Bloom, A. 1991. *The Republic of Plato*, translated with notes and interpretative essay by A. Bloom, 2nd edn. New York: Basic Books.

Blossfeld, H.-P. and Drobnic, S. (eds.) 2001. *Careers of Couples in Contemporary Society: From Male Breadwinner to Dual-Earner Families*. Oxford: Oxford University Press.

Blumer, H. 1969. "Sociological Implications of the Thought of George Herbert Mead," in W. L. Wallace (ed.), *Sociological Theory*. London: Heinemann, pp. 234–244.

Bourgeois, L. J. 1980. "Strategy and Environment: A Conceptual Integration," *Academy of Management Review* 5 (1): 25–39.

Boyd, B. K. 1995. "CEO Duality and Firm Performance: A Contingency Model," *Strategic Management Journal* 16: 301–311.

Brady, D. 2004. "The Brains behind BlackBerry: Research in Motion's Co-CEOs Keep Taking Wireless E-mail to the Next Level," *Business Week*, April 19.

Bremner, B., Edmondson, G., Dawson, C., Welch, D., and Kerwin, K. 2004. "Nissan's Boss," *Business Week*, October 4.

Brockman, J. 1996. *Digerati: Encounters with the Cyber Elite*. San Francisco: HardWired Books.

Brooker, K. 2004. "LOEWS – Like Father, Like Son," *Fortune*, June 28.

Brorsen, J. P. and Strandgaard, J. 2002. "In the Borderland between Art and Business: Knowledge Management in Zentropa." Working Paper, Copenhagen Business School.

Bruch, H. and Ghoshal, S. 2004. *A Bias for Action: How Effective Managers Harness Their Willpower, Achieve Results, and Stop Wasting Time*. Boston: Harvard Business School Press.

Burns, T. 1961. "Micropolitical Mechanisms of Institutional Change," *Administrative Science Quarterly* 6 (3): 257–282.

1977. *The BBC: Public Institution and Private World*. London: Macmillan.

1994. "Preface to the Third Edition", in T. Burns and G. M. Stalker, *The Management of Innovation*, 3rd edn. Oxford: Oxford University Press.

Burns, T. and Stalker, G. M. 1961. *The Management of Innovation*. Oxford: Oxford University Press.

Burt, R. S. 1992. *Structural Holes: The Social Structure of Competition*. Cambridge, MA: Harvard University Press.

1997. "The Contingent Value of Social Capital," *Administrative Science Quarterly* 42 (2): 339–365.

Cadbury, A. 2002. *Corporate Governance and Chairmanship: A Personal View*. Oxford: Oxford University Press.

Callero, P. L. 1994. "From Role-playing to Role-using: Understanding Role as a Resource," *Social Psychology Quarterly* 57 (3): 228–243.

Cannella, A. A. and Monroe, M. J. 1997. "Contrasting Perspectives on Strategic Leaders: Toward a More Realistic View of Managers," *Journal of Management* 23 (3): 213–237.

Cannella, A. A. and Shen, W. 2001. "So Close and Yet so Far. Promotion versus Exit for CEO Heirs Apparent," *Academy of Management Journal* 44 (2): 252–270.

Caplow, T. A. 1956. "A Theory of Coalitions in the Triad," *American Sociological Review* 21: 489–493.

Carter, C. B. and Lorsch, J. W. 2004. *Rethinking Corporate Boards for the Twenty-First Century*. Boston: Harvard Business School Press.

Castro, P. 1991. "Una pareja rentable: Javier y Luis Valls", *Dinero*, February 9.

Champion, D. and Carr, N. G. 2000. "Starting Up in High Gear," *Harvard Business Review* 78 (4): 92–100.

Child, J. and Ellis, T. 1973. "Predictors of Variation in Managerial Roles," *Human Relations* 26 (2): 227–251.

Cianni, M. and Wnuck, D. 1997. "Individual Growth and Team Enhancement: Moving Toward a New Model of Career Development," *Academy of Management Executive* 11 (1): 105–115.

Cifuentes, M. 1989. "El Banco Popular tendrá dos presidentes antes de 1992," *El Periódico*, January 27.

Clegg, S. and Courpasson, D. 2004. "Political Hybrids: Tocquevillean Views on Project Organizations," *Journal of Management Studies* 41 (4): 525–547.

Cockerill, T., Hunt, J. and Schroder, H. 1995. "Managerial Competencies: Fact or Fiction?", *Business Strategy Review* 6(3): 1–13.

Coffey, R. E., Athos, A. G., and Raynolds, P. A. (1968). *Behavior in Organizations: A Multidimensional View*. Englewood Cliffs, NJ: Prentice-Hall

Cohen, A. R. and Bradford, D. L. 1989. *Influence without Authority*. New York: Wiley.

Cohen, I. and Lachman, R. 1988. "The Generality of the Strategic Contingencies Approach to Sub-unit Power," *Organization Studies* 9 (3): 371–391.

Coleman, J. S. 1990. *Foundations of Social Theory*. Cambridge, MA: Harvard University Press.

Collet, V. 2002. "Charmes et mystères du pilotage à deux," *Le Figaro Enterprises*, March 18.

Conrad, J. 2000. *Heart of Darkness*. London: Penguin Books.

Coombes, P. and Wong, S. C.-Y. (2004). "Chairman and CEO – One Job or Two?," *McKinsey Quarterly* 2: 42–48.

Cornelius, P. K. and Kogut, B. (eds.) 2003. *Corporate Governance and Capital Flows in a Global Economy*. New York: Oxford University Press.

Coser, R. L. 1966. "Role Distance, Sociological Ambivalence, and Transitional Status Systems," *American Journal of Sociology* 72 (2): 173–187.

Courpasson, D. 2000. "Managerial Strategies of Domination. Power in Soft Bureaucracies," *Organization Studies* 21 (1): 141–161.

Cox, C. J. and Cooper, C. L. 1989. "The Making of the British CEO: Childhood, Work Experience, Personality, and Management Style," *Academy of Management Executive* 3 (3): 241–245.

Crozier, M. 1964. *The Bureaucratic Phenomenon*. Chicago: University of Chicago Press.

Cubeiro, J. C. 1998. "El mejor superjefe es . . . un tándem," *Actualidad Económica*, July 13.

Cunliffe, A. L. 2001. "Managers as Practical Authors: Reconstructing our Understanding of Management Practice," *Journal of Management Studies* 38 (3): 351–371.

Cunningham, C. R. and Murray, S. 2005. "Two Executives, One Career," *Harvard Business Review* 83 (2): 125–131.

Cyert, R. M. and March, J. G. 1963. *A Behavioral Theory of the Firm*. Englewood Cliffs, NJ: Prentice-Hall.

Daft, R., Sormunen, J., and Parks, D. 1988. "Chief Executive Scanning, Environmental Characteristics and Company Performance: An Empirical Study," *Strategic Management Journal* 9: 123–139.

Daily, C. M., Dalton, D. R., and Cannella, A. A. 2003. "Corporate Governance: Decades of Dialogue and Data," *Academy of Management Review* 28 (3): 371–382.

Daily, C. M. and Schwenk, C. 1996. "Chief Executive Officers, Top Management Teams, and Boards of Directors: Congruent or Countervailing Forces?," *Journal of Management* 22 (2): 185–202.

Dalton, M. 1959. *Men Who Manage*. New York: Wiley.

Daniel, R. D. 1965. "Team at the Top," *Harvard Business Review* 43 (2): 74–82.

Davidson, J. 2001. *Growing Up Harley-Davidson: Memoirs of a Motorcycle Dynasty*. Stillwater, MN: Voyageur Press.

Davis, G. F. and Thompson, T. A. 1994. "A Social Movement Perspective on Corporate Control," *Administrative Science Quarterly* 39 (1): 141–174.

Davis, J., Schoorman, F. D., and Donaldson, L. (1997). "Toward a Stewardship Theory of Management," *Academy of Management Review* 22 (1): 20–47.

De Bruin, A. and Lewis, K. 2004. "Toward Enriching United Career Theory: Familial Entrepreneurship and Copreneurship," *Career Development International* 9(7): 638–646.

De Felipe, F. 1999. *Joel y Ethan Coen: El cine siamés*. Barcelona: Editorial Glénat.

De Jong, G. and Van Witteloostuijn, A. 2004. "Successful Corporate Democracy: Sustainable Cooperation of Capital and Labor in the Dutch Breman Group," *Academy of Management Executive* 18 (3): 54–66.

DeFillippi, R. J. and Arthur, M. B. 1994. "The Boundariless Career: A Competency-based Perspective," *Journal of Organizational Behavior* 15 (4): 307–24.

Dell, M., Rollins, K., Stewart, T. A., and O'Brien, L. 2005. "Execution without Excuses: The HBR Interview," *Harvard Business Review*, March, pp. 102–111.

Delmar, D. R. 2003. "The Rise of the CSO," *Journal of Business Strategy* 24 (2): 8–10.

DiMaggio, P. and Powell, W. W. 1983. "The Iron Cage Revisited: Institutional Isomorphism and Collective Rationality in Organizational Fields," *American Sociological Review* 48: 147–160.

Dobbin, F., Dierkes, J., Kwok, M., and Zorn, D. 2001. "The Rise and Stagnation of the COO: Fad and Fashion in Corporation Titles." Working Paper, Princeton University. http://www.wjh.harvard.edu/~dobbin/cv/unpublished/2001_COO_dierkes.pdf (accessed January 2005).

Donaldson, G. and Lorsch, J. W. 1983. *Decision Making at the Top: The Shaping of Strategic Decision*. New York: Basic Books.

Donaldson, L. 2001. *The Contingency Theory of Organizations*. London: Sage Publications.

Drazin, R. and Sandelands, L. 1992. "Autogenesis: A Perspective on the Process of Organizing," *Organization Science* 3 (2): 230–249.

Drucker, P. F. 1954. *The Practice of Management.* New York: Harper and Brothers.

2004. "What Makes an Effective Executive," *Harvard Business Review* 82 (6): 58–64.

Dumas, A. 1844. *Les Trois Mousquetaires.* Paris: Le Siècle.

Duncan, R. B. 1972. "Characteristics of Organizational Environments and Perceived Environmental Uncertainty," *Administrative Science Quarterly* 17 (3): 313–327.

1976. "The Ambidextrous Organization: Designing Dual Structures for Innovation," in R. H. Kilman, L. R. Pondy, and D. Slevin (eds.), *The Management of Organization.* New York: Elsevier North-Holland, vol. I, pp. 167–188.

Eccles, R. G. and Nohria, N. 1992. *Beyond the Hype.* Boston: Harvard Business School Press.

Eisenhardt, K. M. and Bourgeois, L. J., III. 1988. "Politics of Strategic Decision Making in High-Velocity Environments: Toward a Midrange Theory," *Academy of Management Journal* 31 (4): 737–770.

Eisenhardt K. M. and Schoonhoven, C. M. 1990. "Organizational Growth: Linking Founding Team, Strategy, Environment and Growth among U.S. Semiconductor Ventures 1978–1988," *Academy of Management Journal* 35 (3): 737–770.

Ellis, S., Almor, T., and Shenkar, O. 2002. "Structural Contingency Revisited: Toward a Dynamic System Model," *Emergence* 4 (4): 51–85.

Emerson, R. M. 1962. "Power-Dependence Relations," *American Sociological Review* 27 (1): 31–40.

Endlich, L. 2002. *Goldman Sachs: The Culture of Success.* London: Time Warner Paperbacks.

Ensley, M. D. and Pearce, C. L. 2001. "Shared Cognition in Top Management Teams: Implications for New Venture Performance," *Journal of Organizational Behavior* 22: 145–160.

Etzioni, A. 1961. *A Comparative Analysis of Complex Organizations.* New York: Free Press of Glencoe.

1965. "Dual Leadership in Complex Organizations," *American Sociological Review* 30 (5): 688–698.

Evans, P. 1999. "The Dualistic Leader: Thriving on Paradox," in S. Chowdhury (ed.), *Management 21C.* New York and London: Prentice-Hall/Financial Times.

2000. "Thrive on Paradox," *Executive Excellence* 17 (7): 11.

Evans, P., Pucik, V., and Barsoux, J.-L. 2002. *The Global Challenge: Frameworks for International Human Resource Management.* New York: McGraw-Hill/Irwin.

Farkas, C. M. and Wetlaufer, S. 1996. "The Ways Chief Executive Officers Lead," *Harvard Business Review* 74 (3): 110–123.

Farrell, M. P. 2001. *Collaborative Circles: Friendship Dynamics and Creative Work*. Chicago: University of Chicago Press.

Fiedler, F. E. 1965. "Engineer the Job to Fit the Manager," *Harvard Business Review* 43 (5): 115–123.

Financial Times 2004. "Too Power Hungry" (editorial comment) *Financial Times*, December 10.

Finkelstein, S. 1992. "Power in Top Management Teams: Dimensions, Measurement, and Validation," *Academy of Management Journal* 35 (3): 505–538.

Finkelstein, S. and Boyd, B. K. 1998. "How Much Does the CEO Matter? The Role of Managerial Discretion in the Setting of CEO Compensation," *Academy of Management Journal* 41 (2): 179–199.

Finkelstein, S. and D'Aveni, R. A. 1994. "CEO Duality as a Double-Edged Sword: How Boards of Directors Balance Entrenchment Avoidance and Unity of Command," *Academy of Management Journal* 37 (5): 1.079–1.108.

Finkelstein, S. and Hambrick, D. C. 1996. *Strategic Leadership: Top Executives and Their Effect on Organizations*. St. Paul, MN: West Publishing Company.

Fiol, C. M. and O'Connor, E. J. 2003. "Waking Up Mindfulness in the Face of Bandwagons," *Academy of Management Review* 28 (1): 54–70.

Fligstein, N. 1997. "Social Skill and Institutional Theory," *American Behavioural Scientist* 40 (4): 397–406.

Fligstein, N. and Freeland, R. 1995. "Theoretical and Comparative Perspectives on Corporate Organization," *Annual Review of Sociology* 21 (1): 21–43.

Fombrun, C. J. 1986. "Structural Dynamics within and between Organizations," *Administrative Science Quarterly* 31 (3): 403–421.

Fonda, D. 2003. "He Did So Well, Let's Give Him Two CEO Jobs," *Time Magazine*, December 1.

Fondas, N. 1992. "Understanding Differences in General Management Jobs," *Journal of General Management* 17 (4): 1–12.

Forbes, D. P. and Milliken, F. J. 1999. "Cognition and Corporate Governance: Understanding Boards of Directors as Strategic Decision-making Groups," *Academy of Management Review* 24 (3): 489–505.

Fordham, J. 2002. "Keith Jarett/Gary Peacock/Jack DeJohnette: Always Let Me Go," *Guardian*, November 7.

Foremski, T. 2003. "Doubling Up Helps Chip Away at IT Challenge," *Financial Times*, November 12.

Fournier, V. 1996. "Cognitive Maps in the Analysis of Personal Change During Work Role Transition," *British Journal of Management* 7 (2): 87–105.

French, J. R., Jr. and Raven, B. 1959. "The Basis of Social Power," in D. Cartwright and A. Zander (eds.), *Studies in Social Power*. Ann Arbor: University of Michigan, Institute for Social Research, pp. 150–167.

Friedman, R. 2004. "Editor's Desk," *Fortune*, July 26.

Gabarro, J. J. 1979. "Socialization at the Top – How CEO's and Subordinates Evolve Interpersonal Contracts," *Organizational Dynamics* 7 (3): 2–23.

 1987. "The Development of Working Relationships," in J. W. Lorsch (ed.), *Handbook of Organizational Behaviour*. Englewood Cliffs, NJ: Prentice-Hall, pp. 172–189.

Galbraith, J. R. 1974. "Organization Design: An Information Processing View," *Interfaces* 4 (3): 28–36.

Galbraith, J., Downey, D., and Kates, A. 2002. *Designing Dynamic Organizations: A Hands-On Guide for Leaders at All Levels*. New York: AMACOM.

Galunic, D. C. and Eisenhardt, K. M. 1994. "Renewing the Strategy–Structure–Performance Paradigm," *Research in Organizational Behavior* 16: 215–255.

 2001. "Architectural Innovation and Modular Corporate Forms," *Academy of Management Journal* 44 (6): 1.229–1.249.

Gambetta, D. 1988. "Can We Trust Trust?," in D. Gambetta (ed.), *Trust: Making and Breaking Cooperative Relations*. New York: Blackwell, pp. 213–237.

Garg, V. K., Walters, B., and Priem, R. L. 2003. "Chief Executive Scanning Emphases, Environmental Dynamism and Manufacturing Firm Performance," *Strategic Management Journal* 24 (8): 725–744.

Gargiulo, M. and Benassi, M. 2000. "Trapped in Your Own Net? Network Cohesion, Structural Holes, and the Adaptation of Social Capital," *Organization Science* 11 (2): 183–196.

Garvin, D. A. and Roberto, M. 2001. "What You Don't Know about Making Decisions," *Harvard Business Review* 79 (8): 108–116.

Geisst, C. R. 2001. *The Last Partnerships: Inside the Great Wall Street Money Dynasties*. New York: McGraw-Hill.

Gentile M. and Jick, T. 1987. "Bob Galvin and Motorola (A)." Case 9-487-062, Harvard Business School, Boston.

George, N. 2004. "Nokia Answers the Call for Fresh Leadership," *Financial Times*, December 20, 2004.

Ghoshal, S. and Bartlett, C. A. 1977. *The Individualized Corporation*. New York: HarperBusiness.

Ghoshal, S. and Bruch, H. 2004. "Reclaim Your Job," *Harvard Business Review* 89 (3): 41–45.

Gibson, C. B. and Birkinshaw, J. 2004. "The Antecedents, Consequences, and Mediating Role of Organizational Ambidexterity," *Academy of Journal Management* 47 (2): 209–226.

Glaser, B. G. 1963. "Attraction, Autonomy, and Reciprocity in the Scientist–Supervisor Relationship," *Administrative Science Quarterly* 8 (3): 379–398.

Glover, J. D. and Hower, R. M. 1963. *The Administrator. Cases in Human Relations in Business.* Homewood, IL: Richard D. Irwin.

Glynn, M. A. 2000. "When Cymbals Become Symbols: Conflict over Organizational Identity within a Symphony Orchestra," *Organization Science* 12: 414–434.

Goffman, E. 1990[1959]. *The Presentation of Self in Everyday Life.* London: Penguin Books.

Goñi, J. 1992. "Luis y Javier Valls Taberner: Argamasa y Ladrillos," *El País*, December 13.

Gordon, C. 1976. "Development of Evaluated Role Identities," *Annual Review of Sociology* 2: 405–433.

Gosling, J. and Mintzberg, H. 2003. "The Five Minds of a Manager," *Harvard Business Review* 81 (11): 54–63.

Green, S. E., Jr. 2004. "A Rhetorical Theory of Diffusion," *Academy of Management Review* 29 (4): 653–669.

Greenfeld, L. 1989. *Different Worlds: A Sociological Study of Taste, Choice and Success in Art.* Cambridge: Cambridge University Press.

Greenwood, R. and Empson, L. 2003. "The Professional Partnership: Relic or Exemplary Form of Governance?", *Organization Studies* 24 (6): 909–933.

Greiner, L. 1972. "Evolution and Revolution as Organizations Grow," *Harvard Business Review* 50 (4): 37–46.

Greiner, L., Cummings, T. and Bhambri, A. 2003. "When New CEOs Succeed and Fail: 4-D Theory of Strategic Transformation," *Organizational Dynamics* 32 (1): 1–16.

Gresov, C. 1989. "Exploring Fit and Misfit with Multiple Contingencies," *Administrative Science Quarterly* 34 (3): 431–453.

    1990. "Effects of Dependence and Tasks on Unit Design and Efficiency," *Organization Science* 11 (4): 503–529.

Gresov, C. and Drazin, R. 1997. "Equifinality, Functional Equivalence in Organization Design," *Academy of Management Journal* 22 (2): 403–428.

Gronn, P. 1999. "Substituting for Leadership: The Neglected Role of the Leadership Couple," *Leadership Quarterly* 10 (1): 41–62.

2002. "Distributed Leadership as a Unit of Analysis," *Leadership Quarterly* 13 (4): 423–451.

Grover, R. 1999. "Fixing Disney: Some Unsolicited Advice for Chairman Eisner," *BusinessWeek Online*, November 12. http://www.businessweek.com/bwdaily/dnflash/nov1999/nf91112h.htm (accessed October 20, 2004).

Guillén, M. F. 2001. *The Limits of Convergence: Globalization and Organizational Change in Argentina, South Korea, and Spain*. Princeton: Princeton University Press.

Gunther, M. 2004. "Behind the Shakeup at Viacom," *Fortune*, June 28.

Gupta, A. K. 1984. "Contingency Linkages between Strategy and General Manager Characteristics: A Conceptual Examination," *Academy of Management Review* 9 (3): 399–412.

1986. "Matching Managers to Strategies: Point and Counterpoint," *Human Resource Management* 25 (2): 215–234.

Gupta, A. K. and Govindarajan, V. 1984. "Business Unit Strategy, Managerial Characteristics, and Business Unit Effectiveness and Strategy Implementation," *Academy of Management Journal* 27 (1): 25–41.

Gupta, Y. P. 1991. "The Chief Executive Officer and the Chief Information Officer: The Strategic Partnership," *Journal of Information Technology* 6 (3/4): 128–139.

Hackman, J. R. (ed.) 1989. *Groups that Work (and Those That Don't): Creating Conditions for Effective Teamwork*. San Francisco: Jossey-Bass.

Hackman, J. R. 2002. *Leading Teams: Setting the Stage for Great Performance*. Boston: Harvard Business School Press.

Haleblian, J. and Finkelstein, S. 1993. "Top Management Team Size, CEO Dominance, and Firm Performance: The Moderating Roles of Environmental Turbulence and Discretion," *Academy of Management Journal* 36 (4): 844–863.

Hales, C. P. 1986. "What Do Managers Do? A Critical Review of the Evidence," *Journal of Management Studies* 23 (1): 88–115.

Hall, F. S. and Hall, D. T. 1978. "Dual Careers – How Do Couples and Companies Cope with the Problems," *Organizational Dynamics* 6 (4): 57–77.

1979. *The Two-Career Couple*. Reading, MA: Addison-Wesley.

Hambrick, D. C. 1981a. "Environment, Strategy, and Power within Top Management Teams," *Administrative Science Quarterly* 26 (2): 253–276.

1981b. "Specialization of Environmental Scanning Activities among Upper Level Executives," *Journal of Management Studies* 18 (3): 299–320.

1995. "Fragmentation and the Other Problems CEOs Have with Their Top Management Teams," *California Management Review* 37(3): 110–127.

1998. "Corporate Coherence and the Top Team," in Hambrick, Nadler, and Tushman (eds.), pp. 123–140.

2003. "On the Staying Power of Defenders, Analyzers, and Prospectors," *Academy of Management Executive* 17 (4): 115–119.

Hambrick, D. C. and Cannella, A. A. 2004. "CEOs Who Have COOs: Contingency Analysis of an Unexplored Structural Form," *Strategic Management Journal* 25 (10): 959–979.

Hambrick, D. C., Cho, T.-S., and Chen, M.-J. 1996. "The Influence of Top Management Team Heterogeneity on Firms' Competitive Moves," *Administrative Science Quarterly* 41 (4): 659–684.

Hambrick, D. C. and Finkelstein, S. 1987. "Managerial Discretion: A Bridge between Polar Views and Organizational Outcomes," *Research in Organizational Behavior* 9: 369–406.

Hambrick, D. C. and Lei, D. 1985. "Toward an Empirical Prioritization of Contingency Variables for Business Strategy," *Academy of Management Journal* 28 (4): 763–788.

Hambrick, D. C. and Mason, P. A. 1984. "Upper Echelons: The Organization as a Reflection of Its Top Managers," *Academy of Management Review* 9 (2): 193–206.

Hambrick, D. C., Nadler, D. A., and Tushman, M. L. (eds.) 1998. *Navigating Change: How CEOs, Top Teams, and Boards Steer Transformation.* Boston: Harvard Business School Press.

Harrison, J. R., Torres, D. L., and Kukalis, S. 1988. "The Changing of the Guard: Turnover and Structural Change in the Top-Management Positions," *Administrative Science Quarterly* 33 (2): 211–232.

Hayward, M. L. A., Rindova, V. P., and Pollock, T. G. 2004. "Believing One's Own Press: The Causes and Consequences of CEO Celebrity," *Strategic Management Journal* 25 (7): 637–653.

Hedberg, B., Nystrom, C., and Starbuck, W. 1976. "Camping on Seesaws: Prescription for Self Designing Organization," *Administrative Science Quarterly* 21 (1): 41–65.

Hedlund, G. and Ridderstrale, J. 1997. "Toward a Theory of the Self-Renewing MNC," in B. Toyne and D. Nigh (eds.), *International Business: An Emerging Vision.* Columbia: University of South Carolina Press, pp. 329–353.

Heenan, D. A. and Bennis, W. 1999. *Co-leaders: The Power of Great Partnerships.* New York: Wiley.

Hegedus, C. and Noujaim, J. (Directors) 2001. *Startup.com.* DVD, Pennebaker Hegedus Films, Inc. and Noujaim Films, Inc., An Artificial Eye Release.

Hickson D. J. 1966. "A Convergence in Organization Theory," *Administrative Science Quarterly* 11 (2): 224–237.

Hickson, D. J., Hinings, C. R., Lee, C. A., Schneck, R. E., and Pennings, J. M. 1971. "A Strategic Contingencies Theory of Intraorganizational Power," *Administrative Science Quarterly* 16 (2): 216–229.

Higgins, M. 2005. *Career Imprints: Creating Leaders Across an Industry*, San Francisco: Jossey-Bass.

Hill, L. A. 2000. "Leadership as Collective Genius," in S. Chowdhury (ed.), *Management 21C: Someday We'll Manage This Way*. London: Financial Times/Prentice-Hall.

Hillman, A. J. and Dalziel, T. 2003. "Boards of Directors and Firm Performance: Integrating Agency and Resource Dependence Perspectives," *Academy of Management Review* 28 (3): 383–396.

Hinings, C. R., Hickson, D. J., Pennings, J. M., and Schneck, R. E. 1974. "Structural Conditions of Intraorganizational Power," *Administrative Science Quarterly* 19 (1): 22–44.

Hirsch, P. and Lounsbury, M. 1997. "Ending the Family Quarrel: Toward a Reconciliation of 'Old' and 'New' Institutionalism," *American Behavioural Scientist* 40 (4): 397–406.

Hodgson, R. C., Levinson, D. J., and Zaleznik, A. 1965. "The Executive Role Constellation. An Analysis of Personality and Role Relations in Management." Boston: Division of Research, Graduate School of Business Administration, Harvard University.

Hollenbeck, J. R. 2002. "Structural Contingency Theory and Individual Differences: Examination of External and Internal Person–Team Fit," *Journal of Applied Psychology* 87 (3): 599–606.

Homans, G. 1958. "Social Behavior as Exchange," *American Journal of Sociology* 62: 597–606.

House, J. S., Umberson, D., and Landis, K. 1988. "Structures and Processes of Social Report," *Annual Review of Sociology* 14: 293–318.

House, R. J. 1988. "Power and Personality in Complex Organizations," *Research in Organizational Behavior* 10: 305–357.

House, R. J., Spangler, W. D., and Woycke, J. 1991. "Personality and Charisma in the U.S. Presidency: A Psychological Theory of Leader Effectiveness," *Administrative Science Quarterly* 36 (3): 364–396.

Howard, R. 1992. "The CEO as Organizational Architect: An Interview with Xerox's Paul Allaire," *Harvard Business Review* 70 (5): 107–121.

Huff, A. S. 2000. "Citigroup's John Reed and Stanford's James March on Management Research and Practice," *Academy of Management Executive* 14 (1): 52–64.

Hurley, L. (2000). "Corporate Events Mean Business," *Special Events Magazine*, http://specialevents.com/corporate/meetings_corporate_events_mean (accessed December 26, 2004).

Ibarra, H. 1992. "Structural Alignments, Individual Strategies, and Managerial Action: Elements toward a Network Theory of Getting Things Done," in N. Nohria and R. Eccles (eds.), *Networks and Organizations: Structure, Form, and Action*. Boston: Harvard Business School Press, pp. 165–188.

Inkson, K. and Arthur, M. B. 2001. "How to Be a Successful Career Capitalist," *Organizational Dynamics* 30 (1): 48–61.

Jackall, R. 1988. *Moral Mazes: The World of Corporate Managers*. Oxford: Oxford University Press.

Janis, I. J. and Mann, L. 1977. *Decision Making: A Psychological Analysis of Conflict, Choice, and Commitment*. New York: The Free Press.

Jarvis, P. 1999. "Two's a Company: An Exploration of the Ongoing Relationship between Two People Who Found and Manage Businesses Together and How the Relationship Contributes to the Survival of Their Organisation." Ph.D. thesis, School of Management, Cranfield University, UK.

Jay, A. 1972. *Corporation Man*. London: Jonathan Cape.

Jensen, M. C. 2000. *A Theory of the Firm: Governance, Residual Claims, and Organizational Forms*. Cambridge, MA: Harvard University Press.

Joni, S. A. 2004. "The Geography of Trust," *Harvard Business Review* 82 (3): 82–99.

Kafka, P. and Newcomb, P. 2003a. "Q&A with Jeffrey Katzenberg," *Forbes*, February 20.

2003b. "Q&A with Steven Spielberg," *Forbes*, February 20.

2003c. "Q&A with David Geffen," *Forbes*, February 20.

Kanter, R. M. 1997. *Rosabeth Moss Kanter on the Frontiers of Management*. Boston: Harvard Business Review Books.

1989. "The New Managerial Work," *Harvard Business Review* 67 (6): 85–92.

Kantorowicz, E. H. 1981. *The King's Two Bodies. A Study in Medieval Political Theology*. Princeton: Princeton University Press.

Kaplan, D. A. 2000. *The Silicon Boys and Their Valley of Dreams*. New York: Perennial.

Kaplan, R. E. and Kaiser, R. B. 2003. "Developing Versatile Leadership," *MIT Sloan Management Review* 44 (4): 19–26.

Katz, D. and Kahn, R. L. 1978. *The Social Psychology of Organizations*, 2nd edn. New York: Wiley.

Katzenbach, J. R. 1998. *Teams at the Top. Unleashing the Potential of Both Teams and Individual Leaders*. Boston: Harvard Business School Press.

Kelly, A. 2003. *Decision Making Using Game Theory: An Introduction for Managers*. Cambridge: Cambridge University Press.

Kerr, J. L. 2004. "The Limits of Organizational Democracy," *Academy of Management Executive* 18 (3): 81–98.

Khurana, R. 2002. *Searching for a Corporate Savior. The Irrational Quest for Charismatic CEOs*. Princeton: Princeton University Press.

Kirkpatrick, D. 2004. "Dell and Rollings. The $41 Billion Buddy Act," *Fortune*, April, 19.

Kleiner, A. 2003. *Who Really Matters? The Core Group Theory of Power, Privilege and Success*. London: Currency/Doubleday.

Kotter, J. P. 1982. *The General Managers*. New York: The Free Press.

  1985. *Power and Influence: Beyond Formal Authority*. New York: The Free Press.

  1990. "What Leaders Really Do," *Harvard Business Review* 68 (3): 103–111.

  1996. *Leading Change*. Boston: Harvard Business School Press.

Kotter, J. P. and Heskett, J. L. 1992. *Corporate Culture and Performance*. New York: The Free Press.

Kotter, J. P. and Lawrence, P. R. 1974. *Mayors in Action: Five Approaches to Urban Governance*. New York: Wiley.

Krackhardt, D. 1992. "The Strength of Strong Ties: The Importance of 'Philos' in Organizations," in N. Nohria and R. Eccles (eds.), *Networks and Organizations: Structure, Form, and Action*. Boston: Harvard Business School Press, pp. 216–239.

  1999. "The Ties that Torture: Simmelian Tie Analysis in Organizations," *Research in the Sociology of Organizations* 16: 183–210.

Krackhardt, D. and Kilduff, M. 2002. "Structure, Culture and Simmelian Ties in Entrepreneurial Firms," *Social Networks* 24 (3): 279–290.

Kram, K. E. 1985. *Mentoring at Work: Developmental Relationships in Organizational Life*. Glenview, IL: Scott, Foresman.

Kramer, R. M. 1999. "Trust and Distrust in Organizations: Emerging Perspectives, Enduring Questions," *Annual Review of Psychology* 50 (1): 569–598.

  2001. "Organizational Paranoia: Origin and Dynamics," *Research in Organizational Behavior* 23: 1–42.

Krantz, J. 1989. "The Managerial Couple: Superior–Subordinate Relationships as Units of Analysis," *Human Resource Management* 28 (2): 161–175.

Kraut, A. I., Pedigo, P. R., McKenna, D. D., and Dunnette, M. D. 1989. "The Role of the Manager: What's Really Important in Different Management Jobs," *Academy of Management Executive* 3 (4): 286–293.

Ladika, S. 2004. "When It Comes to Leadership, Two Heads Are Not Better Than One," *Workforce Management* 83 (4): 57–59.

Lank, A. 2000. "Making Sure the Dynasty Does Not Become a Dallas," in S. Birley and D. Muzyka (eds.), *Mastering Entrepreneurship*. London: Financial Times/Prentice-Hall, pp. 193–199.

Lawler, E. J. 2001. "An Affect Theory of Social Exchange," *American Journal of Sociology* 107 (2): 321–352.

Lawler, E. J. and Thye, S. R. 1999. "Bringing Emotions into Social Exchange Theory," *Annual Review of Sociology* 25: 217–244.

Lawler, E. J. and Yoon, J. 1993. "Power and the Emergence of Commitment Behavior in Negotiated Exchange," *American Sociological Review* 58: 465–481.

1996. "Commitment in Exchange Relations: Test of a Theory of Relational Cohesion," *American Sociological Review* 61 (1): 89–108.

Lawrence, P. R. and Lorsch, J. W. 1967. *Organization and Environment*. Boston: Harvard Business School Press.

Le Glay, M., Voisin, J.-L., and Le Bohec, Y. 1996. *A History of Rome*. Cambridge, MA: Blackwell.

Leblanc, F. and Lapierre, L. 2001. "Guy Latraverse and Show Business: A Story of Successful Co-Management," *International Journal of Arts Management* 4 (1): 59–71.

Lee, D. 1976. *Tai Chi Chuan: The Philosophy of Yin and Yang and its Application*. Santa Clarita, CA: Ohara Publications.

Lee, F. and Tiedens, L. Z. 2001. "Is it Lonely at the Top? The Independence and Interdependence of Power Holders," *Research in Organizational Behavior* 23: 43–91.

Leicht, K. T. and Fennell, M. L. 1997. "The changing organizational context of professional work." *Annual Review of Sociology*, 23: 215–31.

Leifer, E. M. 1988. "Interaction Preludes to Role Setting: Exploratory Local Action," *American Sociological Review* 53 (6): 865–878.

1991. *Actors as Observers: A Theory of Skill in Social Relationships*. New York: Garland.

Leonard-Barton, D. 1995a. "Managing Creative Abrasion in the Workplace," *Harvard Business Review* 73 (4): 2–3.

1995b. *Wellsprings of Knowledge: Building and Sustaining the Sources of Innovation*. Boston: Harvard Business School Press.

Levine, D. N., Carter, E. B., and Gorman, E. M. 1976. "Simmel's Influence on American Sociology II," *American Journal of Sociology* 81 (5): 1.112–1.132.

Levinson, D. J. 1963. "Role, Personality, and Social Structure in the Organizational Setting," in Smelser and Smelser (eds.), pp. 428–440.

Levitt, B. and Nass, C. 1989. "The Lid on the Garbage Can: Institutional Constraints on Decision Making in Technical Core of College-Text Publishers," *Administrative Science Quarterly* 34: 190–207.

Levy, L. 1993. "Separate Chairmen: Their Roles and Compensation," *Corporate Board* 14 (79): 10–15.

Lewin, A. Y. and Stephens, C. U. 1994. "CEO Attitudes as Determinants of Organization Design: An Integrated Model," *Organization Studies* 15 (2): 183–212.

Lewis, M. 1989. *Liar's Poker. Rising through the Wreckage on Wall Street.* New York: Norton & Company.

Lewis, M. W. 2000. "Exploring Paradox: Toward a More Comprehensive Guide," *Academy of Management Review* 25 (4): 760–777.

Lewis, R. T. 2002. "New York Times Company President and Chief Executive Officer Russ Lewis on 'The CEO's Lot Is Not a Happy One . . .'," *Academy of Management Executive* 16 (4): 37–43.

Lieberman, S. 1963. "The Effects of Changes in Roles on the Attitudes of Role Occupants," in Smelser and Smelser (eds.), pp. 264–279.

Loomis, C. J. 2003. "The Larger-than-Life Life of Robert Rubin," *Fortune*, December 8.

Lorsch, J. W. and Morse, J. J. 1974. *Organizations and Their Members: A Contingency Approach*. New York: Harper & Row.

Losada Marrodán, C. 2003. "A Contribution to the Study of the Differences in Managerial Function: Political Managers' Function and Civil Service Managers' Function." Doctoral thesis, ESADE, Ramon Llull University, Barcelona.

Luthans, F. 1988. "Successful vs. Effective Real Managers," *Academy of Management Executive* 2 (2): 127–132.

Luthans, F. and Stewart, T. I. 1977. "A General Contingency Theory of Management," *Academy of Management Review* 2 (2): 181–196.

Luthans, F. D., Welsh, H. B., and Taylor, L. A., III 1988. "A Descriptive Model of Managerial Effectiveness," *Group and Organization Studies* 13 (2): 148–162.

Malhotra, D. and Murnighan, J. K. 2002. "The Effects of Contracts on Interpersonal Trust," *Administrative Science Quarterly* 47: 534–559.

Mangalindan, M. 2004. "The Grown-up at Google: How Eric Schmidt Imposed Better Management Tactics but Didn't Stifle Search Giant," *Wall Street Journal*, March 29.

Manzoni, J. F. and Barsoux, J. L. (2002). The Set-Up-to-Fail Syndrome: How Good Managers Cause Great People to Fail. Boston: Harvard Business School Press.

March, J. G. and Cohen, M. 1974. *Leadership and Ambiguity*, 2nd edn. Boston: Harvard Business School Press.

Markham, F. M. H. 1970. "Napoleonic France," in J. M. Wallace-Hadrill and J. McManners (eds.). *France: Government and Society. An Historical Survey*. London: Methuen, pp. 188–206.

Marshack, K. 1998. *Entrepreneurial Couples: Making It Work at Work and at Home*. Palo Alto, CA: Davies-Black.

Marwell, G. and Hage, J. 1970. "The Organization of Role-relationships: A Systematic Description," *American Sociological Review* 35 (5): 884–900.

Mass Mutual Financial Group and Raymond Institute 2003. *American Business Family Survey*. http://www3.babson.edu/ESHIP/ife/upload/American-Family-Business-Survey.pdf (accessed October 19, 2004).

Mayer, R. C., Davis J. H., and Schoorman, F. D. 1995. "An Integrative Model of Organizational Trust," *Academy of Management Review* 20 (3): 709–734.

Mazza, C. 1999. *Claim, Intent, and Persuasion: Organizational Legitimacy and the Rhetoric of Corporate Mission Statements*. Norwell, MA: Kluwer.

Mazza, C. and Alvarez, J. L. 2000. "Haute Couture and Pret-à-Porter: The Popular Press and the Diffusion of Management Practices," *Organization Studies* 21 (3): 567–589.

McAllister, D. J. 1995. "Affect- and Cognition-based Trust as Foundations for Interpersonal Cooperation in Organizations," *Academy of Management Journal* 38 (1): 24–59.

McClelland, D. 1961. *The Achieving Society*. New York: The Free Press.

McDonald, M. L. and Westphal, J. D. 2003. "Getting by with the Advice of Their Friends: CEO's Advice Networks and Firms' Strategic Responses to Poor Performance," *Administrative Science Quarterly* 48 (1): 1–32.

McDonough, E. and Leifer, R. 1983. "Using Simultaneous Structures to Cope with Uncertainty," *Academy of Management Journal* 26 (4): 727–735.

McEvily, B., Perrone, V., and Zaheer, A. (guest editors) 2003a. "Introduction to the Special Issue on Trust in an Organizational Context," *Organization Science* 14 (1): 1–4.

2003b. "Trust as an Organizing Principle," *Organization Science* 14 (1): 91–103.

McLean, B. 2004. "Goldman Sachs: Inside the Money Machine," *Fortune*, September 6.

McNulty, T. and Pettigrew, A. 1999. "Strategist on the Board," *Organisation Studies* 20 (1): 47–74.

Meindl, J. R., Ehrlich, S. B., and Dukerich, J. M. 1985. "The Romance of Leadership," *Administrative Science Quarterly* 30 (1): 78–102.

Merton, R. 1957a. "The Role-Set: Problems in Sociological Theory," *British Journal of Sociology* 8: 110–113.

1957b. *Social Theory and Social Structure*. New York: The Free Press.

1963. "Bureaucratic Structure and Personality," in Smelser and Smelser (eds.), pp. 255–263.

Merz, G. R. and Sauber, M. H. 1995. "Profiles of Managerial Activities in Small Firms," *Strategic Management Journal* 16 (7): 551–564.

Meyer, J. and Rowan, B. 1977. "Institutionalised Organizations: Formal Structures as Myth and Ceremony," *American Journal of Sociology* 83 (2): 340–363.

Meyer, J. and Scott, W. R. 1983. *Organizational Environments: Ritual and Rationality*. Beverly Hills, CA: Sage.

Michel, J. G. and Hambrick, D. C. 1992. "Diversification Posture and Top Management Team Characteristics," *Academy of Management Journal* 35 (1): 9–37.

Micklethwait, J. and Wooldridge, A. 2003. *The Company: A Short Story of a Revolutionary Idea*. New York: Modern Library.

Mieszkowski, K. 1997. "Opposites Attract," *FC [Fastcompany]* 12: 42.

Miles, R. E. and Snow, C. 1978. *Organization Strategy, Structure and Process*. New York: McGraw Hill.

Millás, J. J. 2004. "Almodóvar desconocido," *El Pais Semanal*, March 28.

Miller, A. 2001. *On Politics and the Art of Acting*. New York: Viking Press.

Miller, D. 1981. "Toward a New Contingency Approach: The Search For Organizational Gestalts," *Journal of Management Studies* 18 (1): 1–27.

1991. "Stale in the Saddle: CEO Tenure and the Match between Organizations and Environment," *Management Science* 37 (1): 34–52.

Miller, D. and Dröge, C. 1986. "Psychological and Traditional Determinants of Structure," *Administrative Science Quarterly* 31 (4): 539–560.

Miller, D., Dröge, C., and Toulouse, J. M. 1988. "Strategic Process and Content as Mediators between Organizational Context and Structure," *Academy of Management Journal* 31 (3): 544–569.

Miller, D. and Toulouse, J. M. 1986a. "Chief Executive Personality and Corporate Strategy and Structure in Small Firms," *Management Science* 32 (11): 1389–1409.

1986b. "Strategy, Structure, CEO Personality and Performance in Small Firms," *American Journal of Small Business* 10 (3): 47–63.

Mills, T. M. 1953. "Power Relations in Three-Person Groups," *American Sociological Review* 18 (4): 351–357.

1954. "The Coalition Pattern in Three-Person Groups," *American Sociological Review* 19(6): 657–667.

1958. "Some Hypotheses on Small Groups from Simmel," *American Sociological Review* 23 (6): 642–650.

Mintzberg, H. 1973. *The Nature of Managerial Work*. New York: Harper & Row.

——— 1980. "Structure in 5's: A Synthesis of the Research on Organization Design," *Management Science* 26 (3): 322–341.

——— 1989. *Mintzberg on Management: Inside Our Strange World of Organizations*. New York: Macmillan.

——— 1994. "Rounding out the Manager's Job," *Sloan Management Review* 36 (1): 11–25.

Mitchell, T. R., Holtom, B. C., Lee, T. W., Sablynski, C. J., and Erez, M. 2001. "Why People Stay: Using Job Embeddedness to Predict Voluntary Turnover," *Academy of Management Journal* 44 (6): 1.102–1.121.

Molm, L. D., Takahashi, N., and Peterson, G. 2000. "Risk and Trust in Social Exchange: An Experimental Test of a Classical Proposition," *American Journal of Sociology* 105 (5): 1.396–1.427.

Moore, J. 2001. Interview with J. Moore (Senior Consultant, Executive Development Associates, and Executive Consultant to Sun Microsystems), conducted by Silviya Svejenova, Palo Alto, October 26.

Morten, H., Podolny, J. M., and Pfeffer, J. 2001. "So Many Ties, So Little Time: A Task Contingency Perspective on Corporate Social Capital," *Research in the Sociology of Organization* 8: 21–57.

Moynihan, L. M. and Peterson, R. S. 2001. "A Contingent Configuration Approach to Understanding the Role of Personality in Organizational Groups," *Research in Organizational Behavior* 23: 327–378.

Murnighan, E. and Conlon, D. E. 1991. "The Dynamics of Intense Work Groups: A Study of British String Quartets," *Administrative Science Quarterly* 36 (2): 165–186.

Murray, M. 2000. "Investors Like Backup, but Does Every CEO Require a Sidekick?," *Wall Street Journal Online*, February 24. http://online.wsj.com/PA2VJBNA4R/article_print/0,,SB95135426072 1309341,00.html (accessed January 28, 2004).

Muth, M. M. and Donaldson, L. 1998. "Stewardship Theory and Board Structure: A Contingency Approach," *Scholarly Research and Theory Papers* 6 (1): 5–28.

Nadler, D. A. and Ancona D. 1992. "Teamwork at the Top: Creating Executive Teams that Work," in. Nadler *et al.* (eds.), pp. 209–231.

Nadler, D. A., Gerstein, M. S., Shaw, R. B., and associates (eds.) 1992. *Organizational Architecture: Designs for Changing Organizations*. San Francisco: Jossey-Bass.

Nadler, D. A., Spencer, J. L., and associates (eds.) 1998. *Executive Teams. The Delta Consulting Group*. San Francisco: Jossey-Bass.

Nathan, J. 1999. *Sony: The Private Life*. Boston: Houghton Mifflin.

Nathans, L. with Silverman, G. and Reed, S. 1999. "The Coup at Goldman," *BusinessWeek Online*, January 25. http://www.businessweek.com (accessed January 2005).

Neumann G. A. and Wright, J. 1999. "Team Effectiveness: Beyond Skills and Cognitive Ability," *Journal of Applied Psychology* 84 (3): 376–389.

Neustadt, R. E. 1990. *Presidential Power and the Modern Presidents: The Politics of Leadership from Roosevelt to Reagan*. New York: The Free Press.

Nguyen, Q. 2002. "Emotional Balancing of Organizational Continuity and Radical Change: The Contribution of Middle Managers," *Administrative Science Quarterly* 47 (1): 31–69.

Nicholson, N. 1984. "A Theory of Work Role Transitions," *Administrative Science Quarterly* 29 (2): 172–191.

  2000. *Executive Instinct: Managing the Human Animal in the Information Age*. New York: Crown Business Books.

Norburn, D. 1989. "The Chief Executive: A Breed Apart," *Strategic Management Journal* 10: 1–15.

Norburn, D. and Birley, S. 1988. "The Top Management Team and Corporate Performance," *Strategic Management Journal* 9 (3): 225–237.

Nutt, P. C. 1993. "Flexible Decision Styles and the Choices of Top Executives," *Journal of Management Studies* 30 (5): 695–721.

Ocasio, W. 1994. "Political Dynamics and the Circulation of Power: CEO Succession in U.S. Industrial Corporations, 1960–1990," *Administrative Science Quarterly* 3 (2): 285–312.

Ocasio, W. and Kim, H. 1999. "The Circulation of Corporate Control: Selection of Functional Backgrounds of New CEOs in Large U.S. Manufacturing Firms, 1981–1992," *Administrative Science Quarterly* 44 (2): 532–562.

Osterland, A. 2001. "When Equality Isn't a Virtue," *CFO Magazine*, June 1.

O'Sullivan, M. A. 2000. *Contests for Corporate Control. Corporate Governance and Economic Performance in the United States and Germany*. New York: Oxford University Press.

O'Toole, J., Galbraith, J., and Lawler, E. E., III 2002. "When Two (or More) Heads are Better than One: The Promises and Pitfalls of Shared Leadership," *California Management Review* 44 (4): 65–83.

Padgett, J. F. 1992. "Review Essay: The Alchemist of Contingency Theory," *American Journal of Sociology* 97 (5): 1.462–1.471.

Padgett, J. F. and Ansell, C. K. 1993. "Robust Action and the Renaissance of the Medici 1400–1434," *American Journal of Sociology* 98 (6): 1.259–1.319.

Palmer, D. and Barber, B. M. 2001. "Challengers, Elites, and Owning Families: A Social Class Theory of Corporate Acquisitions in the 1960s," *Administrative Science Quarterly* 46 (1): 87–120.

Palmer, D. A., Jennings, P. D., and Zhou, X. 1993. "Late Adoption of the Multidivisional Form by Large U.S. Corporations: Institutional, Political and Economic Accounts," *Administrative Science Quarterly* 38 (1): 100–131.

Parkhe, A. 1998. "Understanding Trust in International Alliances," *Journal of World Business* 33 (3): 219–240.

Parsons, T. 1956a. "Suggestions for a Sociological Approach to the Theory of Organizations I," *Administrative Science Quarterly* 1 (1): 63–85.

    1956b. "Suggestions for a Sociological Approach to the Theory of Organizations II," *Administrative Science Quarterly* 1 (2): 225–239.

    1960. *Structure and Process in Modern Societies*. Glencoe, IL: The Free Press.

    1968. *The Structure of Social Action*. New York: The Free Press.

Pascale, R. T. 1984. "Perspectives on Strategy: The Real Story behind Honda's Success," *California Management Review* 26 (3): 47–72

    1990. *Managing on the Edge. How the Smartest Companies Use Conflict to Stay Ahead*. New York: Simon & Schuster.

    1996. "The Honda Effect," *California Management Review* 38 (4): 80–91.

Pearce, C. L. 2004. "The Future of Leadership: Combining Vertical and Shared Leadership to Transform Knowledge Work," *Academy of Management Executive* 18 (1): 47–57.

Pearce, C. L. and Conger, J. (eds.) 2003. *Shared Leadership: Reframing the Hows and Whys of Leadership*. Thousand Oaks, CA: Sage.

Pearce J. A., II and Zahra, S. A. 1991. "The Relative Power of CEOs and Boards of Directors: Associations with Corporate Performance," *Strategic Management Journal* 12 (2): 135–153.

Pearson, A. E. 1989. "Six Basics for General Managers," *Harvard Business Review* 67 (4): 94–101.

Pellet, J. 1999. "Are Two CEOs One Too Many?," *Chief Executive*, January–February. http://www.findarticles.com/p/articles/mi_m4070/is_141/ai_54237756 (accessed January 2005).

Pennings, J. M. 1992. "Structural Contingency Theory: A Reappraisal," *Research in Organizational Behavior* 14: 267–309.

Penrose, E. 1972. *Theory of the Growth of the Firm*. Oxford: Blackwell.

Perez, M. 2004. "La Caixa: El fin del triunvirato," *La Vanguardia*, October 31.

Perrone, V., Zaheer, A., and McEvily, B. 2003. "Free to Be Trusted? Organizational Constraints on Trust in Boundary Spanners," *Organization Science* 14 (4): 422–439.

Pescosolido, B. A. and Rubin, B. A. 2000. "The Web of Group Affiliations Revisited: Social Life, Postmodernism, and Sociology," *American Sociological Review* 65 (1): 52–76.

Perrow, C. 1986. *Complex Organizations: A Critical Essay*, 3rd edn. New York: Random House.

Peters, T. and Waterman, R. H. 1982. *In Search of Excellence*. New York: Harper & Row.

Pettigrew, A. 1973. *The Politics of Organizational Decision Making*. New York: Harper & Row.

Pfeffer, J. 1992. *Managing with Power: Politics and Influence in Organizations*. Boston: Harvard Business School Press.

Pfeffer, J. and Salancik, G. R. 1978. *The External Control of Organizations. A Resource Dependence Perspective*. New York: Harper & Row.

Pfeffer, J. and Sutton, R. I. 2000. *The Knowing–Doing Gap*. Boston: Harvard Business School Press.

Piore, M. J. 1995. *Beyond Individualism*. Boston: Harvard Business School Press.

Pitts, R. A. 1980. "Toward a Contingency Theory of Multibusiness Organization Design," *Academy of Management Review* 5 (2): 203–210.

Pocock, J. G. A. 1975. *The Machiavellian Moment: Florentine Political Thought and the Atlantic Republican Tradition*. Princeton: Princeton University Press

Pound, J. 1992. "Beyond Takeovers: Politics Comes to Corporate Control," *Harvard Business Review* 70 (2): 83–94.

   1995. "The Promise of the Governed Corporation," *Harvard Business Review* 73 (2): 89–99.

Pradera, J. 2004. "La tricefalia del PP," *El País*, September 15.

Prahalad, C. K. and Doz, Y. 2001. "El consejero delegado: ¿mano visible en la creación de riqueza?," *Harvard-Deusto Business Review* 103: 4–23.

Prechel, H. 2003. "Historical Contingency Theory, Policy Paradigm Shifts, and Corporate Malfeasance at the Turn of the 21st Century," *Research in Political Sociology* 12: 311–340.

Priem, R. L. and Rosenstein, J. 2000. "Is Organization Theory Obvious to Practitioners? A Test of One Established Theory," *Organization Science* 11 (5): 509–524.

Pucik, V., Judge, T., and Welbourne, T. 1995. *Organizational Transformations: Implications for Career Management and Executive Development in the US, Europe and Asia*. Lexington, MA: International Consortium for Executive Development Research.

Pugh, D. S., Hickson, D. J., Hinings, C. R., and Turner, C. 1969. "The Context of Organization Structures," *Administrative Science Quarterly* 14 (1): 91–115.

Putnam, R. D. 2000. *Bowling Alone: The Collapse and Revival of American Community*. New York: Simon & Schuster.

Pycior, H. M., Slack, N. G., and Abir-Am, P. G. (eds.) 1996. *Creative Couples in the Sciences*. New Brunswick: Rutgers University Press.

Quinn, J. B. 1980. *Strategies for Change: Logical Instrumentalism*. Homewood, IL: Richard D. Irwin, Inc.

Rafaeli, A. and Sutton, R. I. 1991. "Emotional Contrast Strategies as Means of Social Influence: Lessons from Criminal Interrogators and Bill Collectors," *Academy of Management Journal* 34: 749–775.

Ragins, B. R., Cotton, J. L., and Miller, J. S. 2000. "Marginal Mentoring: The Effects of Type of Mentor, Quality of Relationship, and Program Design on Work and Career Attitudes," *Academy of Management Journal* 43 (6): 1.177–1.194.

Rapoport, R. and Rapoport, R. 1965a. "Dual-Career Families: The Evolution of a Concept," in E. Trist and H. Murray (eds.), *The Social Engagement of Social Science*, vol. I: *The Socio-Psychological Perspective*. London: Free Association Books, pp. 351–372.

1965b. "Work and Family in Contemporary Society," *American Sociological Review* 30 (3): 381–394.

1969. "The Dual-Career Family," *Human Relations* 22 (1): 3–30.

Raso, C. 2000. "Two People in the CEO Role: Can It Work?," *Board Leadership. Policy Governance in Action* 48: 1–8.

Rechner, P. L. and Dalton, D. R. 1989. "The Impact of CEO as Board Chairperson on Corporate Performance: Evidence vs. Rhetoric," *Academy of Management Executive* 3 (2): 141–148.

1991. "CEO Duality and Organizational Performance: A Longitudinal Analysis," *Strategic Management Journal* 12 (2): 155–160.

Reger, R. 1997. "Book Review. 'Strategic Leadership: Top Executives and Their Effects on Organizations,' by Finkelstein, S. and Hambrick, D. 1996. Minneapolis: West Publishing Company." *Academy of Management Review* 22 (3): 802–805.

Reitzes, D. C. and Mutran, E. J. 1994. "Multiple Role and Identities: Factors Influencing Self-esteem among Middle-aged Working Men and Women," *Social Psychology Quarterly* 57 (4): 313–325.

Rivero, J. C., and Spencer, J. L. 1998. "Designing CEO and COO Roles," in Nadler, Spencer and associates (eds.), pp. 60–80.

Roberto, M. A. 2005. *Why Great Leaders Don't Take Yes for an Answer: Managing for Conflict and Consensus*. Upper Saddle River, NJ: Wharton School Publishing.

Roberts, J., McNulty, T. and Stiles, P. 2005. "Beyond Agency Conceptions of the Work of the Non-Executive Director: Creating Accountability in the Boardroom," *British Journal of Management* 16, S1: S5–S26.

Ronald, D. D. 1965. "Team at the Top," *Harvard Business Review* 43 (2): 74–82.

Rothschild, W. E. 1993. *Risktaker, Caretaker, Surgeon, Undertaker: The Four Faces of Strategic Leadership*. New York: Wiley.

Rubin, R. E. and Weisberg, J. 2003. *In an Uncertain World*. New York: Random House.

Ruef, M., Aldrich, H. E., and Carter, N. M. 2003. "The Structure of Founding Teams: Homophily, Strong Ties, and Isolation among U.S. Entrepreneurs," *American Sociological Review* 68 (2): 195–222.

Saarel, D. A. 2003. "The 'New Sciences' Framework for Boards and CEOs," *Directorship* 29 (3): 14–17.

Salaman, G. 1980. "Roles and Rules," in G. Salaman and K. Johnson (eds.), *Control and Ideology in Organizations*. Milton Keynes: Open University Press, pp. 128–151.

   1982. "Managing the Frontier of Control," in A. Giddens and G. Mackenzie (eds.), *Social Class and the Division of Labour*. Cambridge: Cambridge University Press, pp. 46–62.

Sally, D. 2002. "Co-Leadership: Lessons from Republican Rome," *California Management Review* 44 (4): 84–99.

Sathe, V. 2003. *Corporate Entrepreneurship: Top Managers and New Business Creation*. Cambridge: Cambridge University Press.

Saunders, C. S. 1990. "The Strategic Contingencies Theory of Power: Multiple Perspectives," *Journal of Management Studies* 27 (1): 1–18.

Sayles, L. R. 1993. *The Working Leader. The Triumph of High Performance Over Conventional Management Principles*. New York: The Free Press.

Schneider, K. J. 1990. *The Paradoxical Self: Toward an Understanding of our Contradictory Nature*. New York: Insight Books.

Schoonhoven, C. B. 1981. "Problems with Contingency Theory: Testing Assumptions Hidden within the Language of Contingency 'Theory'," *Administrative Science Quarterly* 26: 349–377.

Schwartz, N. D. 2004. "Inside the Head of BP," *Fortune*, July 26.

Scott, W. R. 2003. "Introduction to the Transaction Edition: Thompson's Bridge over Troubled Waters," in J. D. Thompson, *Organizations in Action*. New Brunswick: Transaction Publishers, pp. xv–xxviii.

Seers, A., Keller, T., and Wilkerson, J. M. 2003. "Can Team Members Share Leadership? Foundations in Research and Theory," in C. L. Pearce and J. A. Conger (eds.), *Shared Leadership: Reframing the Hows and Whys of Leadership*. London: Sage, pp. 77–102.

Selznick, P. 1957. *Leadership in Administration. A Sociological Interpretation*. Los Angeles: University of California Press.

Senger, J. 1971. "The Co-Manager Concept," *California Management Review* 13 (3): 77–83.

Shen, W. and Cannella, A. A. 2002. "Power Dynamics within Top Management and Their Impacts on CEO Dismissal Followed by Inside Succession," *Academy of Management Journal* 45 (6): 1.195–1.206.

Shenkar, O. and Zeira, Y. 1992. "Role Conflict and Role Ambiguity of Chief Executive Officers in International Joint Ventures," *Journal of International Business Studies* 22 (2): 55–75.

Sheppard, B. H. and Sherman, D. M. 1998. "The Grammars of Trust: A Model and General Implications," *Academy of Management Review* 23 (3): 422–437.

Sibillin, A. 2001. "Bernard Arnault. Capitaliste du jour," *EuroBusiness* 2 (8): 56–66.

Sieber, S. D. 1974. "Toward a Theory of Role Accumulation," *American Sociological Review* 39 (4): 567–578.

Simmel, G. 1902a. "The Number of Members as Determining the Sociological Form of the Group: I," *American Journal of Sociology* 8: 1–46.

1902b. "The Number of Members as Determining the Sociological Form of the Group: II," *American Journal of Sociology* 8: 158–196.

1903. "The Sociology of Conflict: I," *American Journal of Sociology* 9: 490–525.

1950. *The Sociology of George Simmel*, translated, edited and with an introduction by Kurt H. Wolff. New York: The Free Press.

1964. *Conflict and the Web of Group Affiliations*. New York: The Free Press.

Simon, H. A. 1945. *Administrative Behavior: A Study of Decision Making Processes in Administrative Organization*. New York: The Free Press.

Skapinker, M. 2001. "Under Pressure: Why Do Today's Chief Executives Fail to Hold Their Positions for Long?," *Financial Times*, May 31.

Smelser, N. J. and Smelser, W. T. (eds.) 1963. *Personality and Social Systems*. New York: Wiley.

Smith, K. and Berg, D. 1987. *Paradoxes of Group Life*. San Francisco: Jossey-Bass.

Smith, K. G., Smith, K. A., Olian, J. D., Sims, H. P., O'Bannon, D. P., and Scully, J. A. 1994. "Top Management Team Demography and Process: The Role of Social Integration and Communication," *Administrative Science Quarterly* 39 (3): 412–438.

Snook, S. A. 2000. *Friendly Fire. The Accidental Shootdown of U.S. Black Hawks over Northern Iraq*. Princeton: Princeton University Press.

Southwick, K. 1999. *High Noon*. New York: Wiley.

Spiegel, P. 2003. "Arranged Marriage Has Grown into Model Match," *Financial Times*, July 28–August 3.

Spiro, L. N., Silverman, G., and Reed, S. 1999. "The Coup at Goldman," *Business Week Online*, January 25. http://www.businessweek.com/1999/99_04/b3613001.htm?scriptFramed (accessed April 28, 2002).

Spooner, J. 2003. "Reshaping Dell," *News.com*, November 5. http://news.com.com/Reshaping+Dell/2008-1001_3-5102330.html (accessed January 2004).

Stark, M. 2005. "How 'Career Imprinting' Shapes Leaders," Harvard Business School Working Knowledge, February 7.

Stewart, R. 1967. *Managers and Their Jobs: A Study of Similarity and Differences in the Ways Managers Spend Their Time*. London: Palgrave Macmillan.

Stewart, R. 1976. *Contrast in Management*. Maidenhead: McGraw-Hill.

1982. *Choices for the Manager*. London: Prentice-Hall.

1991. "Chairmen and Chief Executives: An Exploration of Their Relationship," *Journal of Management Studies* 28 (5): 511–527.

Stinchcombe, A. L. 1990. *Information and Organizations*. Berkeley: University of California Press.

Strauss, F. 2001. *Conversaciones con Pedro Almodóvar*. Madrid: Ediciones Akal.

Strebel, P. 2004. "The Case for Contingent Governance," *MIT Sloan Management Review* 45 (2): 58–66.

Strodtbeck, F. 1954. "The Family as a Three-Person Group," *American Sociological Review* 19 (1): 22–29.

Sullivan, S. E. 1999. "The Changing Nature of Careers: A Review and Research Agenda," *Journal of Management* 25 (3): 457–484.

Sundaramurthy, C. and Lewis, M. 2003. "Control and Collaboration: Paradoxes of Governance," *Academy of Management Review* 28 (3): 397–415.

Svejenova, S. 2002. "The Autonomy of Ties: Careers and Governance in Creative Project Networks." Unpublished doctoral dissertation, IESE Business School, University of Navarra.

Swedberg, R. 2001. "Sociology and Game Theory: Contemporary and Historical Perspectives," *Theory and Society* 30: 301–335.

Sweet, S. and Moen, P. 2004. "Co-working as a Career Strategy: Implications for the Work and Family Lives of University Employees," *Innovative Higher Education* 28 (4): 255–272.

Synnott, W. R. 1987. *The Information Weapon: Winning Customers and Markets with Technology*. New York: Wiley.

Taylor, A., III 2001. "What's Behind Ford's Fall?," *Fortune*, October 29.

Teather, D. 2004. "Karmazin Quits Viacom After Years of Rivalry," *Guardian Unlimited*, June 2.

Tedlow, R. S. 2001. *Giants of Enterprise. Seven Business Innovators and the Empires They Built*. New York: Harper Business.

Thomas, A. and Ramaswamy, K. 1989. "Executive Characteristics, Strategy and Performance: A Contingency Model," *Academy of Management Proceedings*, 42–47.

Thompson, J. D. 1967. *Organizations in Action. Social Science Bases of Administrative Theory*. New York: McGraw Hill.

2003. *Organizations in Action. Social Science Bases of Administrative Theory*, with an introduction by W. Richard Scott. New Brunswick: Transaction Publishers.

Thompson, M. L. 2002. "Co-CEOs and the Sharing of Power," *Directors and Boards* 26 (2): 36–40.

Thornton, P. H. and Ocasio, W. 1999. "Institutional Logics and the Historical Contingency of Power in Organizations: Executive Succession in the Higher Education Publishing Industry, 1958–1990," *American Journal of Sociology* 105 (3): 801–843.

Thottam, J. 2004. "Martha's Endgame," *Time*, July 26.

Tomlinson R. 2005. "One Company, Two Bosses, Many Problems," *Fortune* (European Edition), January 31.

Toole, J. 2001. "When Leadership is an Organizational Trait," in W. Bennis, G. M. Spreitzerl, and T. G. Cummings (eds.), *The Future of Leadership: Today's Top Leadership Thinkers Speak to Tomorrow's Leaders*. San Francisco: Jossey-Bass, pp. 158–176.

Tosi, H. L. and Slocum, J. W. 1984. "Contingency Theory: Some Suggested Directions," *Journal of Management* 10: 9–26.

Townsend, R. 2000. "Gloria bendita," *El País Semanal*, May 14.

Tushman, M. L. 1977. "A Political Approach to Organizations: A Review and Rationale," *Academy of Management Review* 2 (2): 206–217.

1979. "Work Characteristics and Subunit Communication Structure: A Contingency Analysis," *Administrative Science Quarterly* 24 (1): 82–99.

Tushman, M. L. and Nadler, D. A. 1978. "Information Processing as an Integrating Concept in Organizational Design," *Academy of Management Review* 3 (3): 613–624.

Tushman, M. L. and O'Reilly, C. A. 1996. "Ambidextrous Organizations: Managing Evolutionary and Revolutionary Change," *California Management Review* 38 (4): 8–30.

Tushman, M. L. and Romanelli, E. 1983. "Uncertainty, Social Location and Influence in Decision Making: A Sociometric Analysis," *Management Science* 29 (1): 12–24.

Tyrnauer, M. 2004. "So Very Valentino," *Vanity Fair*, August.

Useem, M. 1999. "Co-Anchoring Viacom: Will It Work? Interview with Warren Bennis," *Wharton Leadership Digest* 3 (12), September. http://leadership.wharton.upenn.edu/digest/09-99.shtml (accessed January 17, 2005).

Uyterhoeven, H. 1972. "General Managers in the Middle," *Harvard Business Review* 50 (2): 75–86.

Uyterhoeven, H., Ackerman, R. W., and Rosenblum, J. W. 1973. *Strategy and Organization: Text and Cases in General Management*. Homewood, IL: Richard Irwin.

Vagnoni, A. 1997. "Creative Teams," *Advertising Age's Creativity* 5 (3): 22–27.

Valls, L. 1989. "Libertad y eficacia," *Actualidad Económica*, July 24.

Van de Ven, A. and Drazin, R. 1985. "The Concept of Fit in Contingency Theory," *Research in Organizational Behavior* 7: 333–365.

Vinacke, W. E. and Arkoff, A. 1957. "An Experimental Study of Coalitions in the Triad," *American Sociological Review* 22: 406–414.

Vogelstein, F. 2003. "Can Google Grow Up?," *Fortune*, December 22.

Von Neumann, J. and Morgenstern O. 1944. *Theory of Games and Economic Behavior*. Princeton: Princeton University Press.

Walsh, J. P. 1988. "Selectivity and Selective Perception: An Investigation of Managers' Belief Structures and Information Processing," *Academy of Management Journal* 31 (4): 873–896.

Wasserman, N. 2003. "Founder-CEO Succession and the Paradox of Entrepreneurial Success," *Organization Science* 14 (2): 149–172.

Wasserman, S. and Faust, K. 1994. *Social Network Analysis. Methods and Applications*. Cambridge: Cambridge University Press.

Wasserman, N., Nohria, N., and Anand, B. 2001. "When Does Leadership Matter? The Contingent Opportunities View of CEO Leadership." Working Paper 01–063, Strategic Unit Working Paper 02–04, Harvard Business School.

Watson, T. and Harris, P. 1999. *The Emergent Manager*. Thousand Oaks, CA: Sage.

Watson, T. J. 1994. *In Search of Management: Culture, Chaos and Control in Managerial Work*. London: Routledge.

1996. "How Do Managers Think? Identity, Morality and Pragmatism in Managerial Theory and Practice," *Management Learning* 27 (3): 323–341.

Weber, M. 1978. *Economy and Society. An Outline of Interpretive Sociology*, edited by G. Roth and C. Wittich. Berkeley: University of California Press.

2001 [1931]. *The Protestant Ethic and the Spirit of Capitalism*. London: Routledge Classics.

Weber, R. J. 1978. "Games Managers Play," in Athos and Gabarro (eds.), pp. 283–289.

Weick, K. E. 1996. "Enactment and the Boundaryless Career: Organizing as We Work," in M. B. Arthur and D. M. Rousseau (eds.), *The Boundaryless Career: A New Employment Principle for a New Organizational Era*. New York: Oxford University Press, pp. 40–57.

Whetten, D. A. 1989. "What Constitutes a Theoretical Contribution?," *Academy of Management Review* 14 (4): 490–495.

2002. "Modelling-as-Theorizing: A Systematic Methodology for Theory Development," in D. Partington (ed.), *Essential Skills For Management Research*. London: Sage, pp. 46–71.

Whisler, T. L. 1960. "The 'Assistant-to' in Four Administrative Settings," *Administrative Science Quarterly* 5 (2): 181–216.

White, H. 1992. *Identity and Control*. Princeton: Princeton University Press.

White, H. C. and White, C. A. 1965. *Canvases and Careers: Institutional Change in the French Painting World*. Chicago: University of Chicago Press.

Whitehead, J. 2002. Interview. Interviewer: Amy Blitz, Harvard Business School Director of Media Development for Entrepreneurial Management. Full video transcript. http://www.hbs.edu/entrepreneurship/video.html (accessed January 17, 2004).

Whitford, D. 2000. "The Two Headed Manager," *Fortune*, January 24.

Whitley, R. 1989. "On the Nature of Managerial Tasks and Skills: Their Distinguishing Characteristics and Organization," *Journal of Management Studies* 26 (3): 209–224.

Williams, M. 2001. "Scenes from a Marriage," *Vanity Fair*, July.

Witt, L. A., *et al.* 2002. "Interactive Effects of Personality and Organizational Politics on Contextual Performance," *Journal of Organizational Behavior* 23 (8): 911–926.

Wootton, A. 2001. Nanni Moretti. Regus London Film Festival 2001 interviews, November 17. http://film.guardian.co.uk/lff2001/news/0,1555,602564,00.html (accessed October 20, 2004).

Worzniak, M. J. and Chadwell, M. 2002. "A Job-Share Model for the New Millennium," *Family Practice Management*, September, pp. 29–32. http://www.aafp.org/fpm (accessed August 14, 2004).

Wrapp, H. E. 1984. "Good Managers Don't Make Policy Decisions," *Harvard Business Review* 62 (4): 8–15.

Yablonsky, L. 1955. "The Sociometry of the Dyad," *Sociometry* 4 (18): 357–360.

Yamaguchi, K. 1996. "Power in Networks of Substitutable and Complementary Exchange," *American Sociological Review* 61 (2): 308–333.

Zajac, E. J. and Westphal, J. D. 1996. "Who Shall Succeed? How CEO/Board Preferences and Power Affect the Choice of New CEOs," *Academy of Management Journal* 39 (1): 64–90.

1998. "Towards a Behavioral Theory of the CEO–Board Relationship," in Hambrick, Nadler, and Tushman (eds.), pp. 256–277.

Zald, M. N. 1969. "The Power and Functions of Boards of Directors: A Theoretical Synthesis," *American Journal of Sociology* 75 (1): 97–111.

1970. *Organizational Change: The Political Economy of the YMCA.* Chicago: University of Chicago Press.

Zaleznik, A. 1963. "The Human Dilemmas of Leadership," *Harvard Business Review* 41 (4): 49–55.

Zelleke, A. 2003. "Freedom and Constraint: The Design of Governance and Leadership Structures in British and American Firms." Unpublished Ph.D. thesis, Graduate School of Arts and Sciences, Harvard University, March 31.

Zorn, D. M. 2004. "Here a Chief, There a Chief: The Rise of the CFO in the American Firm," *American Sociological Review* 69 (3): 345–364.

Zuckerman, E. W., Kim, T., Ukanwa, K., and Rittman, J. von 2003. "Robust Identities or Nonentities? Typecasting in the Feature-Film Labour Market," *American Journal of Sociology* 108 (5): 1.018–1.074.

Zuckerman, H. 1967. "Nobel Laureates in Science: Patterns of Productivity, Collaboration, and Authorship," *American Sociological Review* 32 (3): 391–403.

Index

French, J. R. Jr. 33, 35
Freston, Tom 164
Freud, Sigmund 176
Friedman, Steve 8, 125, 132, 161, 190
friendship 4, 124, 139, 176, 200
Fujisawa, Takeo 118, 130

Gabarro, J.J. 86, 221
Gage, John 156
Galbraith, Jay R. 14, 15, 20, 68
Galvin, Bob 216
game theory 152
games, executive power 45
games, local 79
"Gang of Four," China 148–149
Garavani, Valentino 172–173, 191
Garci, José Luis 19
Gargiulo, M. 2
Gates, Bill 8, 177, 200
Geffen, David 156
Geisst, Charles 124
General Motors, co-CEOs 155
Germany, two-tier board structures 97
Gestalten 62, 74, 75, 107
Ghoshal, S. 50, 68
  roles 72, 74, 74–75, 76, 80
Ghosn, Carlos 88, 89, 98
Giammetti, Giancarlo 172, 191
Gibson, C. B. 67
Glaser, B. G. 187
Glover, J. D. 32
goals 54
  attainment of 36, 51
  displacement of 34, 215
Goffman, E. 150
Goldman Sachs 87, 99
  co-CEOs 7–8, 170, 197–198
  Rubin and Friedman 125, 132, 161
  Weinberg and Whitehead 25, 126, 128–129, 130, 179, 188–190
González, Felipe 9, 140, 198
González, Francisco 188
Google 25, 123, 129, 160–161, 165–168
Gore, Albert 9
Gosling, J. 68, 73, 85
Greenberg, Jerry 126, 129, 130, 132
Greiner, L. 219

Gresov, C. 48, 56, 209
Gronn, P. 117, 132, 136, 187
Guerra, Alfonso 9, 140, 198
Gupta, A. K. 46

Hackman, Richard 11
Haleblian, J. 44
Hales, C. P. 75
Hambrick, D. C. 1, 31, 49, 68, 103
  leadership 3, 21, 44, 45
  CEO–COO dyads 12–13, 122, 140
  COO role 89, 94
Harley-Davidson Motor Company 156, 177
Harley, William 156, 177
Harris, P. 221
Harrison, J. R. 98, 120, 121
Harvard Laboratory of Social Relations 151
Haskett, J. L. 37
Hedlund, G. 67
Heenan, D. A. 13, 15
Hegedus, Chris 111–113
Herman, Tom 111, 124, 200
Hertrich, Rainer 130
Hewlett, William R. 8, 177, 200
Hewlett-Packard Company 8, 177
Hickson , D. J. 56
Higgs Report 52
high-technology industry 8
Hill, Linda 99
Hirsch, P. 77
Hirshberg, Jerry 6, 196
Hodgson, R. G.
  dyads 119, 130, 151, 206
  executive constellations 24, 74, 103, 118
Hollenbeck, J. R. 44
Honda, Soichiro 118, 130
horizontal structures 49, 101
  design of 3, 33, 45, 54, 205–210
hostile takeovers 17
Hower, R. M. 32
Humphrey, S. E. 44
Hungate, Alex 8

Ibuka, Makoto 191
Ibuka, Masaru 25, 107, 179, 180, 190–193, 201
identity, supra-individual 150, 209

small-numbers structures (*cont.*)
  contingencies and 204
  corporate governance and 194,
    205
  explanations for 22, 30
  integration in 101
  longevity of 194
  processes involving 195, 196–198
  roles and relationships in 108
Smith, Winthrop H. 8
Snow, C. 68
social capital 4
social networks 36, 86, 115, 149
social psychology 152
social reform 223
social responsibility, corporate 34, 41
Sogestalt Télévision 176
solo management 63–81, 205–206,
    214, 217, 220
Sony Corporation 25, 105, 179, 180,
    190–193
Sony Pictures Classics 7
Southwick 137
Spencer, J. L. 72, 72–73, 96, 119
Spiegel 8
Spielberg, Steven 156
splitting 65
stakeholders 82
Stalin 148
Stalker, G. M. 10, 57
  contingencies 53, 56, 58, 59
  mechanistic structures 88, 96
Startup.com 111–113
Stephens, C. U. 3, 44, 47, 59
Stewart, Martha 16, 100
Stewart, R. 2, 5, 10, 15, 18, 22
Stewart, T. I. 40
Stinchcombe, A. L. 50
strategies 24
  arbiter 160
  divide et impera 24, 160, 160,
    162–163, 165, 171
  integrator 160, 161, 163, 168–169,
    171
  legitimator 160, 160–161, 163,
    165–168, 171
  mediator 160, 161–163, 164, 171,
    208
  tertius gaudens 24, 160, 160,
    162–163, 164–165, 171

strategy, responsibility for 43–44, 50,
    52, 56, 61
Strebel, P. 47
string quartets 158–159
Strodtbeck, F. 151
structures, and contingencies 47
sub-roles 89, 89, 99
succession 123
Sufrategui, Paz 183
Sullivan, S. E. 201
Sun Microsystems 24, 95, 134,
    134–138, 156

Takeshima, Hiroshi 130
Taylor III, A. 100
team composition 45, 46
Teather, D. 133
technology (as a contingency) 42
tertius gaudens strategy 24, 160, 160,
    162–163, 164–165, 171
Thompson, James 36–38, 38, 50, 54,
    57
  contingencies 40, 51, 64
  dominant coalitions 1, 12
  integration 57
  paradox of administration 37, 64
Thompson, T. A. 60, 211
threesomes and foursomes 24
Tidens, L. Z. 140
time-frames, short- and long-term 50,
    64, 77
Tisch, Andrew and Jonathan 161,
    168-169
Tisch, James 161, 168
Tisch, Larry and Bob 168–169
Torres, D. L. 98, 120, 121
Toulouse, J. M. 48, 49
transitions, intra-role 174
Treuba, Fernando 19
triads 24, 25, 143–163, 208–210
  affection 150
  CEO role in 158
  decision-making in 159
  distribution of power in 152, 171
  and dyads 151
  equal 159
  hierarchical 159
  origins of 149
  in the politics regime 216
  and professional duos 149–152

Wetlaufer, S. 73, 82
White, H. 80
Whitehead, John 25, 138, 179,
    188–190, 201
  origins of co-CEO role 128–129,
    130, 180, 200
Whitford, D.
Whitley, R. 75, 82
van Witteloostuijn, A. 211
Wozniak, Steve 8, 200
Wnuck, D. 196
Wrapp, H. E. 79

Yablonsky , L. 140
Yahoo 129
Yang, Jerry 129

Ybarra, Emilio 188
Young Men's Christian Association
    (YMCA) 34

Zajac, E. J. 16
Zald, M. N. 34, 35, 211
Zaleznik, A.
  dyads 130, 151
  executive constellations 24, 74, 103,
    118
Zander, Edward 134, 134–138
Zelleke, A. 11, 49, 121–122
Zorn, D.
  CFO role 91, 94, 95
  COO role 94, 122
Zuckerman, H. 114